TRUTH UNDER ATTACK

VOLUME 1

Deviations from biblical Christianity

TRUTH UNDER ATTACK

VOLUME 1
Deviations from biblical Christianity

DR ERYL DAVIES

EVANGELICAL PRESS

EVANGELICAL PRESS
Faverdale North Industrial Estate, Darlington, DL3 0PH,
England

Evangelical Press USA
P. O. Box 825, Webster, New York 14580, USA

e-mail: sales@evangelicalpress.org
web: www.evangelicalpress.org

First published 2004

**British Library Cataloguing in Publication Data
available**

ISBN 0 85234 574 7

Printed and bound in Great Britain by Creative Print &
Design Wales, Ebbw Vale, South Wales.

CONTENTS

Section B: Unitarian churches and movements

Section C: Personal and pastoral challenges

Postscript: Summary of major Bible doctrines

PREFACE

I am grateful to the editors of *Evangelical Times* for inviting and encouraging me to write regular monthly articles under the title *Concerning Cults*. Although onerous at times, this commitment has stimulated ongoing research and the response of *ET* readers has been rewarding over the past five years. Many of those *ET* articles have been incorporated into these three volumes.

Mrs Chris Connor has again undertaken a great deal of secretarial and liaison work in preparing these chapters for publication. I am indebted to her and also to my wife for proof reading the material. In these ways I have been relieved of a lot of necessary but tedious work.

As usual, Evangelical Press directors were also encouraging as they waited for me to complete the writing of these volumes. I appreciated their patience, especially when I failed, because of the pressures of college teaching and wider ministry, to observe agreed submission dates. The suggestions of EP directors concerning the structuring of the three volumes along with detailed comments on the text were also invaluable.

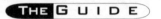

PREFACE

For any mistakes which remain, I assume responsibility. However, I have endeavoured consistently to be accurate and gracious in what I have written.

Eryl Davies
Evangelical Theological College of Wales
Bridgend
December 2004

INTRODUCTION AND OUTLINE OF THE THREE-VOLUME SERIES

For over three decades I have researched the complex subject of cults and new religious movements. My reasons for doing so have been three-fold.

Firstly, in the context of evangelism I met increasing numbers of people belonging to the cults. In sharing the gospel of grace with them I found it helpful to acquaint myself with their teaching. Evangelism, therefore, has always been for me a primary reason for researching this subject.

Secondly, but closely related, was the fact that my own church members were often confused as a result of talking to cult members who called at their homes or approached them in shopping areas. Here was a challenge to instruct Christians more adequately in the Scriptures and also to mobilize them in personal evangelism.

A third reason for continuing this research, especially in recent years, has been the regular requests for help from missionaries, pastors and individual Christians troubled by cult activities in their situations. On occasions, some have been distressed over the involvement in a cult by a close relative or even infiltration of a Bible-believing church by cult members thus causing division and confusion.

INTRODUCTION

This volume, originally published under the title *Truth Under Attack* in two editions in 1990 and 1995, has undergone major revision, updating and expansion with several new groups included. Volumes 2 and 3, to follow soon, are being prepared in a similar way. An outline of all three volumes is included below. The three volumes together are intended to provide Christians, churches, schools and colleges with a reliable introduction to, and overview of, the contemporary Western cult scene from a biblical perspective.

Whether you are a Christian, a searcher or a cult member, I appeal to you to read regularly and understand 'the holy Scriptures, which are able to make you wise for salvation through faith in Christ Jesus' (2 Timothy 3:15).

VOLUME 1: DEVIATIONS FROM BIBLICAL CHRISTIANITY

Introduction to the three-volume series

Section A: Deviations from biblical Christianity in Trinitarian churches/movements

You may find some surprise inclusions in this section. Concerning the Worldwide Church of

God, for example, I have decided to include it — and place it first — only as a most unusual instance of a cult returning to orthodox Bible teaching. I no longer regard it as a cult and warmly welcome the reformation which has occurred, and continues, amongst its leaders and members.

At a time when Protestants and Roman Catholics often co-operate, even worship together, the inclusion of Roman Catholicism here may offend some readers. I assure you that my primary concern is to be faithful to biblical teaching; that, not sentimentality, must be our criterion for assessing any church or movement, irrespective of whether it is Protestant or Roman Catholic.

Section B: Unitarian churches and movements

It is important to recognize that in addition to the movement that calls itself 'Unitarian', there are Unitarian-type cults like the Jehovah's Witnesses, Christadelphians and also others such as The Way International and 'Jesus-only' movements. Unitarian views have also spread extensively into many Protestant, and other, churches. While there are significant differences between Arians and Unitarians, I have included them together in this section as there are some common features.

Section C: Personal and pastoral challenges

Postscript: Summary of major Bible doctrines

VOLUME 2: CULTS AND SECTS

Section D: What are cults and sects?

Introduction
1. Reflections: the term 'sect'
2. Reflections: the terms 'cult' and 'NRM'
3. Reflections: shared features relating to cults; tests
4. Reflections: a contemporary, worldwide problem
5. Reflections: MI5 and cults
6. Christ's death and cults

Section E: Case studies and issues arising

Introduction
7. MI5 and 'Concerned Christians' (1)
8. Concerned Christians (2)
9. Waco: Branch Davidians
10. Waco: the challenge of Koresh
11. Waco: danger signals
12. Waco: Waco and religious liberty

Section F: Established cults

Introduction
13. Mormons
14. Christian Science or Church of Christ, Scientist

OUTLINE

OUTLINE

HOW TO USE *THE GUIDE*

Truth under attack is the latest book in a new series called *The Guide*. This series covers books of the Bible on an individual basis, such as *Colossians and Philemon*, and relevant topics such as *Christian comfort*. The series' aim is to communicate the Christian faith in a straightforward and readable way.

Each book in *The Guide* will cover a book of the Bible or topic in some detail, but will be contained in relatively short and concise chapters. There will also usually be questions at the end of each chapter for personal study or group discussion, to help you to study the Word of God more deeply.

An innovative and exciting feature of *The Guide* is that it is linked to its own web site. As well as being encouraged to search God's Word for yourself, you are invited to ask questions related to the book on the web site, where you will not only be able to have your own questions answered, but also be able to see a selection of answers that have been given to other readers. The web site can be found at www.evangelicalpress.org/TheGuide. Once you are on the site you just need to click on the 'select' button at the top of

HOW TO USE THE GUIDE

the page, according to the book on which you wish to post a question. Your question will then be answered either by Michael Bentley, the web site co-ordinator and author of *Colossians and Philemon*, or others who have been selected because of their experience, their understanding of the Word of God and their dedication to working for the glory of the Lord.

Many other books have already been published in this series. These include *The Bible book by book, Job, Ecclesiastes, Esther, Revolutionary forgiveness* and *Christian comfort;* many more will follow. It is the publisher's hope that you will be stirred to think more deeply about the Christian faith, and will be helped and encouraged in living out your Christian life, through the study of God's Word, in the difficult and demanding days in which we live.

THE **GUIDE**

SECTION A:

DEVIATIONS FROM biblical CHRISTIANITY IN TRINITARIAN CHURCHES/MOVEMENTS

CHAPTER ONE

WORLDWIDE
CHURCH
OF GOD

A BRIEF HISTORY

A major U-turn: that is the only way you can describe it. Such U-turns occur often in the world of politics, business, sport and other areas of society. And we have now witnessed a major U-turn in the cult world; well, at least, with regard to one major cult. I am referring to the Worldwide Church of God (WCG), founded by Herbert Armstrong (1892-1986).

Professor Eddie Gibbs, Fuller Theological Seminary, Pasadena, claims that 'the transformation of the WCG represents a unique phenomenon in church history'. Ruth Tucker of Calvin Theological Seminary agrees: 'Never before in the history of Christianity has there been such a complete move to orthodox Christianity by an unorthodox fringe church.'[1] An exaggeration? Possibly, but both writers are drawing attention to a change that is at least rare, if not unique, in church history.

The U-turn has been recognized officially by many evangelicals in the United States of America. For example, in the spring of 1997 the National Association of Evangelicals (NAE) there issued an important press release from Wheaton concerning the WCG. The NAE leaders 'overwhelmingly' agreed to accept the WCG into membership but only after detailed examination of doctrinal changes which had taken place within the group.

NAE President, Don Argue, was in no doubt on the matter: 'I respect Joseph Tkach and the leadership of the Worldwide Church of God who did not rest in the refuge of their historically held doctrines, but sought the Truth through careful study of the Scriptures, even at significant cost to the denomination.'

There was a cost too. WCG once had as many as 90,000 members in the United States alone, but now the figure has dropped to under 50,000. Worldwide membership of the WCG is currently about 74,000 and there are 802 'churches'. Over half of these 'churches' are in the United States together with 678 ordained WCG ministers out of a total of 1,046 ministers. Despite the membership loss, the doctrinal changes in WCG are viewed by NAE President Argue as an answer to prayer: 'We see the dramatic changes that have occurred among our friends as God's continuing efforts to bring renewal and revival for His glory.'

The changes were certainly dramatic and unexpected; so much so, that Dr John MacArthur, pastor of Grace Community Church, California, USA, was caught out when his 12 January 1998 radio broadcast *Grace to You* included a dated negative reference to WCG. When challenged, the programme's director explained that the programme had been recorded eight years previously and they had failed to check then update its content. The director agreed to edit the programme accordingly.

One further example of the acceptance by orthodox Christians of WCG is included here in order to underline the way in which the group has changed.

Albert Mohler is the president of the Southern Baptist Theological Seminary in Louisville, Kentucky, and he reviewed in *Preaching Magazine* a book written by WCG leader Joseph Tkach entitled *Transformed by Truth*. Mohler is full of praise for the book, claiming, 'One of the most fascinating stories in modern American religious life is the transformation of the group established by Herbert Armstrong, the Worldwide Church of God, into an orthodox Christian tradition.' In the book, Mohler explains how Tkach 'offers his testimony of his group's rejection of the teaching of Herbert Armstrong and its progressive embrace of historic Christianity'. He adds, 'As this group embraces orthodox Christianity, we can see the almost unprecedented development of a religious cult into a distinctive Christian tradition ... the group still has serious issues to resolve.'

We now need to retrace our steps and see how and when these dramatic changes occurred. The story begins, of course, with Herbert W. Armstrong. Influenced by his wife in the late 1920s, Armstrong embraced Seventh Day Adventist ideas, particularly concerning Saturday as being 'God's Sabbath'. In 1933 he was ordained as a minister within the sabbatarian movement and a year later launched his influential Radio Church of God, then his *Plain Truth* magazine and, in 1947, his Ambassador College.

His organization was renamed the Worldwide Church of God in 1968, but only six years later a major division occurred when forty ministers and thousands of members left WCG on doctrinal and moral grounds. Even his own son, Garner Ted, formed his own breakaway organization under the name the Church of God International.

By the 1970s, Herbert Armstrong announced that he was God's apostle for the last days, but following financial problems and lengthy court battles he died in 1986 at the age of 94. His moral life left a lot to be desired.

Armstrongism

The doctrines promulgated by Armstrong were un-orthodox and bizarre. There is convincing evidence that he also plagiarized extensively. What did he teach? The doctrine of the Holy Trinity, he insisted, was 'false' because God was a 'family', a 'group in which there are two separate and individual Persons'. Sadly, Armstrong taught that Jesus Christ only became the Son of God when born of the virgin Mary and could sin like anyone else.

Salvation is by grace, according to Armstrong, but plus water-baptism and the keeping of commands such as the seventh-day Sabbath and tithing. Sabbath observance is essential for salvation. Racism was implicit in his teaching and an irresponsible interpretation of Bible prophecy led him to embrace British-Israelism. This discredited theory claimed that the USA, Russia, UK, Germany, France and other Western European nations were the descendants of the lost ten tribes of Israel!

Armstrong even predicted the end of the world on several specific dates such as 1975. Like other exclusive cults, Armstrong also believed that the WCG was the only true church; only members of WCG could be saved.

Beware

During and since Herbert Armstrong's ministry, it is claimed by the present WCG leader, Joe Tkach Jr, that over 100 groups 'split off' from the WCG. Such breakaway groups include the United Church of God, the Philadelphia Church of God and the Global Church of God. After being disciplined for immoral behaviour, Armstrong's son, Garner Ted, also founded his own Church of God International with 'a liberal version of Armstrongism'.

Changes

How did WCG change doctrinally? One man used significantly in this process of change was

HISTORY

Earl Williams, who in the 1990s began to preach Christ fearlessly and to emphasize salvation by grace without human obedience to the law. His message was fruitful and the leadership began to approve what Williams preached.

Already in the early 1990s it emerged that the WCG leadership had been looking to revise radically its doctrine of God. Discussions were held with faculty members of Trinity Evangelical Divinity School in 1991 and a year later WCG leaders were able to affirm the deity and personality of the Holy Spirit. This was a major shift from Armstrong's teaching and in 1993 the movement made a clear orthodox statement concerning the Trinity: '...the Father, the Son and the Holy Spirit are co-equal, co-eternal...'

It was a major U-turn indeed, especially in view of the fact that Joseph Tkach Sr upheld Armstrong's teaching when he assumed WCG leadership in 1986. His famous 1994 Christmas Eve sermon was a further step in securing doctrinal reform: 'We cannot assume that any part of the Old Covenant is binding on us today simply on the basis of it being the old package of laws,' he insisted. He also denied in this sermon that only Sabbath-keepers were true Christians. From 1995, Tkach's son has led the WCG and consolidated these doctrinal changes. Soon after assuming the leadership, he apologized to all who had been misled by Armstrongism: 'We earnestly desire their understanding and forgiveness,' he added.

We can rejoice in this new Trinitarian emphasis on divine grace and the centrality of the Saviour's unique sacrifice for sinners. After all, Christ and Christ alone is our only hope. That is the testimony of Conrad Comoau, a former WCG member and a pilot for the Armstrongs. After years in the movement he acknowledged: 'We cannot possibly save ourselves… It is only by the grace of God… So we must turn directly to God and not to any man.' That is the true gospel.

Welcoming visitors, the UK and Ireland web-page urges us to 'Worship and praise God, hear the Gospel of our Lord Jesus Christ expounded, and fellowship with us.' The main WCG home page claims that its goal is 'to proclaim the gospel of Jesus Christ' and adds, 'The gospel is the message that God is reconciling the world to himself and offering forgiveness of sin and eternal life through Jesus Christ.' Concerning its mission, we are informed that 'as a result of our heritage and tradition as a church', the following 'spiritual gifts and distinctives' are offered: 'emphasis on the absolute sovereignty and centrality of Jesus Christ … insistence on salvation by grace through faith, reverence and commitment to God's Holy Scriptures … willingness to be continually transformed by the Holy Spirit … the certainty and importance of the second coming [of Christ]' as well as 'responsible stewardship'.

The WCG doctrines of God, Scripture, Christ, salvation, justification and grace are now adequate, reflecting a major movement away from Armstrong's strange and unbiblical teachings.

The Scriptures are 'the accurate record of God's revelation' and 'constitute ultimate authority in all matters'. It is refreshing to learn that they officially view grace as 'the free, unmerited favour God bestows on a sinner who repents' while justification 'is God's gracious act of pronouncing a believer righteous in his sight' on the ground of Christ's sacrificial death.

Maintaining its seventh-day 'tradition and practice', the WCG officially declares that 'physical sabbath keeping is not required for Christians'. On 24 December 1994, Tkach spoke in Big Sandy, Texas, on the reality of the Christian life under the New Covenant. Quoting Colossians 2:16-17, he claimed, 'Paul's point is that to bring the physical figure back in, as a requirement for salvation, is to minimize the value of the true reality. We are not saved by grace through faith in Christ plus the Sabbath, or plus circumcision, or plus the sacrifices, or plus anything. We are saved by grace through faith in Christ.' It is well spoken, but in the *Watchman Expositor*, Phillip Arnn reported that some WCG members complained 'about remaining Old Testament language and practices' in that Holy Days, Saturday worship and tithing are 'still observed', even 'enforced' for some.

What about the respect still given by some to Armstrong? Tkach acknowledges: 'We've distanced ourselves as far as we can from him', his spending, lifestyle, behaviour, false teachings and claims; yet,

CHALLENGES

he adds, 'Armstrong was sincere' although 'his interpretation of scripture, even his reading of history was in error. And so he made errors.' This official stance towards Armstrong is ambivalent.

There are many books in the United States exposing the former leader; also many ex-members and their web sites are angry towards Armstrong for having deceived them. They feel they are 'victims' who have gone for years through something even worse than rape. There is a magazine called *The Painful Truth* which exposes Armstrong and monitors WCG progress.

In his useful book, *The Liberation of the World-wide Church of God*, J. Michael Feazell, a senior WCG leader, only spends eight pages (pp. 96-103) discussing 'Coping with the role of the Founder'. Armstrong, the author emphasizes, 'was not what he claimed to be' (p. 97). He was proud, condemnatory of others and 'taught a good-sized chunk of heresy' (p. 100).

But is that all? What about Armstrong's abuse of power and the gross inconsistency of his life? Feazell's reply is that 'Herbert Armstrong's judgement is not my business; it is the Lord's' (p. 96). I agree, but a thorough account of Armstrong's life and work is required. What is more, WCG should not hesitate to recognize their founder as a false prophet.

Michael Feazell illustrates well the new gospel emphasis of WCG in terms of his own spiritual experience. Asked in early 1991 by his ageing, godly grandmother as to whether he loved Jesus, Feazell was deeply challenged. 'I knew a lot *about* him', he confessed. 'But I didn't yet know *him*' (p. 49).

However, the transformed WCG still faces problems. There has been a shortage of gospel-preaching pastors (p. 122); WCG lost more than half of its pastors and members as well as over 85% of its annual income during the period of theological reformation.

And Feazell is realistic: 'Our current financial challenges', he admits, 'and generally flagging morale may finally prove irreversible' (p. 130).

But whatever the future holds for WCG, he testifies that by God's grace, 'we have already received the greatest gift imaginable' — the rediscovery of the gospel of grace. For Feazell, that is a key element in the WCG U-turn; other elements are rediscovery of the doctrines of the Triune God and the personality of the Holy Spirit (p. 135), as well as leadership experiences of the gospel which were 'like the light of day and like shouts of rescue to hopeless souls, beaten, starved, and imprisoned in darkness' (p. 139). Other key elements specified by the author are the rediscovery of the priesthood of believers (p. 140) and outreach.

There is no doubt now that WCG has become a Trinitarian, Christ-centred, gospel-loving and biblically-oriented church. The changes are dramatic and prayers have been answered.

CHAPTER TWO

SEVENTH-DAY ADVENTISTS

A BRIEF HISTORY

The story of this movement begins in America with a military captain named William Miller (1782-1849), who left the army in 1812 to work as a farmer. He was not a Christian at this time but was determined to study the Bible thoroughly. His resolve was somewhat weakened by some cynical friends but in 1816 he was converted, joined the local Baptist church and reapplied himself diligently to the study of the Bible, using only *Cruden's Concordance* as an aid.

Prophecy soon absorbed his interest and after two years he was convinced that the coming of Christ was imminent and that the Lord would set up his kingdom in America. Anxious to find out when this would occur, Miller made the serious error of date-fixing. By misusing certain verses in Daniel and Revelation he announced publicly in 1831 that the Lord's return would take place on 10 October 1843. For months before the specified date there was great excitement amongst his followers. When the Lord's return did not occur on this date, Miller blamed himself for making an error in his calculations, so 22 October 1844 was then proposed as the correct date.

Several weeks before this date many of the 'Millerites' left their jobs and there was considerable anticipation of the Lord's return. In one shop-window in Philadelphia the following message was displayed:

> This shop is closed in honour of the King of
> Kings, who will appear about the 22 October.
> Get ready, friends, to crown him Lord of all.

Needless to say, the Lord did not return and Miller acknowledged his mistake, remarking that 'To contend that we were not mistaken is dishonest. We should never be ashamed frankly to confess our errors.' Until his death in 1849 Miller remained a keen Bible student and a godly believer.

His successor in the movement was Mrs Ellen White, a 'prophetess' who frequently claimed to have visions and revelations directly from God. She was convinced, even as a seventeen-year-old, that Miller was right in his prediction regarding the date of the Lord's return. When on the morning following 'the great disappointment' she saw in a vision the heavenly sanctuary in need of cleansing and Christ standing there, she regarded this as the revelation explaining the true significance of Miller's prophecy. Christ had come in 1844, but he had come to his heavenly, not earthly, sanctuary!

Mrs White exercised a great influence on the development of Adventism and since her death in 1915 her writings are frequently appealed to as authoritative and divine expositions of Scripture.

A chequered history

Seventh-Day Adventism has had a chequered history. The early years, 1844-1888, were difficult years characterized by a failure to appreciate and accept justification by faith. 'The almost universal position' in this period was, according to Australian researcher G. J. Paxton, that 'Acceptable righteousness before God is found through obeying the law with the aid of the Spirit of God.'[1]

1888 was a watershed in the movement's history. Talks given by E. J. Waggoner and Mrs White at the General Conference Session of 1888 in Minneapolis helped to re-establish the doctrine of justification by faith to a position of prominence in the movement. They stressed the impossibility of human obedience satisfying the law of God and also underlined the necessity of a mediator who was both God and man to satisfy the law on behalf of sinners. Only through faith, they added, could this righteousness be received.

There was opposition to this new emphasis in the conference and subsequently some leaders were strongly criticized by Mrs White for their antagonism to the doctrine of justification by faith. The years 1901-1920 witnessed expansion and consolidation of the movement despite a crisis over the teaching and influence of pantheism, i.e., the theory that God is identifiable with the forces of nature and with natural substances.[2]

In subsequent years the controversy over the meaning and importance of justification and its relation to sanctification deepened and the decade of the seventies was a period of profound crisis with differing emphases and interpretations.

Adventist scholars like Desmond Ford, Geoffrey Paxton and Robert Brinsmead argued strongly for the Reformation principle of justification by faith alone; they insisted that sanctification is not the basis of salvation. Others, however, like Hans K. La Rondelle, disagreed. As the debate continued in the late 1970s, an official committee was appointed to study the question. Sadly, this committee issued an ambiguous, compromising statement which did little to clarify the official Adventist position concerning the crucial doctrine of justification by faith. La Rondelle, for example, had rejected the Reformation gospel as the norm for the Adventists' understanding of the apostolic gospel, while Fritz Guy affirmed, 'One of the most important elements in our Adventist heritage is the notion of "present truth" — truth that has come newly alive and has become newly understood and significant because of a new experience, a present situation. What is important, then, theologically and experientially, is not whether our understanding is just like that of the Reformers; what is important is whether our beliefs are true.'[3]

With the establishment of Adventist research centres in the 1960s and 1970s, attention also focused on the nature and authority of Ellen White's writings. As a result of this historical research, three points were established. First of all, Ellen White borrowed a lot of her material from other sources; secondly, she was fallible; and, thirdly, she was conditioned by late nineteenth-century American culture.

Recent controversy

In September 1980 church leaders disciplined one of the movement's leading theologians, Australian Desmond Ford, removing him from ministerial and teaching posts within the movement. Having gained his doctoral degree in New Testament studies in Manchester under Professor F. F. Bruce, Ford had been head of the theology department of the Adventists' Avondale College in New South Wales, Australia, for sixteen years. Ford challenged some of the most cherished Adventist traditions, including the status of Mrs White's writings and the 'Investigative Judgement'. He claims, 'You can't find the investigative judgement in the Bible. You can get it out of Ellen White. The fact is, she got it out of Uriah Smith, an early Adventist writer.'

Prior to his dismissal, Desmond Ford was given a six-month leave of absence in order to research the question of the 'sanctuary' doctrine and other related issues. He published the findings of his research in the summer of 1980 in a manuscript called *Daniel 8:14, The Day of Atonement and the Investigative Judgment*.[4] In this lengthy document, Ford denied the traditional Adventist teaching that Christ entered the Most Holy Place in 1844 to start upon his work of investigative judgement. Ford then underlined the biblical truth, namely, that Christ has been interceding for his people as High Priest since his ascension. What then, according to Ford, was the significance of 1844? It was the time, he declared, 'when God, in heaven and on earth, raised up a people to whom he entrusted his last, everlasting gospel of righteousness by faith in Christ, for the world'.[5]

The official Adventist response was disappointing. In numerous articles and editorials in the *Adventist Review* it was argued that the traditional sanctuary doctrine was an essential article of faith. Richard Lesher, for example, insisted: 'These landmark doctrines are to be received and held fast, not in formal fashion but in the light of divine guidance given at the beginning of the movement and made our own. Thus we become part and parcel with the movement, and the beliefs that made the original Seventh-day Adventists make us Seventh-day Adventists too.'[6]

Ford's manuscript was then studied by the 'Sanctuary Review Committee', where the majority of members decided that the 'Adventist tradition was the norm for interpreting the Bible, rather than the Bible for tradition'.[7]

A few weeks later the General Conference recommended that Ford should be disciplined and the Australian Division took the appropriate steps. Almost immediately, however, a new magazine called *Evangelica* was launched to defend and propagate Ford's teaching.

Ford's influence on Adventism both in America and Australia has been extensive. One Adventist reported that in the U.S.A., 'There is a vast youth movement in the church identifying with the evangelistic gospel [as a result of Ford]. There's a renewed excitement about the cross.'[8] Some, like John Toews, the Californian pastor, withdrew their churches from the movement; Pastor Toews renamed his church the South Bay Gospel Fellowship. 'We feel,' he explains, 'we want to move into the mainstream of Christianity now because we feel that Adventism is very definitely way off to the side.'[9] He predicted that many more pastors would resign.

Underlying this debate is the nature of Christ's death; was it sufficient and final? Their 'sanctuary' teaching detracts from these two aspects of the Saviour's sacrifice. For example, they speak of the Lord entering the inner sanctuary of heaven in 1844 to finish his work of atonement for sin. This is called his 'investigative judgement', that is, examining and revealing the life records of people to the Father and blotting out the sins that are still recorded against the believers in heaven.

Evangelicals and Adventists

Many evangelicals, however, now insist that Adventism should be regarded as a Christian church rather than a cult.

A dialogue was held in 1955-6 in America between leading evangelicals like Donald Grey Barnhouse (a Presbyterian minister in Philadelphia and editor of the influential evangelical magazine *Eternity*) and Adventists. Walter R. Martin had also been commissioned by Zondervan to write a book exposing Adventism as a cult, but after his discussions with Adventist theologians he concluded they were Christians and that Adventism was not a non-Christian cult. Dr Barnhouse and his son agreed with Martin and their conclusion was reported in *Eternity*. Martin then wrote a book called *The truth about Seventh-Day Adventism*[10], in which he demonstrated how Adventists believe all the crucial biblical truths which are necessary for salvation. Areas of disagreement, too, were pinpointed by Martin, including Adventist teachings on conditional immortality, the seventh-day sabbath, the investigative judgement, the heavenly sanctuary and the claim that Ellen White was a divinely appointed messenger of God. In his conclusion, Martin wrote, 'We trust that evangelical Christianity as a whole will extend the hand of fellowship to a group of sincere, earnest fellow Christians, distinguished though they are by some peculiar views, but members of the Body of Christ and possessors of the faith that saves.'[11]

Several Adventist ministers and members have written to me in recent years providing useful evidence that they accept unreservedly central doctrines such as justification by faith alone. Their formal statement is: 'This faith which receives salvation comes through the divine power of the Word and is the gift of God's grace. Through Christ we are justified...' It is 'the divine act by which God declares a penitent sinner righteous'.

This is further explained by a minister: 'When this declaration takes place the righteousness of Christ is imputed to the believer ... justification is by faith alone and does not have anything to do with works or merits.'

These statements are unambiguous in showing that Adventists formally embrace the biblical doctrine of justification by faith which, as Calvin observed, is 'the hinge on which all true religion turns'.

I also want to clarify the Adventists' attitude towards date-fixing in relation to the personal return of the Lord Jesus Christ in glory. While the Millerites set dates for the second coming of Christ, since their establishment as a separate movement in 1863, Seventh-Day Adventists have consistently refused to set such dates. They have taken seriously the teaching of Matthew 24:36, 42; it is wrong to link Adventists in any way with the earlier date-fixing of the Millerites or that of the Jehovah's Witnesses. However, Adventists usually reject other Calvinistic teaching like election.

The movement in the world today

Official statistics reveal that there are over 3,500,000 Adventists spread over 189 countries. A breakdown of this figure in terms of geographical location is interesting. 76% of the total membership live in Third World countries, 16% in North America, 6% in Europe and only 1% in Australia and New Zealand. By 1980 almost half of Adventist missionaries came from the Third World. Adventists maintain 433 hospitals or health-care institutes, fifty publishing houses and have the largest Protestant school system in the world. They have also been active in Britain since 1878 and now have 420 workers here. Their membership in Britain in 1970 was 12,145 and this increased to 16,831 in 1987, with an estimated membership of 22,700 in the year 2004. It was the Adventists who first used the Dial-a-Prayer for the lonely, and Five-Day Clinics for those wanting to abandon smoking; these clinics have been used now in over 100 towns and cities in Britain. They also run Britain's leading health-food company, Granose, and are involved in several health-food retail businesses. In addition, they maintain old people's homes at Oulton Broad, Norfolk; and Lundin Links, Fife; a large nursing home in Crieff, Perthshire; seven junior schools; a secondary school; and a college which prepares students

for BA and M. Div degrees. Their British headquarters stands in a large area of parkland near
the Watford exit of the M1 and they also own the
New Gallery Theatre in 123 Regent Street which
they use, among other things, as an evangelistic
centre. They also have, or use, numerous conference or youth camp centres in various parts
of Britain.

RELEVANT COMPARISONS

**Seventh-Day
Adventists**

The Bible

Adventists accept the or-
thodox biblical teaching
concerning the Trinity,
the deity and incarnation
of the Lord Jesus, including his virgin birth, the
Lord's bodily resurrection
and ascension to heaven,
and the prospect of his
personal return to earth
in glory. The sinfulness of
human nature, salvation
through Christ alone and
the necessity of the new
birth are also affirmed by
them.

There are, however,
some deviations in their
teaching, as set out here.

DEATH OF CHRIST

A distinction is made between receiving forgiveness here and the ultimate, final blotting out of sins from our records in heaven. Apart from Daniel 8:14, this view is based on Leviticus 16:14, namely, that on the Day of Atonement the sin-stained blood was taken into the Holy of Holies, but there was still need for sin to be removed by the blood which, Adventists claim, Christ has been doing in heaven since 1844.

Hebrews 9:11-12 indicates the sufficiency and finality of what Christ did on the cross (cf. v. 26).

Christ entered heaven not in 1844, but in his ascension, 'to appear for us in God's presence' (Hebrews 9:24).

'And the blood of Jesus, his Son, purifies us from all sin' (1 John 1:7). It is not past sins only that are forgiven, nor a partial forgiveness, that is obtained at Calvary.

While Hebrews 8 teaches that there is a heavenly sanctuary where Christ is the priest, it also shows that Christ has sat down there, having completed the work of atonement. Even if 'azazel' in Leviticus 16:8 refers, as Adventists claim, to Satan or an evil spirit, this does not prove that the scapegoat is Satan.

According to verses 20-22, after atoning for his personal and then for the nation's sins, Aaron as high priest put his hands on the goat while confessing the sins of Israel. These sins are symbolically laid on the head of the second goat, which is then sent into the wilderness, never to return. The symbolism is deeply significant. Through

COMPARISONS

the death of the first goat a full atonement for the people was made, typifying the sacrifice of Christ, while in the sending away of the second goat they are shown that the curse upon them due to their sins is removed for ever (see Isaiah 53:6; 2 Corinthians 5:21; Galatians 3:13).

INVESTIGATIVE JUDGEMENT

One Adventist informs me that the term 'investigative judgement' has been 'sometimes unfortunately set out' by them. However, the term is not intended to imply divine ignorance as to what happens on earth. It is for the benefit of the whole universe: 'A kind of publication of the company accounts, so to speak, for the shareholders' benefit, rather than that of the managing director ... to whom the details will be known already.' A scriptural reference used is Genesis 18:20-21 where God is described as going down to Sodom and Gomorrah to see whether what he had heard was true.

1. This term is not biblical either in terminology or content. Genesis 18:20, 21 does not support the theory at all. Notice the following points:

a. The reason for telling Abraham is not because he had a relative in Sodom but because 'all nations on earth will be blessed' through him (v. 18). The blessing to come to Lot's family, saved out of Sodom, was to come through Abraham's intercession, so Abraham needed to be informed of impending judgement.

b. Genesis 18:20-21; 19:1-29 record a temporal judgement on earth, not an investigative judgement in heaven.

Verses 17-19 indicate it was for Abraham's benefit for God 'wanted Abraham to see that he was manifestly just in what he did'. It is claimed that Christ entered the inner sanctuary of heaven in 1844 to examine and reveal the life records of people to the Father and to blot out sins still recorded against believers in heaven.

c. It is at the Final Judgement, when the Lord returns, that the whole universe will see the vindication of God's righteousness (see, for example, Romans 2:5-10, 16; 1 Corinthians 4:5; Matthew 25:31-46).

2. The distinction between 'receiving forgiveness here and now, and the ultimate blotting out of sins when things are finally wound up' is unbiblical because:

a. Justification is a judicial pronouncement by God as Judge in which he pardons all the sins of a believer because of Christ's substitutionary sacrifice and his righteousness imputed to the believer (Romans 8:30-34; 4:4-8).

b. God continues on earth to forgive the sins of those that are justified (Matthew 6:12; 1 John 1:7-9; 2:1-2).

c. The believer will always be justified (e.g. Luke 22:32; John 10:28; Hebrews 1:14).

PERSEVERANCE OF BELIEVERS

Believers can fall from grace and be eternally lost.

'I give them eternal life, and they shall never perish; no one can snatch them out of my hand' (John 10:28; cf. John 6:37-40; Romans 8:35-39; Philippians 1:6; 1 Peter 1:5).

COMPARISONS

DEATH

Between death and the resurrection the souls of believers 'sleep'.

'We ... prefer to be away from the body and at home with the Lord' (2 Corinthians 5:8).

'...desire to depart and be with Christ, which is better by far' (Philippians 1:23; cf. Psalm 73:24; Luke 16:22-31).

FUTURE STATE OF UNBELIEVERS

Satan and unbelievers will be annihilated.

'Then they will go away to eternal punishment, but the righteous to eternal life' (Matthew 25:46).

'They will be tormented day and night for ever and ever' (Revelation 20:10).

SABBATH

Mrs White claimed that in a vision she saw the ark and the Ten Commandments in heaven, but a halo of light surrounded this fourth commandment. She concluded that this was a message to stress a commandment which had been greatly neglected. On studying the history of the sabbath she concluded that Sunday observance was 'the mark of the beast' (Revelation 13), the beast being the pope.

Hebrews 4:1-10 teaches that the Sabbath rest is fulfilled when believers cease from their works.

In the New Testament there is a change from the seventh to the first day of the week as the Christian sabbath, largely because on this day the Lord both rose from the dead (John 20:1) and made his resurrection appearances to the disciples (John 20:19, 26; cf. Acts 20:6-7; 1 Corinthians 16:2; Revelation 1:10).

SECOND COMING OF CHRIST

'The Saviour's coming will be literal, personal, visible, and worldwide.'

'When he returns, the righteous dead will be resurrected and, together with the righteous living, will be glorified.'

Yes, his personal and visible return will be glorious indeed (see Matthew 24:30-31; 25:31-46; 1 Thessalonians 4:16-17).

a. Believers who die go immediately to be with the Lord (Luke 23:43; Philippians 1:21-24; 2 Corinthians 5:8).

b. The resurrection of the dead, believers and unbelievers, is clearly taught in the Bible (John 5:28-29; 1 Corinthians 15:35-58; Philippians 3:21).

'The wicked will be slain by the glory of his coming.'

Eternal, conscious punishment in hell awaits unbelievers (Matthew 25:46; Luke 16:23, 24; Revelation 14:11; 19:3; 20:10).

For a more detailed treatment, read the author's *Condemned for Ever* (Evangelical Press).

Note: Miller decided on his first date, 1843, by using Daniel 8:14 and assuming the 2,300 days here to be years. 2,300 years would elapse then before the sanctuary would be cleansed at his return. The 'seventy weeks' reference in Daniel 9:24 was interpreted as seventy weeks of years, that is 490 years before the Messiah would die

Date fixing is wrong: 'No one knows about that day or hour, not even the angels in heaven, nor the Son, but only the Father' (Matthew 24:36).

'Therefore keep watch, because you do not know on what day your Lord will come' (Matthew 24:42).

in A.D. 33. Working back 490 years Miller arrived at the date of 457 B.C. and he then added the 2,300 years of Daniel 8:14 which gave him A.D. 1843!

THE GUIDE

CHAPTER THREE

PROTESTANT CHURCHES: MODERNISM AND POST-MODERNISM

A BRIEF HISTORY

'I'm confused,' remarked a middle-aged man after attending a Protestant church service one Sunday morning. 'The preacher told us he did not believe in the Bible. He did not even believe that Jesus Christ was God or that he performed any of the miracles recorded in the Gospels.' The man was clearly upset. 'What am I to believe?' he asked. 'Who is right? I was always taught by my family and Sunday school teachers that Christ was God and that he fed the 5,000 miraculously and turned the water into wine at the wedding in Cana of Galilee.' His distress was real indeed. Eventually, however, he shrugged his shoulders and, before going into his house, said, 'I don't like all these new theories.'

Or think of a different situation. A young married couple were watching a religious discussion programme on the television. They were interested in finding out more about Christianity and how it related to their lives. Their reaction, however, was one of astonishment as the three clergymen on the programme proceeded to give their views about God, Jesus Christ, the atonement and life after death. One of them, a bishop, did not believe in the virgin birth of the Lord Jesus and could not accept the fact that the Lord Jesus had risen physically from the dead. The other two clergymen were just as sceptical. 'God is not outside or up there,' one insisted, 'but he is merely the "depth" inside your personality.' Another clergyman was unsure whether there was a heaven or hell after death. 'Perhaps, when we die,' he said, 'we just cease to exist.' At the end of the programme, the young woman turned to her husband and exclaimed, 'I thought those men were supposed to believe all those things, not deny them! Who and what are we to believe?'

The same sad story can be repeated many, many times. The winds of change have blown through many Protestant church denominations causing havoc and confusion concerning the truth. Who or what is responsible? In a word, 'modernism'. The rest of this chapter will explain what 'modernism' is and how it has affected Protestant churches.

What is modernism?

The terms 'modernism' or 'liberalism' are used to describe a critical and rational approach to the Bible which originated in Germany early in the nineteenth century and slowly extended its influence until by the early decades of the twentieth century almost the whole of Protestantism in Western Europe, and more recently Roman Catholicism, had embraced its dangerous presuppositions, methods and conclusions.

The history of modernism

One must really go back to the German phil-
osopher Immanuel Kant (1724-1804) in order
to appreciate the rise of modernism. For Kant,
knowledge must always be related to what we can
perceive by our senses (the phenomenal); but the
noumena, that is, objects like God or questions
such as immortality and salvation, are beyond
the scope of our experience and knowledge and
therefore must remain incomprehensible to us
or, at best, are matters of faith about which there
can be no certainty. The implications of this for
biblical Christianity were devastating. For example, Christian doctrines were removed from
the spheres of history and knowledge, the verbal
inspiration of the Bible was regarded as being
impossible, and attention was diverted away
from God to the individual and his or her knowledge, so that the door was respectably opened
for a thorough-going sceptical and subjective
approach to Christianity. While the Deists[1] of
the eighteenth century had denied all the supernatural elements in the Bible, and scholars like
Lessing (1729-1781) published sceptical accounts
of the life of Jesus which were later to influence
Albert Schweitzer and others, it was Kant and
his followers who gave to modernism the necessary philosophical framework and impetus in
order to develop and win the eventual approval
of Christendom.

An important landmark was the *Life of Jesus* written by the German theologian D. F. Strauss in 1835-36. Strauss's Jesus was a human, fallible person around whom the early Christians had built numerous myths in order to project him as a kind of hero-god. In 1863 J. E. Renan published a similar *Life of Jesus* in which Christ was depicted as a zealous revolutionary with a martyr complex. At the same time Albrecht Ritschl (1822-1889), the newly-appointed theology professor at Göttingen, wholeheartedly embraced Kant's philosophy and ridiculed, for example, the doctrine of Christ's atoning death and the Bible.

Near the end of the nineteenth century the church history specialist, Adolf van Harnack (1851-1930), was lecturing to enthralled audiences at Berlin University under the general title, 'What is Christianity?' Once again he viewed Jesus as an ordinary man but one who was at peace with himself and thereby able to help others as he proclaimed a moral life of love in the context of God's fatherhood.

In Britain in 1910 Arthur Drews wrote his devastating book, *The Christ Myth*, in which he claimed that the entire gospel was fictitious. During this period, Albert Schweitzer (1875-1965) became popular both as an academic and a missionary, but his *Quest of the Historical Jesus*, published in 1906, projected the image of the Lord as a sincere believer who dabbled in politics and made a mess of things as well. Schweitzer had no time for the supernatural elements in the Bible.

By the end of the nineteenth century 'higher criticism'[2] of the New Testament was firmly entrenched through the work of men like C. H. Weisse, C. G. Wilke, B. F. Westcott and H. J. Holtmann, while in the field of Old Testament study equally disastrous results emerged as Julius Wellhausen and others subjected the sacred text to a critical and sceptical analysis. For example, the authorship of most biblical books was questioned (e.g. the Mosaic authorship of the Pentateuch[3]); the historicity of Genesis chapters 1-11 was denied; and Israel's history was interpreted exclusively in terms of man's progressive search for God and for absolute standards.

Protests against modernism

We must not imagine, however, that these radical views were advocated without protest or opposition. One of the outstanding Old Testament scholars of the nineteenth century was Ernst Wilhelm Hengstenberg (1802-1869) who, after his conversion as a student in Basle, devoted himself to the study and defence of the Old Testament. Although his writings received little attention, Hengstenberg answered the critics most competently and wrote many helpful commentaries which are still in use.

In Princeton Theological Seminary, too, Charles Hodge (1797-1878), B. B. Warfield (1851-1921) and then Gresham Machen did invaluable work in expounding and upholding the biblical faith amidst great opposition.

John Urquhart also published an important book in defence of the Bible in 1895 entitled *The inspiration and accuracy of the Holy Scripture*. 'Criticism', he affirms in the preface, 'has reached certain conclusions regarding various books of Scripture. The older narratives are declared to be mere legends, and the history generally is described as tradition tinctured by the time when it was put into writing. Certain books of the Old Testament are said to fall below even this low level. They are declared to be fictions … and all these conclusions are placed before the public as genuine scientific discoveries.'[4] But Urquhart was not content merely to trace the development of this critical approach and question some of its conclusions. More importantly he deemed it 'essential to ascertain, first of all, what the scriptural view of inspiration is. How did inspired men regard the words which they and others have handed on to us and, above all, how did our Lord receive them? A clear and full answer to that question is the need of the hour. Once got, it would settle this controversy for many.'[5]

Concluding his discussion of the Lord's endorsement of the Old Testament, Urquhart writes, 'If our Master is to be judge in this matter, or if we are to give heed to the testimony of His apostles and of the Scriptures… doubt is no longer possible as to the reality or the extent of the Inspiration of the Bible. The Book has God for its Author. Its every utterance and its every word are His. But this testimony is openly set aside or silently ignored

WHAT MODERNISM TEACHES

by those who claim to be heard as authorities in the Christian Church. The so-called Higher Criticism sits unchallenged in our Divinity Halls, our Colleges, and our Universities. It is moulding the future ministry of every denomination in the land. It is issuing textbooks, commentaries, treatises, and magazine articles in which the public is informed that the former teaching regarding the Bible can no longer be maintained.'[6]

Modernism asserts its stranglehold

Despite the defence of the faith by such competent men, modernism continued to consolidate its stranglehold on Christendom in the first half of the twentieth century. In Britain, for example, men like A. S. Peake, W. R. Inge, Wheeler Robinson, J. Baillie and C. H. Dodd were prominent, while on the Continent theologians such as Paul Tillich and Karl Barth refined the new theology (in radically different ways). Rudolf Bultmann's influence on New Testament studies has been devastating, with his insistence that the Gospels (which he says were glamourized by the early church) must be demythologized before we can discover the authentic meaning of the text. His antagonism to orthodox, biblical Christianity is uncompromising. 'The task of theology', claims Bultmann, 'is to imperil souls,

to lead men into doubt, to shatter all naïve credulity...
I often have the impression that my conservative New
Testament colleagues feel very uncomfortable for I see
them perpetually engaged in salvage operations. I let
the fire burn.' When asked who Jesus was and what he
was like, Bultmann replied, 'I do not know and do not
want to know.'[7]

Tillich, too, rejected orthodoxy in favour of a sceptical, existentialist approach to truth. Deriding the
biblical teaching of God's wrath, he wrote that people
receive forgiveness in spite of the Saviour's death, not
because of it, while the claim that God has become
man he regards as not just paradoxical but actually
nonsensical. Tillich regards the New Testament narratives of the crucifixion of the Lord as 'contradictory
legendary reports' and the resurrection, too, is deprived
of all historicity and interpreted in psychological terms
as the Lord's restoration to dignity in the minds of the
disciples. While pursuing a distinguished academic
career, Tillich lived an immoral life and when he was
dying he not only spoke at length about the *Tibetan
Book of the Dead*, but he refused to have the Bible read
to him.[8]

First in a newspaper article and then in a small
paperback entitled *Honest to God*, published in March
1963, the views of Tillich, Bultmann and Bonhöffer
were popularized by the then Bishop of Woolwich, Dr
John A. T. Robinson. According to the bishop, Jesus
was God only in the sense that he gave us insights
into God at work, whereas the atonement was the

complete self-surrender of Jesus to people, in love, rather than a sacrifice for sin. Similarly he explains prayer away as a 'listening, when we take the otherness of the other person most seriously'. Nor does he believe in the objective commands of God as expressed, for example, in the Ten Commandments. He prefers to advocate 'situation ethics', in which the rightness or wrongness of stealing, adultery and murder must be decided personally in each situation.

Within the mainline churches, the situation has continued to deteriorate, as is evidenced by the publication of books like *The Myth of God Incarnate* in 1977, in which the deity of Christ was again rejected by important church dignitaries. This book was a collection of essays by seven British theologians, edited by John Hick, who also wrote the concluding essay, 'Jesus and the world religions'. Here Hick rejects the traditional Christology of Chalcedon and Nicæa as 'mythical … traditional language'; for Hick, Christ was only a man. To be precise, Hick regards Jesus as the largely unknown man of Nazareth. He regards the claim to deity as part of the 'mythical' structure of the New Testament; its true meaning, he says, is not literal but poetic and symbolic.

This argument is really a rehash of what other critical scholars have taught for decades and it evidences Hick's liberal approach to Scripture and his denial of the supernatural. John Hick is now one of the leading proponents of the view that 'God' alone, not Christ, is at the centre of religions, including Christianity. He insists that all religions and 'holy' books are equally valid for they express man's search for the one universal God.

In the late 1980s the Rt Rev. Dr David Jenkins, the then Bishop of Durham, denied major Christian doctrines including the physical resurrection of Christ. His Easter message in 1989 affirmed that Christ's resurrection was only 'spiritual not physical... It means a spiritual resurrection, a transforming resurrection.' While many Bible-believing Anglicans were outraged over the bishop's remarks, the Bishop of Manchester came to his colleague's defence by saying that Dr Jenkins was not alone in his beliefs. Sadly, modernism is still deeply entrenched and influential in Protestant churches at the beginning of the twenty-first century.

Postmodernism

Today, however, it is not 'modernism' which troubles the church but rather 'postmodernism'. The latter has been an insidious, undermining influence on the Christian Church and its message over the last couple of decades at least. To put it simply, postmodernism has lots of assumptions; the major assumption, however, is that ultimate, objective truth does not exist. There are no absolutes at all for postmodernists; no absolute, final revelation, no absolute truths and certainly no universal or absolute values and laws which are binding on people.

The question now has changed. It is no longer a question of whether something is true or false. That is not a proper question. Rather, the question becomes relative: do I like it and want it? Morals are now a matter of personal 'desire' and convenience, rather than conforming to objective laws and certainly not divinely given laws.

Strangely, there are those who prefer to be identified as 'post-evangelical'. One example of this is Dave Tomlinson in his book *The Post Evangelical*.[9] What, according to Tomlinson, do post-evangelicals believe? 'For evangelicals,' he informs us, 'truth is a very clear cut issue', whereas post-evangelicals 'find themselves instinctively drawn towards an understanding of truth which is more relative' (p. 87). He adds: 'Doctrinal correctness matters little to God and labels matter less; honesty, openness and a sincere searching for truth, on the other hand, matter a great deal' (p. 61).

Not only is this postmodernist approach controversial; it is unbiblical.

Decline in the churches

Neither modernism nor postmodernism has attracted people to church in Britain or overseas.

Consider, for example, the plight of Canada's largest Protestant denomination, the United Church of Canada (UCC). Reginald Bibby, the head of the sociology department at the University of Lethbridge, Alberta, made a detailed survey early in 1982 of religious life in the country and particularly among members of the UCC (a project supported by the UCC, the Canadian Government and the Canadian Broadcasting Corporation). 'Organized religion in Canada is experiencing a dramatic drop-off,' reports Bibby, 'churches are losing many of their once active members and adherents, while failing to replenish such losses…' Only about 40% of UCC members claim to believe in the existence of God and the deity of Christ, and only a small proportion attend church regularly and practise private prayer, while personal Bible-reading is 'virtually non-existent'. The survey shows that whereas in 1956 61% of Canadians said they had attended church during the previous week, only 35% had done so in 1978 and Sunday school attendance slumped from 570,000 to 242,000. The decline has continued unabated.

The story is no better in Britain. The steady decline in Protestant church attendance and membership has turned in recent years into a dramatic collapse, with the result that many churches have either closed or are unable to support a full-time ministry. For example, between 1960-2000 church membership in Britain fell as much as 40% with 6,000 churches closing. At its peak in 1930, the ten-million-plus church members were 31% of the adult population, whereas by 2000 it had fallen to 12%. Protestant and Catholic churches have an acute shortage of ministers and an increasing number of churches are grouped together under the pastoral care of a single minister.

Since the early 1970s many Christians, including pastors, have felt compelled to withdraw from churches and denominations where the Bible is not taught faithfully and a significant number of new evangelical churches have been established throughout England and Wales. In this respect the work of the Universities and Colleges Christian Fellowship among students,[10] the more varied ministry of the Evangelical Movement of Wales,[11] the publishing work of the Banner of Truth Trust and Evangelical Press, and the powerful preaching ministry of the late Dr Martyn Lloyd-Jones have all had a formative influence in the establishing of Bible-teaching churches and the propagation of biblical truth.

However, even amongst evangelicals there is disturbing evidence of a growing departure from orthodoxy and this is reflected in different ways. Some scholars have conceded too much to the critical approach, whereas the charismatic movement tends to affirm the primacy of experience at the expense of biblical doctrine. Others have qualified and redefined the doctrine of Scripture in order to allow for what they consider to be errors and contradictions, while yet others are focusing attention on annihilation rather than the eternal punishment of unbelievers. More than ever before, believers today must 'contend for the faith that was once for all entrusted to the saints' (Jude 3), and this involves rejecting modernism in whatever form it appears.

In the 2001 Census, more than thirty-seven million people in England and Wales claimed Christianity as their religion. Caution is needed in responding to this statistic because it includes all denominations, including nominal 'Christians' and even those who may not go to church but see themselves for various reasons as 'Christian'.

However, the statistic is encouraging because Britain is not such a multi-faith society as has been claimed and the majority of the population felt more affinity with Christianity. Here is a challenge and encouragement to engage more wholeheartedly in biblical evangelism.

RELEVANT COMPARISONS

Modernism/ postmodernism	The Bible

GOD

God is love and is incapable of wrath.	God's wrath is the controlled and necessary reaction of his holy nature against all sin, necessitating the punishment of sin (Habakkuk 1:13; Romans 1:18-23; 2:5-16). There is no contradiction in the Bible between the love and wrath of

COMPARISONS

God is the 'God above God', with the result that man can never define or describe him in any objective or absolute way. 'He is the Ground of Being. God is present in all those activities which unite people rather than divide them, which call upon persons to transcend self-interest through brotherhood and sisterhood.'[12]

The Trinity is only a symbol originally introduced to safeguard and express man's diverse but unified experience of the Father, Son and Holy Spirit. John T. Robinson, for example, denies any objective validity to the doctrine and interprets it exclusively and subjectively as 'entering into a shared life with others and God'.[13]

God, for even at Calvary, where God's love was supremely manifested, God's wrath also fell upon Christ when he died as our substitute (Romans 3:25-26; Galatians 3:13-14; 1 John 4:10).

Finite creatures like ourselves cannot comprehend the infinite (Job 11:7), yet God has revealed himself to us in his perfections (i.e. power, holiness, love, etc.) in creation and especially in the Bible so that we have an accurate though not exhaustive knowledge of God. To deny this leads inevitably to scepticism and subjectivism.

Within the one Godhead, there are three distinguishable but equal persons.

'Hear, O Israel: The LORD our God, the LORD is one' (Deuteronomy 6:4).
'... baptizing them in the name of the Father and of the Son and of the Holy Spirit' (Matthew 28:19).

BIBLE

A human book, full of mistakes, which describes man's experience of, and thinking about, God.

Because it was written in a cultural context, its statements are relative and personal, being 'the natural by-products of a community's struggle with questions of meaning and faith'.

Reason rather than the Bible is the supreme authority.[14]

'All your words are true' (Psalm 119:160).

'Your word is truth' (John 17:17).

'Men spoke from God as they were carried along by the Holy Spirit' (2 Peter 1:21).

CREATION

The creation narratives in Genesis 1 and 2 are 'myths' and are not in any sense historical or literal. Man has evolved over billions of years.

'Haven't you read, that at the beginning the Creator "made them male and female"?' (Matthew 19:4).

'Through him all things were made; without him nothing was made that has been made' (John 1:3).

PERSON OF CHRIST

A significant number of modernists now question or deny the deity of Christ. Some have used the phrase 'emptied himself' (NASB) from Philippians 2:7 to suggest that the Lord laid aside his deity so that while on earth he was fallible and frequently in error in his

According to Philippians 2:7 and other Scripture references, the Saviour remained God even after his incarnation. He made himself nothing or 'emptied' himself in the sense of veiling his visible glory as God the Son when he voluntarily assumed our human nature and

COMPARISONS

teaching. This is called the 'kenosis theory'.

submitted himself to the Father and the law.

VIRGIN BIRTH OF CHRIST

Untrue and impossible! 'To say that new life was fathered and quickened in Mary by the Spirit of God, is a profound way of expressing an inner truth about Jesus. It is to say that his birth and life cannot simply be thought of as biological events: his significance lies much deeper than that ... we are not bound to think of the Virgin Birth as a physical event in order to believe that Jesus's whole life is "of God"'.[15]

'For nothing is impossible with God' (Luke 1:37).

'The Holy Spirit will come upon you, and the power of the Most High will overshadow you. So the holy one to be born will be called the Son of God' (Luke 1:35; cf. Matthew 1:20).

MIRACLES OF CHRIST

The miracle stories are all 'myths' which teach and remind us of that which 'becomes possible when the power of love is really let loose'.[16]

The healing of Peter's mother-in-law in Mark 1:30-31 is explained in this way: 'She was just fed up with Peter spending all his time going around with Jesus instead of looking after her daughter. But when Jesus

Three words are used by Luke in Acts 2:22 to describe the miracles of the Lord Jesus. The first word, translated 'miracles', comes from the Greek word *dunamis*, meaning 'powerful works', and emphasizes the extraordinary manifestation of divine power on these occasions. They were not psychological or ordinary happenings in nature.

The second, 'wonders',

came to her house and she saw the sort of person he was, she wanted to get up and do things for people. There's the power of love, overcoming resentment and the physical protest in which it found outlet. And that's why Jesus saw that so often what was needed was a spiritual miracle — the putting right of a person's whole inner outlook on life.'

Dr Schweitzer explained the feeding of the 5,000 in John 6 as a mere sharing of the boy's food so that all present had at least a crumb or taste of food! John Robinson also calls it the 'miracle of sharing'.[17]

describes the astonishment of the people when they witnessed these miracles (e.g. Mark 2:12; Luke 5:9; Matthew 15:30-31), whereas the third word, 'signs', emphasizes the purposefulness of the miracles: they had deep spiritual significance and pointed to himself (see Luke 7:22; John 2:11; 3:2; 5:36; 9:35-38).

DEATH OF CHRIST

Apart from expressing God's love and setting an example to us in love and patient suffering, the Saviour's death has no saving value.

'Since we have now been justified by his blood, how much more shall we be saved from God's wrath through him! For if, when we were God's enemies, we were reconciled to him through the death of his Son, how much more, having been reconciled, shall we be saved through his life' (Romans 5:9-10).

The doctrine of salvation through the 'blood of Christ' is regarded as offensive and immoral.

'How much more, then, will the blood of Christ, who through the eternal Spirit offered himself unblemished to God, cleanse our consciences from acts that lead to death, so that we may serve the living God!' (Hebrews 9:14).

'But when this priest had offered for all time one sacrifice for sins, he sat down at the right hand of God ... because by one sacrifice he has made perfect for ever those who are being made holy' (Hebrews 10:12-14).

In Genesis 9:4; Leviticus 17:11 and Deuteronomy 12:23 we are told that the blood is the life (of the flesh) so that blood shed is a witness to physical death. In the New Testament the phrase 'blood of Christ' is mentioned nearly three times more often than the 'cross' and five times more frequently than the 'death' of Christ. The phrase, 'blood of Christ', therefore is the most frequent way of referring to the Saviour's sacrifice and it witnesses to the physical, sacrificial death of the Lord Jesus as he bore away our sin (Romans 3:25; 5:9; Ephesians 1:7; 1 Peter 1:18-19; Revelation 1:5; 5:9).

RESURRECTION OF CHRIST

We can never know what happened to the Lord's body.

Various views are held. For example, Christ arose in spirit only, not bodily or, more radically, he did not rise at all except in the minds of the early believers, so the resurrection narratives need to be demythologized.

Read carefully Luke 24:39-44; John 2:19-22; 20:27-28; Acts 2:23-32; 1 Corinthians 15:4-7.

'If Christ has not been raised, your faith is futile; you are still in your sins... But Christ has indeed been raised from the dead' (1 Corinthians 15:17-20).

ASCENSION OF CHRIST

Christ did not literally and physically ascend into heaven; Luke fabricated the story. 'The truth of the ascension is that Christ after his resurrection is a necessary part of the true idea of God and ... controls the entire universe so the ascension is the most political of all Christian doctrines.'[18]

'He appeared in a body, was vindicated by the Spirit, was seen by angels, was preached among the nations, was believed on in the world, was taken up in glory' (1 Timothy 3:16).

'...who has gone into heaven and is at God's right hand' (1 Peter 3:22; cf. Acts 1:9-11; 2:32-36).

SALVATION

Faith in Christ is not essential to salvation. Atheists and people of all religions will be saved. Missionary work is discouraged or regarded primarily as humanitarian.

'Salvation is found in no one else, for there is no other name under heaven given to men by which we must be saved' (Acts 4:12).

CHURCH

All churches, whatever their beliefs, are equally valid and members and adherents are assumed to be Christians in

'To the church of the Thessalonians in God the Father and the Lord Jesus Christ' (1 Thessalonians 1:1) — a people in

COMPARISONS

virtue of their attendance and activities.

spiritual fellowship with God, converted (1:9) and examples to others (1:6; cf. 1 Corinthians 1:2; Colossians 1:2-8).

HELL

A revolting, pagan doctrine; God does not punish sinners.

'For wide is the gate, and broad is the road that leads to destruction, and many enter through it. But small is the gate and narrow the road that leads to life, and only a few find it' (Matthew 7:13-14).

'Then they will go away to eternal punishment, but the righteous to eternal life' (Matthew 25:46).

SECOND COMING OF CHRIST

It is 'the greatest phantasmagoria in the whole collection of mumbo jumbo that goes under the name of Christian doctrine... The Second Coming ... stands for the conviction that — however long it takes — Christ must come into everything. There's no part of life from which he can or will be left out.'[19]

'They will see the Son of Man coming on the clouds of the sky, with power and great glory' (Matthew 24:30; cf. 1 Thessalonians 4:16-17; 2 Peter 3:3-13).

'The Spirit clearly says that in later times some will abandon the faith and follow deceiving spirits and things taught by demons...' (1 Timothy 4:1; cf. 2 Timothy 4:3-5).

Bibliography

The following books have been used as representative samples of contemporary modernist and post-modernist teaching:

John A. T. Robinson, *But that I can't believe!* Collins, 1967.

The Nature of Christian Belief: A statement and exposition by the House of Bishops of the General Synod of the Church of England, Church House Publishing, London 1986.

David Edwards with John Stott, *Essentials*, Hodder & Stoughton, 1988.

Paul Badham, *The Contemporary Challenge of Modernist Theology*, University of Wales Press, 1998.

Dave Tomlinson, *The Post Evangelical*, SPCK, 1995.

A helpful biblical response is provided by:

David F. Wells, *No Place for Truth*, IVP, 1993.

CHAPTER FOUR

ROMAN CATHOLICISM

A BRIEF HISTORY

'Today for the first time in history a bishop of Rome sets foot on English soil and I am deeply moved at this thought,' declared Pope John Paul II as he spoke in Westminster Cathedral on 28 May 1982. *The Times* described this visit as 'Pope John Paul's historic pilgrimage of faith'. It was certainly a historic visit. He was also the first pope to visit Canterbury Cathedral and his agreement with Archbishop Runcie to study and pursue further the union of their respective churches has had, and will continue to have, a radical impact on the future of interchurch relationships. Again, the celebration of the mass by the pope in Coventry before an estimated congregation of 350,000 was the 'largest known gathering of Roman Catholics in England', and the papal mass in Cardiff on 2 June before a crowd of 100,000 was the largest Roman Catholic gathering ever held in Wales. The tumultuous welcome given to the pope earned him the titles 'the first pop-star pope', 'the top of the popes' and the 'people's pope'.

In the wake of this historic papal visit, some may accuse me of being ungracious and unfair in including the Roman Catholic Church in this book alongside the more obviously heretical groups of churches such as Jehovah's Witnesses or the Unitarian Church. Such disquiet is expressed in several ways and we must briefly consider two of these objections before we discuss in detail the errors of Rome.

For example, in this ecumenical age when churches are coming closer together, is it right to be critical of Roman Catholicism? Should we not accept and respect each other's positions and work together in love for church unity?

In support of this objection, one can point to the considerable improvement in church relationships at local and national levels. For example, the British Council of Churches has established more than 300 ecumenical projects in England and Wales where buildings, ministries, Sunday schools and day schools are shared by different denominations. Addressing the General Synod of the Church of England in February 1982, Dr Runcie, the Archbishop of Canterbury, called on all Christians to welcome the pope and be optimistic about the prospect for unity and not to give way to prejudice and insularity. 'The pope's willingness to attend the service at Canterbury', he affirmed, 'has already made a contribution to the seriousness and urgency of our search for unity.' Speaking in Canterbury on 29 May 1982, the pope himself replied in a similar way: 'I appeal to you in this holy place, fellow-Christians and especially members of the Church of England and the Anglican Communion throughout the world, to accept the commitment to which Dr Runcie and I pledge

WHAT IT TEACHES

ourselves anew before you today … praying and working for ecclesiastical unity.'

When the pope later met Protestant church leaders in Cardiff he expressed publicly his pleasure in learning of the co-operation between different denominations in Wales, as this bore 'witness to the desire to fulfil God's will for our unity with him and each other in Christ'. Clearly *The Times* was correct in stating that 'The ecumenical movement has been given a boost beyond anyone's expectations because of the pope's visit and because of the way the pope conducted himself while he was here,' and we have entered a new era of openness and of more deliberate and determined plans for the merging of mainline denominations.

Dare we go against the stream, then? Ought we to criticize a church that is seeking closer links with Protestantism? My answer is a positive one. Christian unity is important and it is the duty of the Lord's people to maintain, express and develop the unity which the Holy Spirit has established between believers (Ephesians 4:3). However, such unity must never be sought at the expense of truth. When, therefore, a church is in error concerning key doctrines such as sin, the atonement, justification by faith etc., and thereby propagates a gospel different from that of the New Testament we can neither co-operate with such a church nor support it. Our supreme test here is not sentiment or popular opinion but the Bible.

The objection is expressed differently, too. Are there not radical changes occurring within the Roman Catholic Church — changes both in outlook and in dogma? If this is so then, it is argued, we should not dismiss Rome as being heretical.

Changes are certainly taking place within the Roman Catholic Church and nowhere is this seen more dramatically than in the largest Catholic order, the Society of Jesus, founded originally in 1540 to counter the Protestant Reformation. This society, popularly known as the Jesuits, has a world membership of 26,000 and 600 priests. Their devotion both to the pope and Roman Catholic dogma has been proverbial and exemplary since the Counter-Reformation, but in the past thirty years, particularly since Vatican II, they have led in the more progressive and radical developments within the church by championing such things as new forms of liturgy, liberation theology in Latin America and modernist theology, in which some have even questioned the deity of Christ. Some Jesuits have also adopted a more 'relaxed' sexual lifestyle and regard celibacy as inappropriate outside the monastery. Jesuits are reported as being active in revolutionary movements in Guatemala, El Salvador and Nicaragua, while in the Philippines a Jesuit priest was accused of plotting to undermine the government. These alarming trends have troubled recent popes, but Pope John Paul II has rebuked the Jesuits and has appointed a man of his own choice, Paola Dezza, as the superior-general of the order with the purpose of bringing its members to heel.

These developments and changes among the Jesuits are reflected more widely throughout the Roman Church. The modern critical approach to the Bible, for example, outlawed by the pope in 1907 and in disfavour until the late 1950s, is now openly espoused by the majority of Catholic scholars, while a few, like Hans Küng, now reject the dogma of papal infallibility. There is also a strong charismatic faction under the leadership of Cardinal Suenens, who has helped to accommodate the Catholic charismatic renewal to formal Catholic dogma and polity.

Rather than signalling a return to Bible doctrines, these changes and developments within the Roman Catholic Church have served to undermine the Bible and to encourage the reinterpretation of the gospel in political or sacramental terms. Despite his charisma, the present pope belongs to the conservative or traditional wing of the church which seeks to propagate, not change, its unbiblical teachings.

One of our responsibilities as believers in our contemporary situation is that of contending 'for the faith that was once for all entrusted to the saints' (Jude 3) and distinguishing between 'the spirit of truth and the spirit of falsehood' (1 John 4:6). For this reason the teachings of the Roman

Catholic Church are here tested by the supreme standard of the Bible, and readers will quickly discover the error of Rome on many key doctrines. Concerning such important issues we dare not compromise or be silent, whatever people may think or say.

When the pope went to Scotland on 1 June 1982 to meet his flock of 820,000 he was welcomed in the courtyard of New College, Edinburgh, by the Moderator of the Church of Scotland and the brief ceremony took place under the shadow of the statue of the Scottish Protestant Reformer, John Knox. Was that significant? Certainly. The gospel preached by John Knox was thoroughly biblical, apostolic and Christ-exalting but radically different from that which the pope brought to Britain. Sadly, however, such differences are no longer important to many Protestants in Britain and are regarded as ancient and irrelevant disputes. Is the Roman Catholic Church in error? Are these differences of secondary importance? Read the following section carefully and discover for yourself what God declares in his infallible Word, and then make the Bible your supreme standard by which you judge truth and error. Do not be afraid of being thought narrow.

'Yes,' writes Dr Martyn Lloyd-Jones, 'we do think that we are right; but we are not alone. The great stream of evangelical witness runs down through the centuries of Church history. The gates of hell have not prevailed and will not finally prevail against it. We believe as our evangelical forefathers did, and we must be prepared for the reproaches of "intolerance" and "bigotry" which they also bore... The charge of intolerance is a compliment. For, surely, if your position is that in which God has ordained His elect should stand, we must necessarily be intolerant of all that would divert us from it. We believe and hold to it. We must be prepared to sacrifice everything for it. We must be like Martin Luther when he stood alone against the authority of the Roman Church...We must be like the Puritans, who were prepared to forsake their emoluments rather than to compromise on such principles. We must be humbly aggressive in propagating the true faith, and patiently adamant in the true gospel's defence — if need be, to the utmost degrees of sacrifice.'[1]

Over the past thirty years, however, some conservative evangelicals like J. I. Packer have sought to identify areas of doctrinal agreement with the more conservative Anglo-Catholics.[2] Furthermore, there has been dialogue also between some evangelicals and Roman Catholics. For example, between 1977 and 1984 there was a joint, unofficial dialogue on mission; evangelical participants included Martin Goldsmith, David Wells, Harvie Conn and John Stott. They were not committed to organic unity but rather to 'a search for such common ground as might be discovered between Evangelicals and Roman Catholics which harm our witness to the gospel, contradict our Lord's prayer for unity of his followers, and need if possible to be overcome'.[3]

Important theological differences were recognized but the report suggested co-operation in Bible translation and publishing, the use of media, community service, social thought and action, dialogue then informal prayer groups.

This dialogue, but in different contexts, has continued. In the United States during the early 1990s, Charles Colson, the Prison Fellowship Ministry leader, and Richard Newhans, the editor of the Catholic journal *First Things*, launched a new movement seeking to network leaders from different Christian traditions. Acting unofficially, they published three documents under the names of both Evangelical and Catholic leaders. The first document was published in 1994 under the title *Evangelicals and Catholics Together* and its initials ECT are used now to identify this movement.

Their second document in 1997, *The Gift of Salvation*, argued — unsuccessfully — that the two communities are agreed on the doctrine of justification by faith alone! In 2002, the third document, *Your Word is Truth*, appeared and it was concerned with the authority of Scripture.

One feature of the three documents is that they discuss doctrinal differences in an open and non-confrontational manner. However, all three documents demonstrate that there is no fundamental agreement on gospel Christianity.

Sadly, we fear that gospel distinctives are being blurred by co-operation on the part of some evangelicals and Roman Catholics. For example, Scripture Union recently appointed Jim Donnan, a practising Roman

Catholic, as its General Director in the Republic of Ireland. Both Donnan and Rev. David Bruce, the Northern Ireland S. U. Director, were signatories to the 1998 *Evangelicals and Catholics Together in Ireland* document.

Another example of co-operation between Catholics and Evangelicals that causes distress to many Protestants is the decision of Scripture Gift Mission to include a practising Roman Catholic as a member of its Irish Council.

RELEVANT COMPARISONS

BIBLE

The Bible plus the fifteen books of the Apocrypha and tradition as interpreted by the Roman Catholic Church are equally authoritative.

1. The sixty-six canonical books of the Bible are a sufficient revelation of God to man and sufficient for all matters of faith and conduct (cf. 2 Timothy 3:15-16; Luke 16:29; Acts 17:11).

2. Whenever the Lord Jesus spoke of tradition, he condemned it and warned his people against it (see Matthew 15:3,6,9; Mark 7:8-9, 13; cf. Deuteronomy 4:2; Colossians 2:8; Revelation 22:18-19).

3. The church both in the Old and New Testaments submitted itself to the Word of God proclaimed by the prophets and apostles.

4. Concerning the Apocrypha:

a. There is no record of Christ quoting from or referring to it. This is surprising as he would have known about the existence of at least some of these writings.

b. There were two versions of the Old Testament in circulation at the time of the Lord's earthly ministry, namely, the Hebrew Old Testament (without the apocryphal books) and the Greek translation of the Hebrew Old Testament made in Alexandria and called the Septuagint, which included twelve or more apocryphal books. While this 'Septuagint' translation was popular in Palestine the Lord did not endorse the apocryphal section or refer to it.

c. It was almost 2,000 years after the completion of the Old Testament that the Roman Catholic Church (at the Council of Trent in 1546) 'added' the apocryphal books to the Old Testament. Several members in this council disagreed with the decision.

d. The apocryphal books are inferior in content, style and reliability, and teach unbiblical ideas such as purgatory and salvation by works.

Everywhere in the Bible the sufficiency of the Old and New Testaments is assumed — they alone are authoritative, final and adequate, thus determining all matters of faith and conduct so that no extra-biblical tradition is required.

POPE

The pope (from the Latin papa meaning 'father') is regarded as the vicar of Christ on the earth, taking the place of Jesus Christ in the world. He is also the ruler of the world and supreme over all.

It was the emperor Phocas in A.D. 604 who first used and applied the title of 'pope' to Gregory I. While Gregory established the power and supremacy of the Bishop of Rome, he refused to accept the title 'pope', but a successor, Boniface III, accepted it and it has been used ever since to describe the Bishop of Rome.

Vatican I in 1870 claimed supreme authority and infallibility for the pope in all aspects of

1. The Lord Jesus warns us not to call any man 'father' — that is, in a spiritual context.

2. The position of a pope as an overlord ruling over all believers is forbidden in 1 Peter 5:3.

3. Concerning the apostolic succession of bishops, the Bible teaches: firstly, the uniqueness of the apostles as eyewitnesses of the resurrection (Acts 1:21-22); secondly, apostolic succession means believing and teaching only what the Lord and the original apostles taught. The test is doctrinal and biblical (Galatians 1:8-9; Ephesians 2:20; 1 Timothy 6:3-5; 2 Timothy 1:13-14).

faith and morals, particularly when he speaks ex cathedra, that is, officially. Vatican II, in its decree on the constitution of the church called the *Lumen Gentium*, modified the authority of the pope somewhat, claiming that when the bishops as successors of the apostles act together to define questions of faith and morals they thus teach infallibly. At present some Catholic scholars, like Hans Küng in his book *Infallible?*, have questioned this traditional doctrine of papal infallibility.

PETER

On the basis of Matthew 16:13-19, they wrongly claim that Christ appointed Peter as the first pope and Bishop of Rome.

'And I tell you that you are Peter, and on this rock I will build my church...' (Matthew 16:18).

While the Greek word 'Peter' here is masculine (*Petros*) and refers to a person, the word 'rock' (*Petra*) is feminine, referring not to Peter but to his confession that Jesus is 'the Christ, the Son of the living God' (v. 16). Christ builds his church not upon a man but on the truth that Peter confessed (cf. 1 Corinthians 3:11; Ephesians 2:20).

'I will give you the keys

COMPARISONS

of the kingdom of heaven; whatever you bind on earth will be bound in heaven, and whatever you loose on earth will be loosed in heaven' (Matthew 16:19).

According to verses 1 and 18 in Matthew 18 this authority was given to all the disciples, not only to Peter. The authority our Lord speaks of here is that of opening the kingdom of heaven to people through the preaching of the gospel. This was not an absolute power to exclude or admit people to heaven but a declarative power only, that is, authority to proclaim the conditions on which God is prepared to forgive and save sinners.

In Acts 2:14-42 (see especially v. 21) Peter did this through preaching, and later in Acts 10:34-43 he had the privilege of preaching the same gospel to Cornelius, thus opening the door to the Gentiles, but such authority, or 'keys', was given to all the apostles, then to others like evangelists and pastors.

Note also:

1. Peter nowhere claims in the Bible to be a bishop or pope in Rome (see 1 Peter 1:1; 5:1-3; Acts 10:25-26).
2. Paul was called to be an apostle independently of Peter (see Galatians 1) and that Peter was not more important than Paul is evident in 2 Corinthians 12:11 and Galatians 2:7, 11-14. Again, it was not Peter but James who chaired the church council in Jerusalem in Acts 15.
3. There is no evidence that Peter was ever in Rome, and even Paul's letter to the Romans includes no reference at all to Peter, which would have been strange if Peter was a bishop there.
4. Neither are the words, 'Strengthen your brothers,' in Luke 22:31-32 unique to Peter, as Rome teaches. Luke uses the words to describe Paul's work in Acts 14:22; 15:32, 41; 18:23.

Similarly, the command to 'feed the flock' in John 21:15-17 was not exclusive to Peter, for Paul uses one of the words in describing the work of elders at Ephesus in Acts 20:28.

THE GUIDE

COMPARISONS

PRIESTS

The priest is a special person who, by the sacrament of ordination, receives special grace and authority to act in the place of Christ, communicating spiritual life and grace to people. He is able, for example, to hear confession and forgive sins, to offer Christ as a sacrifice in the mass, to baptize and hereby make children or adults Christians. He also has the task of administering 'extreme unction' before individual Catholics die.

Without the help of the priesthood, salvation is impossible and the church would be unable to fulfil her divine mission.

In the New Testament there is only one priest, namely, Jesus Christ, the great High Priest who offered himself as the sufficient and final sacrifice for sins (Hebrews 7:17, 24-27; 10:12-14). Christ is, therefore, the only mediator between God and men (1 Timothy 2:5), so there is no need for priests to mediate for us.

The Old Testament priesthood, like the system of sacrifice and temple worship, was temporary. It pointed to, and found its fulfilment in, Christ, so after the Lord's incarnation and sacrifice the priesthood was abolished.

Church officers are never described as 'priests' in the New Testament and even the apostle Peter described himself as a 'fellow-elder' (1 Peter 5:1) and not as a priest. While the book of Acts, for example, refers to the establishing of many Christian churches, there is no reference at all to a sacrificing priesthood. The Swiss Catholic theologian

Hans Küng has shown convincingly that the theory of the Roman priesthood emerged and developed between the fifth and thirteenth centuries.

According to 1 Peter 2:5, 9 and Revelation 1:6, all believers are priests and have the privilege of direct access to God through Christ (Hebrews 10:19; 4:16), the right and duty of praying for others (Ephesians 6:18) and offering, not an atoning sacrifice, but spiritual sacrifices of praise (Hebrews 13:15), monetary gifts (Hebrews 13:16) and themselves in service to God (Romans 12:1).

This biblical truth of the priesthood of all believers was rediscovered in the Protestant Reformation of the sixteenth century and needs to be re-emphasized today.

TRANSUBSTANTIATION

This doctrine, first formulated in the ninth century and officially accepted in 1215, refers to the communion, when the priest claims to change the bread and wine into the physical body and blood of Christ; even individual particles of bread or drops of wine become the entire Christ.

1. The Lord was still present in the flesh when he spoke the words, 'This is my body', so there could have been no literal identification of the bread with his own body (Matthew 26:26).
2. Many other sayings of the Lord, such as 'I am the door', must be interpreted symbolically, not literally.

3. Even after Jesus said, 'This is my body', he still regarded the wine a few moments later only as wine and certainly not as his literal blood (see Matthew 26:29; Luke 22:18).

4. Nor does John 6:33 support the teaching of Rome, for in verse 63 the Lord stresses that the words have a spiritual meaning. To eat and drink is to trust Christ, as in verse 35.

5. Before Christ ascended to heaven he promised to come to us not in the sacrament of the mass but by the Holy Spirit (John 16:7), but at the end of the world he will return personally and visibly to the world (Acts 1:11). In the Lord's Supper, therefore, we proclaim the Saviour's death 'until he comes' (1 Corinthians 11:26).

6. At the Council of Constance in 1415 it was agreed to withhold the cup from the congregation lest the wine — or, for the Roman church, the literal blood of the Lord — be spilt. This was not,

however, the practice in the New Testament. Our Lord told his disciples, 'Drink from it, all of you' (Matthew 26:27), and Mark records, 'They all drank from it' (14:23). The Corinthian believers also all drank of the wine (1 Corinthians 11:25-29).

MASS

The most important part of Roman Catholic worship is the mass when the priest is supposed to offer Christ as a sacrifice to God the Father on behalf of the living and the dead. It is the same sacrifice as Calvary but offered differently.

1. The Lord's Supper must be observed 'in remembrance' of Christ (1 Corinthians 11:25) and not as a sacrifice for sin.

2. At the Last Supper, our Saviour was not offering a sacrifice through the bread or wine but giving the bread and the wine to the disciples as symbols of his own body and blood to be broken and shed on Calvary.

3. The significance of this ordinance is explained by Paul in 1 Corinthians 11:26 as 'proclaiming' or 'heralding' the death of Christ; there is no sacrificing of Christ in it.

4. The Lord's sacrifice was final and perfect and he died 'once' and 'once for all' (Hebrews 9:12; 10:10, 12, 14, 18). The mass implies the inadequacy of the Saviour's sacrifice and the need to repeat it indefinitely, but his cry from the cross, 'It is finished!' (John 19:30), means

that the work of our salvation was accomplished at Calvary, so that the mass is both unscriptural and unnecessary.

CHRISTIANS

Children and adults are made Christians in water baptism by the power of the Holy Spirit operating through an authorized priest.

'Whoever believes in him is not condemned, but whoever does not believe stands condemned already' (John 3:18).

'Believe in the Lord Jesus, and you will be saved' (Acts 16:31; see also John 1:12).

'Now this is eternal life: that they may know you, the only true God, and Jesus Christ, whom you have sent' (John 17:2-3).

PENANCE

Rome distinguishes between greater or 'mortal' sins and lesser or 'venial' sins. Examples of the former include the breaking of the Ten Commandments and also pride, lust, anger, sexual offences and failure to attend mass. Speaking hastily or being slothful in doing one's religious duties are examples of venial sins.

The Bible does not distinguish between 'mortal' and 'venial' sins.

COMPARISONS

In Roman Catholic confession, a distinction is also made between 'attrition' and 'contrition'. The motive in the former is the fear of sin's consequences, such as shame, imprisonment or hell, etc. While this is regarded as adequate for 'lesser' sins, 'contrition' is required for greater sins and such contrition or repentance includes a resolve to confess to a priest as soon as possible.

Confessing sin before a priest in order to obtain pardon is a sacrament binding on all Catholics. The priest, they argue, does more than declare God's forgiveness; he actually has the power also to forgive or retain sins and impose penance as a means both of testing the genuineness of the person's confession and of making a satisfaction to God for that sin.

Only contrition is true repentance and a good example of this is seen in Psalm 51.

There is a need at times to confess, not to a priest, however, but to fellow believers if we sin against them (James 5:16), but as a general practice sin must only be confessed to God (1 John 1:9), for God alone has the power to forgive (Mark 2:7-10).

Furthermore, no good works we do by way of penance will ever satisfy God, but sinners can be accepted and forgiven on the sole ground of Christ's sacrifice, through which alone the justice and wrath of God against sin have been satisfied (Romans 3:25; Ephesians 2:8-9; 1 John 2:2).

INDULGENCES

The punishment of sins is met partly by penance and partly by sufferings in purgatory after we

Church discipline sometimes demands suspension of an individual from communion but

die. For this reason, Rome teaches, indulgences are necessary for they reduce the temporal punishments for sin imposed by God. Indulgences are available because the Roman Church claims to have a great wealth of unused merit accumulated through Christ's sufferings and also through the holy, unselfish lives of Mary and the saints who did more than God's law required of them.

the church can reduce or remove this discipline when there is evidence of repentance. This, however, is not an indulgence nor an action of merit or satisfaction to God (see for example, Matthew 18:15-18; 2 Corinthians 2:6-8).

It is impossible for any human being to obey God more than is necessary. The Lord says, 'So you also, when you have done everything you were told to do, should say, "We are unworthy servants; we have only done our duty"' (Luke 17:9-10; 1 Corinthians 15:10; 1 Timothy 1:15).

MARY'S PERPETUAL VIRGINITY

After giving birth to the Lord, Mary continued as a virgin for the rest of her life.

See Matthew 1:24-25. We are not told here the reason why Joseph and Mary abstained from sexual intercourse until after the birth of the Saviour. Was it meant as additional, irrefutable evidence that the child was conceived miraculously by the Holy Spirit and not by man? But notice the following details of Scripture which contradict Rome's teaching of Mary's perpetual virginity:

1. We read in Matthew 1:25 that Joseph 'had no union with her until she gave birth to a son,' i.e. full physical union began and continued after the Saviour was born.

2. Our Lord had brothers and sisters, according to Mark 6:3.

3. Jesus is described as Mary's 'firstborn son', which suggests that she had other children (Luke 2:7).

4. Marriage is a divinely ordained ordinance within which sexual intercourse is legitimate.

IMMACULATE CONCEPTION OF MARY

In 1854 the pope declared, 'The most holy virgin Mary was, in the first moment of her conception, by a unique gift of grace and privilege of Almighty God, in view of the merits of Jesus Christ the Redeemer of mankind, preserved free from all stain of original sin.'

Although Genesis 3:15 is used by Rome in support of the immaculate conception, the verse actually teaches that the 'offspring of the woman' (Christ), not the woman herself, will overcome Satan. Luke 1:28 is also misused, especially the words, 'Hail, favoured one!', or as in the NIV: 'Greetings, you who are highly favoured!'

'Hail' was a word of greeting commonly used (Matthew 26:49; 28:9; Acts 23:26), whereas the word translated 'favoured' is also used in Ephesians 1:6 to describe the elect people of God, who are far from being sinless! This verse does not therefore teach or imply the sinlessness of Mary.

But what of the words in Luke 1:42, where Elizabeth says of Mary, 'Blessed are you among women...'? Certainly Mary was greatly privileged to be chosen as the mother of the Lord, but this does not mean she was sinless. Later, in verse 45, Elizabeth shows it was Mary's faith that marked her out as being blessed: 'Blessed is she who has believed that what the Lord has said to her will be accomplished.'

Two other details provide conclusive evidence of the error of Rome at this point. Mary calls the Lord 'my Saviour' in Luke 1:47 (cf. Matthew 1:21), and after the Lord's birth she obeyed the Old Testament law of purification by making a sin-offering (Luke 2:22; Leviticus 12:6-8). If she had been perfect, there would have been no need of this offering. In fact, Mary is included with all other people in the statement of Romans 3:23.

BODILY ASSUMPTION OF MARY

This dogma, formally announced as recently as 1950 by Pope Pius, maintains that at the end of her life Mary's body and soul were taken directly to heaven.

There is no biblical support for this erroneous teaching.

MARY, QUEEN OF HEAVEN

Mary is enthroned in heaven as queen where she prays for her church. Her special relationship to Christ makes her prayers valuable and effective.

Recent popes have gone on to claim: 'Nothing ... comes to us except through Mary ... nobody can approach Christ except through the Mother...' Mary dispenses 'all gifts which Jesus has acquired for us by his death and his blood...'; she is 'the mediatrix with God of all graces'.

Christ invites sinners to go directly to him as Saviour: 'Come to me, all you who are weary and burdened...' (Matthew 11:28; cf. John 7:37).

Again, Christ is the only mediator, as verses like 1 Timothy 2:5 and John 14:6 teach. We have only one advocate in heaven, namely, 'Jesus Christ, the Righteous One. He is the atoning sacrifice for our sins...' (1 John 2:1-2), and he is certainly sympathetic in his intercession for us (Hebrews 4:15).

WORSHIP OF MARY

A distinction is made between the 'adoration' of God, the 'veneration' of saints and the 'special veneration' given to Mary.

This distinction is not found in the Bible and, clearly, only God should be worshipped (Matthew 4:10). Both Peter (Acts 10:25-26) and Paul (Acts 14:15) refused to accept veneration or worship from people, while the wise men worshipped the Lord Jesus, not Mary (Matthew 2:11).

Roman Catholics tend to give as much honour to Mary as to the Lord himself. The rosary, for example, which was invented in 1070, demands the reciting of the Lord's Prayer and the Gloria fifteen times each, but there are 150 Hail Marys. In other words, there are ten times as many prayers to Mary as there are to the Father, and not one prayer to Christ.

In Luke 11:27-28 a woman was so impressed by the Lord's teaching that she exclaimed, 'Blessed is the mother who gave you birth and nursed you.' But Christ did not allow any special veneration of Mary, for he went on to say, 'Blessed rather are those who hear the word of God and obey it.' Mary's blessedness consisted primarily in the fact that she received and obeyed the divine Word.

PURGATORY

While some distinguished and 'holy' people in the Roman Catholic Church go directly to heaven after death, and non-Catholics Some of the verses appealed to in support of purgatory are:

1 Corinthians 3:13. Here the reference is to ministers

or unbelievers go to hell, the majority of Catholics go to purgatory where their venial and mortal sins are purged and punished.

of the gospel and their responsibility to do their work well in view of the scrutiny of their work in the Final Judgement. There is no reference at all here to purgatory.

1 Peter 3:19-20. The 'disobedient' here refers to the unbelieving people in the days of Noah to whom Christ preached through Noah before the Flood. Again, there is no reference to purgatory here.

Matthew 5:21-26. William Hendriksen summarizes these verses most helpfully: 'It is as if Jesus were saying, "Be not surprised about the urgency of my command that you be reconciled; for, should it be that you were to pass from this life with a heart still at variance with your brother, a condition which you have not even tried to change, that wrong would testify against you in the day of judgement. Moreover, dying with that spirit of hatred still in your heart, you will never escape from the prison of hell."'[4]

Rather than going to purgatory, the Bible teaches that believers go directly to heaven when they die (Luke 16:19-31; 23:43; John 5:24; Philippians

1:21; Revelation 14:13), and unbelievers go immediately to hell (Luke 16:22-23); there is no intermediate or preparatory place such as purgatory.

Bibliography

BIBLIOGRAPHY

In addition to newspapers and periodicals/ journals, I have consulted several books, including:

Giuseppe Alberigo, (ed.), *The Reception of Vatican II*, Burns and Oats, 1987.

Herbert McCabe, *The Teaching of the Catholic Church: A New Catechism of Christian Doctrine*, Catholic Truth Society, 1985.

CHAPTER FIVE

QUAKERS: THE RELIGIOUS SOCIETY OF FRIENDS

WHO ARE THEY?

A BRIEF HISTORY

You may be surprised that the Quakers are included in this book, and if so I understand your reaction. For example, the Quakers are usually very kind and sincere people; some are converted and love the Lord Jesus Christ deeply. In the United States, some of the Quaker groups are more thoroughly biblical and evangelical. These facts I gladly acknowledge as well as their valuable humanitarian work throughout the world.

What we are concerned with in this book, however, is the Bible. To what extent do Quakers still adhere to the Bible and the foundational truths which the Bible teaches? Sadly, their distinctive conviction concerning the inward illumination and authority of the Spirit has led many Quakers to a more open and less biblical position on important truths. Their strong biblical heritage is now being eroded.

Who are the Quakers? How did they begin? What do they believe? These questions will be answered in this chapter.

How did they begin?

Whatever picture is conjured up in your mind by the name 'Quaker', you need to remember that it was originally a nickname given to the followers of George Fox in the middle of the seventeenth century. The nickname was given partly because some members 'quaked' in meetings, and partly because of a joke made by a judge in 1650 when George Fox faced a charge of blasphemy. When Fox told the judge he should 'tremble at the word of the Lord', the judge proceeded to call Fox and his followers 'Quakers'. The official title of the movement, however, is 'The Religious Society of Friends' but members are still popularly referred to as 'Quakers' or 'Friends'.

At the age of nineteen the founder of this society, George Fox (1624-1691), was invited to a drinking party by some religious friends. He was disgusted at their behaviour at the party, and as a result turned away from the recognized churches in his search for truth and spiritual reality. Three years later he had a conversion experience in which he claims that Christ was revealed directly to him by means of an 'inner light'. Within a year Fox began his public ministry and the first Quaker community was established in Preston Patrick in 1652, while by 1654 there were groups in London, Bristol and Norwich. A strong missionary zeal helped to spread the Quaker message quickly as far as Germany, Austria, Holland, the West Indies and America.

The effects of persecution

Until freedom of worship was introduced by Parliament in the Toleration Act of 1689, Quakers as well as other Dissenters were persecuted severely. Unlike most Congregationalists and Presbyterians, they refused to meet secretly and consequently about 400 Quakers died in prison during this period and many more were impoverished by heavy fines. To escape from such suffering and poverty, many emigrated to America when William Penn offered them a home in his new colony in Philadelphia in 1681. One writer estimates that between 4,000-5,000 'Friends' left their native Wales for America and numbers in Britain fell so much that the Yearly Meeting for Wales (1797) appealed regularly for their numbers 'not to run away to America'.[1] In the late eighteenth and nineteenth centuries it was nonconformity, signally blessed by God with numerous outpourings of the Holy Spirit, which won many of the British people, including some Quakers, to the kingdom of Christ.

Today the world membership of the Society of Friends is approximately 203,000.

The 'inward illumination'

Fox and his early followers felt that they had re-discovered primitive Christianity and that 'Christ had come to teach his people himself', directly. Despite a powerful conversion to Christ and a deep love of the Bible, Fox tended to emphasize the inward illumination and authority of the Spirit at the expense of the Bible. In the late seventeenth century, one of the society's most illustrious members, William Penn, could write, 'It is not opinion, or speculation, or notions of what is true, or assent to, or the subscription of articles or propositions, though never so soundly worded, that makes a man a true believer...' We can concur wholeheartedly with this statement, but when Penn goes on to describe a believer as one who lives 'according to the dictates of this Divine principle of light and life in the Soul',[2] we must disagree, for he has now abandoned the objective and supreme authority of the Bible.

This subjective emphasis has gradually led the Quakers away from biblical truth. While Quakers in the United States are still evangelical, nevertheless the society has become more liberal and unorthodox in its teaching.

'Concern' and practice

Another strong Quaker conviction is that their 'concern' must be translated into practice, and this concern is channelled, for example, into the Samaritan movement, the Marriage Guidance Council, the Local Council of Churches and, more especially today, into various peace and international organizations like the United Nations Association and Amnesty International.

RELEVANT COMPARISONS

Non-evangelical Quakers	The Bible

COMPARISONS

GOD

'Friends' are cautious about using the name of God, partly because it has been misunderstood and used, often exclusively, as an intellectual concept. They have no official or formal doctrine of God. The Quaker awareness of God 'is discovered in response and commitment to the deep meaning of life'.

'Who among the gods is like you, O LORD? Who is like you — majestic in holiness, awesome in glory, working wonders?' (Exodus 15:11).

'Now to the King eternal, immortal, invisible, the only God, be honour and glory for ever and ever' (1 Timothy 1:17; cf. 1 Chronicles 29:11-12; Psalm 96:4-10).

BIBLE

The Bible is 'a remarkable collection of writings covering the history and experience of countless ordinary, fallible men and women ... who had a great capacity to reflect upon the inwardness of this experience and to interpret it to their fellows in such a way as to command respect for their insights... These insights were expressed in the thought forms and assumptions of the day.'

'For prophecy never had its origin in the will of man, but men spoke from God as they were carried along by the Holy Spirit' (2 Peter 1:21).

The authority of the Bible does not rest on an external and infallible guarantee of its truth but 'on its ability to arouse the response and trust of men'.

Among modern 'Friends' the Bible, while still greatly treasured, is not as widely known as in previous generations, but 'Where some of the time previously given to the study and devotional use of the Bible is spent on other sources of religious insight, the life of the Society will be enriched.'[3]

'Jesus answered, "It is written..."' (Matthew 4:4, 7, 10; cf. John 17:17).

'Let the word of Christ dwell in you richly as you teach and admonish one another...' (Colossians 3:16; cf. Deuteronomy 6:5-7; 2 Timothy 3:15).

JESUS CHRIST

'Friends' vary in their views but the more common position is that the historical Jesus was an outstanding religious teacher whose absolute trust and commitment to love give us 'a window into God', for 'In his life the love that is God is most clearly seen.' The biblical account of Christ's person is unimportant: 'What matters is the greatness of his personality and his spiritual insight.'

'Your attitude should be the same as that of Christ Jesus: who, being in very nature God, did not consider equality with God something to be grasped...' (Philippians 2:5-8; cf. John 1:1; Colossians 1:15-19).

DEATH OF CHRIST

No atonement was necessary. The Jews killed Jesus because they were afraid of him, but

'In fact, the law requires that nearly everything be cleansed with blood, and without the

the Lord's creative attitude of love and forgiveness radically changed this act of human wickedness into an event that releases love and forgiveness into the world. Such love can overcome evil and this knowledge has freed many people to live meaningful lives.

shedding of blood there is no forgiveness... so Christ was sacrificed once to take away the sins of many people...' (Hebrews 9:22-28).

RESURRECTION OF CHRIST

Many 'Friends' are sceptical about the New Testament accounts of the physical resurrection of Jesus. They would agree that the essential meaning behind the Easter story is 'that death could not destroy all that was of real value in the earthly life of Jesus'.

'If Christ has not been raised, your faith is futile; you are still in your sins... But Christ has indeed been raised from the dead' (1 Corinthians 15:17-20).

MAN

Man is a unique and individual person, made in the image of God. 'That of God in every man' is a popular Quaker phrase and means that each person has the capacity to experience 'mystical awareness' and the 'inward light'.

Man is essentially good.

'God created man in his own image, in the image of God he created him' (Genesis 1:27).

'For all have sinned and fall short of the glory of God' (Romans 3:23).

DEATH

Life has a timeless quality and death cannot destroy love. Quakers do not dogmatize about what happens after death. Some are convinced there is an afterlife, while others believe death is the end of our existence.

'Just as man is to die once, and after that to face judgement' (Hebrews 9:27).

'... I desire to depart and be with Christ...' (Philippians 1:23; cf. Job 19:25-27).

CHAPTER SIX

EXCLUSIVE BRETHREN — 'TAYLORITES'

A BRIEF HISTORY

Aberdeen, July 1970

Does this date and location have any significance for you? Probably not. However, for those readers who were, or still are, members of the Exclusive Brethren then the above date may be significant. And the reason? Aberdeen, July 1970, was a milestone for many Exclusive Brethren; it was a crisis and a turning point in their movement.

I will explain what happened but I need to warn you that there has been a conspiracy on the part of some people to withhold and deny the facts.

Bad behaviour

Basically, the facts concerning Aberdeen '70 are as follows. The American, James Taylor Junior (1899-1970), was leader of an Exclusive Brethren group at the time and he was in the United Kingdom during the summer of 1970 for a series of conferences known as *Three day meetings*, as they commenced on a Friday and continued until the Sunday. Taylor addressed three such conferences in Reigate, Manchester and Aberdeen. Sadly, he had become an alcoholic, at least from 1965, and his general behaviour on occasions was shameful and distressing.

And that was what happened in Aberdeen. In a private home from 23-25 July there was 'adulterous behaviour' on the part of Taylor, witnessed by a number of people, as well as 'obscene language and gestures' in a meeting on 25 July. The Aberdeen brethren, supported by many from other places, withdrew from Taylor and reported the incidents with the appropriate evidence (including tapes) to Taylor's assembly in New York.

The report was denied both by Taylor and his followers. What was worse, they refused to investigate the matter. Immediately, all those in membership with the Taylor assemblies had to commit themselves, under pressure and without reservation, to Taylor.

You can imagine at least part of the sequel to this incident. Leaders tried to suppress the facts, hundreds of brethren worldwide were pressurized to support Taylor while some left in disgust and others were disfellowshipped or 'withdrawn from' for their attitude to Taylor. And that was painful and cruel, as I will illustrate later. But in October that same year, 1970, Taylor died.

Open or exclusive

At this point it is necessary to pause and view the Aberdeen incident within the broader Brethren background.

HISTORY

It was in 1820 that the 'Plymouth Brethren' movement started when a group of Christians met in Plymouth, Devon, in England, for worship and the breaking of bread without the support or use of ordained ministers.

A man who dominated the movement in the early years was J. N. Darby (1800-1882), but in 1848 there was a deep division between Darby and the Plymouth Brethren. The latter became known as 'Open Brethren' while Darby and his followers were identified as 'Exclusive Brethren'.

The differences between the two groups were not insignificant. Darby insisted on separating from people who disagreed with his interpretations of Scripture, and a significant number of believers endorsed Darby's policy and followed him. They believed in a universal worldwide network of fellowships with strong central leadership and a tight control of members.

In contrast, for Plymouth Brethren, or 'Open Brethren' as they were later called, each local assembly is independent. The fellowship enjoyed between assemblies is spontaneous and spiritual without impinging on the autonomy of the local assembly. The believers locally are themselves directly responsible to the Lord, not a human leader. This represents a major difference between the two sections of the Brethren movement.

Open Brethren commended

I now need to emphasize that I am in no way referring to the Open Brethren in what I write here. They are themselves facing some contemporary issues such as the appointment of a salaried 'worker' or even pastor, the audible participation of women in meetings, the process of appointing elders and the length of the appointment, the use of musical instruments in services, modern music, the exclusive use of the Authorized Version, the rightness of forming a recognized denomination as well as maintaining their ties with historic denominational churches.

Another practical issue is whether visitors should be received to the breaking of bread only on the basis of a formal letter of introduction from the home assembly. Varying attitudes are adopted towards these issues and one welcomes a new openness on the part of many of these assemblies towards other Christians and to co-operation in genuine evangelical activities.

What is also pleasing about Open Brethren is their commitment to missionary work. It is estimated, for example, that one per cent of the total number of members in Brethren assemblies are serving on the mission field. By modern standards, this is in excess of almost every Christian denomination.

Operation World reports that Brethren fellowships in Canada, USA, UK, Australia and New Zealand together have 1,223 missionaries. But, in addition, there are many national workers as well as workers from other countries involved in world mission. The position is that several thousand members are currently working in mission. These facts are encouraging and I repeat that I am in no way criticizing the 'Open Brethren' in this book.

Exclusive heresies?

Let me pick up the story again regarding the Exclusive Brethren. F. E. Raven assumed the leadership of this section of the Brethren when Darby died in 1882 but within eight years, in 1890, a major division took place over Raven's teaching.

The heresies which Raven was accused of teaching were:

1. Denial that each true believer in Christ necessarily has eternal life as a present possession;
2. Denial of the unity of Christ's person;
3. Denial of the full humanity of Christ.

There is agreement that Raven's teaching was unclear and unsound but there was considerable confusion as well as misunderstanding (not to mention misrepresentation) in the ensuing discussions. It seems, however, that Raven taught the pre-existence of Christ but that he only became the Son at his incarnation.

It is suggested by some that Raven's wish to 'study Scripture less and pray more' freed him and his followers eventually from subscribing to the traditions and teachings of his forebears. Did this lead to the present approach, where the leader makes whatever rules he pleases for the members? Those who disagreed with Raven formed an assembly known as the Tunbridge-Wells Brethren as distinct from the 'Raven Brethren'.

Further discussions

After Raven's death in 1903, the leadership of his group was taken by James Taylor Senior (1870-1953). His contribution was distinctive for two main reasons.

1. He perpetuated, especially after 1929, Raven's teaching that Jesus only became the Son of God *after* his incarnation.
2. He insisted that 'the ministry', namely the discussions of the brethren in formal assembly, were equivalent in importance to Scripture.

Further divisions occurred in 1920, 1935, 1951 and 1960-61. In 1970 the Aberdeen dissidents became known as the 'Strange-Walker Brethren' and later united with the 'Ilford Fellowship' and 'Frost Group'. A number of small groups, as well as many of the 'Grant-Kelley meetings', also reunited in 1973.

WHAT THE 'TAYLORITES' TEACH

It is the Raven/Taylor group, or Taylorites, on which we will now focus. James Taylor Sr was succeeded by his son James Taylor Jr, who died in 1970. James Symington then assumed the Taylorite leadership, and Symington was followed in turn by John Hales of Australia.

How strong is this Exclusive Raven/Taylor group?

There are assemblies in 288 cities in the world and approximately 27,000 members worldwide. They are mostly of European descent. Meetings are held in the following countries: the UK, Ireland, Germany, Holland, Sweden, Denmark, France, Italy, Spain, South Africa, Argentina, Trinidad, St Vincent, Barbados, Jamaica, USA, Canada, New Zealand, Australia and India. All meetings, whatever the native language, must be conducted in English.

Why call this group a cult?

1. Members must give total allegiance to their leaders.

Jim Taylor Sr died in 1953 and six years later his son established himself as his successor.

Until this time, the group's official teaching was that of Christ's sole headship of the church. While the Taylorites still embrace this principle in theory, they deny it in practice. Consider the evidence.

In recent years they have taught that the Lord directs the group through one man. Again, some significant titles are attributed to their leader such as 'the Lord's representative', the contemporary 'Paul', and 'great man' whose position is 'apostolic in character'. James Symington, group leader from 1970 until 1987, was known as 'God's representative on earth'. His successor, John S. Hales, was described publicly as 'the personification of the Holy Spirit'. This status was bolstered by the claim that 'new light' was being given by God, uniquely through him, to members. As a consequence, the leader's interpretation and application of Scripture were regarded as binding on members.

Most members would not dare to question such a 'man of God'! And Aberdeen July 1970 is only one illustration. Consider, for example, Jim Taylor Jr's adultery there with the young wife of a member. Two independent persons witnessed the adultery. Astonishingly, the wife's husband spoke later to reporters, expressing support for her. Their opinion? Well, it was 'quite suitable' behaviour. Why? Because she was 'ministering' to Taylor. A second reason? Yes, Taylor was a 'pure man'!

There is more. In what was called a Bible reading in Aberdeen, Taylor indulged in spells of hysterical laughter and whistling; he also frequently used obscene language. The response? Many who attended the meetings left the group in disgust. About eighty out of the 850 present decided to support Taylor because, they believed, as God's man, God would not allow him to do wrong or that it was proper for 'a pure man doing God's will' to act in such ways!

The cultic aspect here is frightening. An individual is elevated as leader, then his status is strengthened by claims of 'new light' mediated through him. His actions, however wrong, are denied or justified by members. The leader is beyond criticism. Control of 'the whole thinking pattern of the membership' is maintained on this formula in a Waco-type relationship between leader and members. Allegiance is total. To quote Mark Gillingham, a former Taylorite excommunicated in 1990, members have 'a slavish and fanatical loyalty to the "men of God"'.

Professor Peter Caws (University Professor of Philosophy at the George Washington University in Washington) and Roger Stott both grew up among the Exclusive Brethren in England. In a letter to the *Evangelical Times* editor, they wrote:

> Taylor's fall into disgrace and degradation, through drunkenness and lasciviousness, at Aberdeen could not be hushed up in Scotland, where almost all the Brethren

left the sect. Elsewhere the Brethren spin doctors interpreted the events at Aberdeen as a 'divine ambush', insisting that the Man of God had taken on the 'appearance of evil' in order to discover who were his true followers and who were merely 'assenting mentally'. Absolute, unquestioning loyalty to Taylor was made a condition of remaining in fellowship.

2. *Tight control is exercised over members.*

The practice of disciplining members is often described by them as 'shutting up' and it is based on instructions in Leviticus chapters 13 and 14. In the context of Leviticus, a person or house where leprosy was suspected would be 'shut up', that is, isolated or expelled. At intervals, priests visited to establish whether or not the leprosy had spread. This Scripture was misapplied by Taylor to mean that a member suspected of sin or breaking Taylor's directives was banned both from meetings, and from contact with all other members, even close relatives. The 'priests' were assembly leaders who visited these individuals and decided their fate.

And there are many horror stories. One husband was 'shut up', that is, expelled, and banned fifteen years ago from living with his wife and children. Neither his brother nor his wife knew the reason for the decision but they were submissive to the leaders. Such practices place considerable power in the hands of the leadership.

3. *The group undermines the supreme authority and sufficiency of the Bible.*

In theory, Taylorites rightly acknowledge the Bible's authority but in practice they compromise it. One needs to go back to an early Exclusive Brethren leader, F. E. Raven, to appreciate this compromise. Raven wrote, '…if I had to live over again I would study Scripture less and pray more. The great thing for a Christian is to get into his closet and pray. Prayer and meditation.'[1] The statement appears impressive but this emphasis tends subtly towards subjectivity and places the thoughts of a man above the Word of God.

The Bible's sufficiency is also undermined. For example, James Taylor Sr taught that the Holy Spirit is speaking in meetings of the brethren *in addition* to what was inspired and recorded in the Bible. In other words, we need continuing revelation. The same man insisted that the Holy Spirit is giving us truth today which was not given to the apostles. This is the significance of their emphasis on 'new light' but it weakens the authority of the Bible over the lives and consciences of the members.

He also insisted that they should not reject the teaching given by the 'man of God'. This is plain error. Nothing should be added to the Bible. There is no new revelation. And we do not need any, for revelation was given finally to the apostles and 'once for all entrusted to the saints' (Jude 3). All beliefs and practices, even those of prominent leaders, must be tested by the supreme standard and authority of the Bible.

4. *Members are enslaved in legalism.*

Exclusive Brethren teaching on 'separation' is based partly on 2 Corinthians 6:17 and Amos 3:3. Taylor Jr developed this teaching, appealing to 2 Timothy 2:19-22 as their 'Magna Carta'. These verses are regarded as the divinely-given basis for disassociating oneself from 'evil'. Separation is compulsory, especially where there is disagreement concerning doctrine and practice as taught by the 'man of God'. Contact with those in the world should be minimal. This point is justified by reference to James 4:4: '…friendship with the world is hatred towards God…'

In 1959 Taylor Jr began to develop the 'separation' teaching, urging that members should not eat with non-members. Ten years later a member estimated that Taylor had given 150 new 'directives'; others were later added. The result is legalism with consciences bound to human regulations rather than to the Bible.

Examples of legalism

Members must not attend religious services outside their exclusive movement or join a trade union or a professional association. Nor must they live in the same building with non-members; even a semi-detached house is unacceptable as they share a common wall! This is applied to paths or driveways to houses and even a sewer. Business links are also prohibited. Sadly, a member must be legally and physically separate from a husband or wife if they have been put out of fellowship.

There are many more rules! TV, films, radio, novels, public swimming, a mobile phone or CB radio are all banned. Nor can they buy life insurance or have a house pet. Beards and moustaches are forbidden, as is dating. A couple who want to court and marry must obtain the approval of the 'man of God'. Computers as well as faxes are outlawed. In 1982 their leader, James Symington, maintained that computers are linked to the antichrist; as a result, many members changed careers to comply with this 'truth'.

Freedom in Christ

'Freedom' is how Mark Gillingham describes life outside the 'prison' of the Taylor cult. Rehabilitation was gradual and, at times, difficult. 'The greatest release of all' he reports as a Christian is the realization that he has the ability 'to live a fulfilled Christian life and to worship God acceptably...' He continues: 'I was given to understand there was no other divinely approved body of Christians…' but, he adds, 'I can assure you that they are just about everywhere. I discovered I was free to find them, eat and drink with them and worship with them.'

Gillingham likens the group to the Pharisees in the New Testament period who 'grossly distorted and added' to the Old Testament Law, 'placing a great burden on the lives of simple Jews … so many of our lives', he acknowledges, 'have been blighted with legalistic sectarianism'. However, he sounds the joyful note that 'deliverance can be found in Jesus Christ'.

The Clarke family left the group in 1970 over the Aberdeen issue. Sarah was eighteen at the time and trusted in Christ personally in 1967. What has been her experience? 'The worst is losing valued friends and relatives,' she reports, 'the best is rediscovering the joy of fellowship with my Saviour and learning to appreciate the worth of all believers, regardless of "brand" name.' Salutary words indeed. And words which centre on the glorious gospel of Christ, intimate spiritual union with Christ and the unity of believers.

RELEVANT COMPARISONS

The Taylorites	The Bible

JESUS CHRIST

The Taylorites	The Bible
Taylor Senior perpetuated Raven's teaching that Jesus only became the Son of God after his incarnation.	Not only was Christ pre-existent (John 8:58; 17:5, etc.), but he was eternally the Son of God (Philippians 2:6; Colossians 2:9; Isaiah 6:1; cf. John 12:41).

COMPARISONS

SUFFICIENCY AND AUTHORITY OF THE BIBLE

'The ministry' (i.e. the discussions of the brethren in formal assembly) is equivalent in importance to the Bible.

'New Light', given by the Holy Spirit, is also claimed for today, which weakens the authority of Scripture.

No new revelation is provided by God and there is no need for it. The reason? Revelation was given finally to the apostles and 'once for all entrusted to the saints' (Jude 3).

SEPARATION

Misusing 2 Corinthians 6:17, Amos 3:3 and especially 2 Timothy 2:19-22, they insist on a minimal contact with the world which results in legalism and human, not divine, regulations.

Read Colossians 2:20-23. In 2 Timothy 2:19-22 the context concerns Timothy's responsibilities with regard to the false teaching in the church. A prominent note is 'peace'.

Note that the Greek imperatives in verses 14 and 16 relate to teachings as well as 'evil' in verse 19.

Unlike those advocating false teaching, Timothy must not quarrel, but be kind to all, gently correct with a view to their repentance. He himself, too, must turn from wickedness and pursue godliness.

CHAPTER SEVEN

INTERNATIONAL CHURCH OF CHRIST

⟨A BRIEF HISTORY⟩

The story is a familiar one. And often it can be a distressing and even tragic story. In order to illustrate the point, here are two real situations which occurred recently and are known to the writer. A young lady recently studied in a college in England for three years and enjoyed her course. In the second year of studies, she was approached on campus by a stranger who invited her to a small Bible-study group. She was then pressured to join their Sunday services, was baptized and became a member. The group slowly began to control her beliefs and lifestyle; she became frightened and depressed, then left the group.

Similar stories can be repeated from other UK universities and city areas, especially London. For example, a twenty-one-year-old male student in London, together with his graduate pal working in city finance, were approached on an underground train by an ICC member. The next day they received a phone call and invitation to a meal as well as a Bible study. Slowly they were dragged into the ICC net, baptized and heavily involved themselves in recruiting for the group.

It was nearly two years before they both recognized how deceptive and manipulative the ICC had been. To the relief of their families, they have now left that church, but at a price: they are disillusioned and emotionally wounded.

In order to understand more about the ICC, I want now to answer a number of key questions concerning its background, beliefs and activities.

Who are they?

Their new name is 'International Church of Christ'. However, it is confusing because they also use other names. Their normal practice has been to use the name of the city in which they operate so they have called themselves the 'London (or Birmingham, or Boston, etc.) Church of Christ'. If the name is already used by another group or denomination, then they use similar titles like 'Church of Christ Jesus', 'Christian Church' or 'Disciples of Christ'. One suspects that a major reason for using different names is to cause confusion and make people think that they are an ordinary, orthodox church. And there certainly has been confusion both in Edinburgh and London. In the English capital, the group was previously known as the Central London Church of Christ, whereas it is now known as the International Church of Christ. To make it more confusing, their branches in London use additional titles like London City Fellowship. Beware!

How big are they?

This is not an easy question to answer. Since 1981 the movement launched an aggressive, international mission programme and sent out teams of people to form churches. Such churches were established in many major cities including London (1981), Chicago (1982), New York City (1983), Tokyo (1985), Johannesburg, Paris and Stockholm (1986), Mexico City, Hong Kong, Bombay and Cairo (1987-1988). Today there are churches in each continent and total membership is estimated between 50,000 and 85,000 worldwide. Nevertheless, the group is far more influential than this statistic suggests. ICC has been regarded both in the United States and in the United Kingdom as the fastest growing religious cult. In the UK there are branches in Birmingham, Bristol, Cardiff, Leeds, Liverpool, Oxford, Manchester, Edinburgh and Belfast. UK membership is estimated at between 2,000-2,500 with the largest group located in London. Alongside the Church of Scientology and the Moonies, the ICC is rated as belonging to the three cults that cause the greatest concern in Britain at present.

When did they start?

There is a long complicated history dating back to Christians in the early 1800s who protested against denominations and institutionalized forms of Christianity. People belonging to this movement wanted only the Bible but without creeds, constitutions and organization. These different voices merged later to form what is known as the nineteenth-century Restoration Movement with leaders like Barton Stone, Thomas and Alexander Campbell. This movement later included groups like the Disciples of Christ and the Churches of Christ, the latter being a conservative, Protestant group of churches. From within the Churches of Christ, there emerged in the later 1960s the 'Crossroads Movement', which concentrated on campus evangelism and used the same basic methods as are now being used by the ICC.

1979 was an important year for the movement and it can be claimed with justification that this was the beginning of the ICC. It was in that year that the ICC leader, Kip McKean, with a small group, took over a small Church of Christ in Lexington, Boston. The church grew rapidly but became isolated from other churches in the denomination. 1987 marked the formal separation of the Boston Church of Christ and some supporting churches from the official group. It was the Boston church which established the London church in 1981 and the Birmingham church in 1989.

Are they clear about the gospel?

No. In fact, they distort the gospel of Christ. The problem largely relates to whether baptism is essential in order for an individual to be saved. ICC answers loud and clear: yes. One must be baptized in water into Christ in order to receive the forgiveness of sins; that is the teaching of the ICC. They insist that saving faith itself is not enough — baptism is also essential, but it must be baptism administered by their leaders.

The Bible is clear in its teaching regarding salvation. Christ achieved our salvation. How did he do it? He 'died for sins once for all, the righteous for the unrighteous, to bring you to God...' (1 Peter 3:18). The same message is emphasized throughout the New Testament. 'God was reconciling the world to himself in Christ...' (2 Corinthians 5:19). This reconciliation was achieved only and entirely 'through the death of his Son' (Romans 5:10) when he took our place by suffering the punishment due to us for our sin.

Notice carefully, that God's work of reconciliation must be accepted personally by us in faith. You cannot earn it and all you must do is to trust in Christ. That was the message of the Apostle to the jailer when he asked how he could be saved: 'Believe in the Lord Jesus, and you will be saved...' (Acts 16:31). Although the man was baptized later it was not necessary for obtaining salvation. In fact, nothing that we do can contribute to the obtaining of salvation: 'To the man who does not work but trusts God who justifies the

wicked, his faith is credited as righteousness' (Romans
4:5). Does not John 3:5 support ICC teaching? No, for
'water' here is a picture of cleansing and forgiveness
based on Ezekiel 36:25-27. What about Acts 2:38?
Baptism is an external sign that we are already saved
by grace through faith. As John Calvin says, baptism,
as a seal, 'is a help to confirm and increase our faith'.

ICC recruits tend to be young but usually middle-
class and intelligent. They are often either students or
professionals, with social and personal needs. Another
example is a marine engineer, Bill, who moved from
Sheffield to Surrey to take up a new job. Two girls
then befriended him and telephoned him regularly to
invite him to go to their church. Needing a social life,
he eventually accepted their invitation, although he
had no interest in Christianity. 'My first impression',
he described later, 'was that it was a load of rubbish
— people dancing around, clapping and singing "Jesus
will fix it"'. But it was their friendship that really won
him. Within six months he reported, 'There was nothing else in my life. I had completely lost interest in my
career and family.'

Older people, however, are drawn into the ICC cult
and not just in the UK or USA. Francis Mbugua, for
example, was fifty-two years old and had been brought
up by godly parents in Kenya. His father was a pastor
in the African Inland Church. It was in April 1996 that
Francis attended the Nairobi Christian Church (NCC),
affiliated to ICC. He was in turmoil due partly to family
problems, and he longed for genuine friendship and

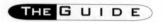

WHAT THEY TEACH

encouragement. In the first sermon the NCC was introduced as God's movement, consisting only of disciples who taught the Bible and who would evangelize the world by AD 2000. The claim, 'we preach only what the Bible teaches', impressed and deceived Francis. In the service, he heard 'vibrant singing, lengthy emotional prayers and frenzied preaching', and then he was welcomed, befriended and lured into the cult, where he remained until 1997. But now Francis testifies, 'I am closer to my God now that I am no longer in the ICC… There is life after NCC/ICC. In fact, a far better life without stress, mind control and stumbling blocks, but the scars take a long time to heal.'

Where do they meet?

They meet usually on Sundays in rented rooms or halls, hotels, conference centres and, where possible, schools or colleges. They tend to change their location at regular intervals. During the week, members meet in small groups called 'House Churches' and then again in even smaller groups called 'Bible Talks', consisting of six to fifteen people. Each member is expected to bring at least one stranger each week to these meetings. The purpose of the two smaller groups is to encourage sharing on an informal basis and to show visitors their need to be 'converted'.

What do they believe?

They accept the Bible as their authority for what they
believe and do. They also believe in one church and
teach that denominations are sinful. From the Great
Commission (Matthew 28:18-20), they insist that all
Christians should be involved in aggressive evangelism and disciple-making. One must also be baptized
in water in order to receive salvation. They claim that
baptism is essential and, of course, it must be administered by their leaders.

What is wrong with ICC beliefs?

Baptism is not essential to salvation, but it is an ordinance to be honoured by those who are saved. It is only
by grace that we are saved, through faith (Ephesians 2:8-
9). This gospel of grace has been distorted by the ICC.
The group is also exclusive in its claim that the ICC is
the only true church in this generation. From this they
conclude that only ICC members can be saved.

From Acts 11:25-26 they also try to link the words
'disciple' and 'Christian', claiming that you have to
teach people about Jesus as Paul and Barnabas did, in
order to be a Christian. They ask, 'Who were called
Christians?' And, of course, people respond by saying,
'disciples', because the verses say so. 'And what did they
do?' comes the rejoinder. In this way they try to show
that witnessing to Jesus is involved in *becoming* as well
as in *being* a Christian. But this twists the two verses in

an irresponsible and dishonest way. Why? Look again at the meaning of the text — Barnabas brought Saul to Antioch so that they could share together the burden of teaching publicly a young, growing and multi-racial church. It was the ministry of the Word to the church, not 'witnessing' to unbelievers, that Saul and Barnabas were engaged in at Antioch. The emphasis of their ministry would have been on the life, death and exaltation of Jesus Christ and it was probably this that gave rise to the nickname 'Christian' being given to believers. Remember, too, the fact that Saul and Barnabas were already converted. This points to the error of the ICC interpretation. The teaching and witnessing of the two preachers did not *make* them Christians. Not at all!

Are there other concerns?

Yes, there are. They practise compulsory tithing of the gross income of members of the church, and strictly monitor and record such giving. This practice puts some people into considerable debt. Again, young people are targeted and exploited, particularly students. In 1992, for example, all ten halls of residence belonging to University College, London, had ICC members resident in them. The cult describes such places as an 'evangelistic paradise'.

Their recruiting methods also cause concern. Such methods involve 'tubing' (talking to folk on the underground) and 'blitzing' (talking to people in the high streets and shopping centres), as well as offering friendship as a bait to attract people to their meetings. There is an element of deception here. When invited to their meetings, you will usually be told that they are informal Christian gatherings of a non-denominational flavour. The bait may even be a party, concert or games evening, but the intentions behind the invitation are concealed. More seriously, they make recruits 'confess' sins to their leader ('discipler') and share confidential, private matters. This confidentiality is sometimes broken to get a person to obey the leaders. The ICC exert a considerable level of control over the lives of their members and this leads to psychological and spiritual abuse. For example, even dating, courting and marrying come under the complete control of the cult.

How can we help friends or relatives in ICC?

- Keep in touch with them by writing and phoning, even if there is no response.
- Make sure your manner is calm and caring. You need to be warm and helpful in your approach.
- Find out in a low-key way why the person joined the cult.
- Obtain more information about the cult.
- Pray regularly for the person and visit, if possible.

Is there a challenge for Christians?

There certainly is. We need to warn our young
people and children about the group. They
should not accept invitations from strangers to
a meeting nor should they disclose their address
or phone number to them. Are we failing our
youngsters? Do we teach the Bible at an appropriate level and deal with the questions they are
asking? Have we a prayerful, pastoral concern
for them as individuals?

There is one final challenge, namely, we must
make clear what the gospel is. 'It is God who
justifies' (Romans 8:33), and reconciles sinners
to himself. And he does it by grace alone. Here
is the secret. 'Grace' means that God's mercy is
completely undeserved. Salvation is free, wholly
from God and without any human contribution,
not even baptism or witnessing. Here is the significance of Calvary. Christ's righteousness is
reckoned to us personally when we trust in the
Lord Jesus, for our sins were laid on him when
he died as our substitute.

This is the heart of the Christian gospel. Be
clear about it yourself, then tell as many people
as possible. That is the challenge.

CHALLENGE

RELEVANT COMPARISONS

The International Church of Christ	The Bible

PREDESTINATION

This is a 'false doctrine' invented in the fifth century A.D.

'And those he predestined, he also called...' (Romans 8:30; cf. 9:11-18).

'...he chose us in him before the creation of the world...' (Ephesians 1:4).

'from the beginning God chose you to be saved...' (2 Thessalonians 2:13).

ORIGINAL SIN

A misleading and false teaching invented in the early centuries of the church.

'Surely I was sinful at birth, sinful from the time my mother conceived' (Psalm 51:5).

'Just as through the disobedience of the one man the many were made sinners, so also through the obedience of the one man the many will be made righteous' (Romans 5:19).

BAPTISM

This ordinance must be observed as a condition and means of salvation.

'References to baptism in the patristic literature abound! It is extremely clear that for the first few centuries everyone was

'For it is by grace you have been saved, through faith — and this not from yourselves, it is the gift of God' (Ephesians 2:8).

Salvation is planned, accomplished and applied

COMPARISONS

in agreement that baptism was for the forgiveness of sins, and was the only way to be saved.'[1]

to us by the Lord; faith is the means by which we receive this salvation as we rest upon the Lord Jesus (Romans 5:1; 1:16).

Believers' baptism is an act of obedience on the part of the believer to Christ and is an outward sign of an inner spiritual change and of entry to the church. Baptism has no efficacy in itself (Matthew 28:19; Acts 2:41).

FALLING FROM GRACE

Salvation is never secure in this life and members can be lost again even after baptism and a reasonable life of commitment.

'I give them eternal life, and they shall never perish; no one can snatch them out of my hand' (John 10:28).

'...he who began a good work in you will carry it on to completion until the day of Christ Jesus' (Philippians 1:6; cf. Romans 8:35-38; 1 Peter 1:3-5).

CHAPTER EIGHT

A NAMELESS GROUP: 'GO-PREACHERS'

A BRIEF HISTORY

Who are they?

That was the question put to me some time ago by an anxious Christian. His concern? Well, in his rural area of England a tent-mission had just been held. His concern initially was that the organizers were unwilling to identify themselves, appearing secretive. Clearly they did not belong to any denomination or a recognized evangelical agency. Nor did they want to co-operate with Bible-teaching churches in the area. Their tent-mission meetings were poorly supported by 'outsiders'.

My contact went along to a meeting in order to investigate further. Their hymn book was different, but the people themselves appeared serious, respectable and sincere. They emphasized the Bible but their views seemed to be off-centre. The Christian felt extremely uneasy. But who are they?

Names

We soon discovered the answer to the question. The tent mission had been arranged by a group which officially does not have a name. However,

the group has been given many names such as The
Nameless House Church, the Friends, the Dippers, the
Secret Sect, Pilgrims, Tramp Preachers, the Jesus-Way,
Reidites and Irvinites. The group is sometimes called
'Cooneyites' after one of its early leading preachers,
Edward Cooney, who came from Enniskillen, Northern
Ireland. They are also called 'Go-Preachers' based on
Matthew 10:7 where Jesus told his disciples, 'As you
go, preach...' Another name given them is 'The Two-by-
Twos'. This name relates to Mark 6:7 where we are told
that after the Lord called the Twelve to him, 'he sent
them out two by two...' (see also Luke 10:1).

    While the group registered with the UK Government
in 1914 as 'The Testimony of Jesus' and in 1942 with
the USA Government as 'Christian Conventions' and in
Australia and New Zealand as 'Christian Assemblies',
they still pride themselves in not having a name. But
why? They claim that they are the 'true' and 'original'
New Testament Church started by Jesus. For this reason
some followers have referred to the group as 'The Truth'
or 'The Way'. For convenience, I will refer to them as
'the group' although there have been serious divisions
among the members. A much smaller part of this group
can be more easily identified as Cooneyites. But more
of this later.

Where do they meet?

Their 'fellowship meetings' are held in the homes of
members and only members are allowed to attend.

WHAT THEY BELIEVE

They are opposed to the use of church buildings and regard their use as pagan for 'the Most High does not live in houses made by men' (Acts 7:48; 17:24). Houses are regarded as the New Testament norm for their meetings. An annual convention is held and at intervals they invite outsiders to their missions, which are held in tents or rented halls.

Do they condemn other churches?

Yes, they condemn all other churches and clergy. There are several reasons for this.

- They think they hinder both the sincere and hypocrites from being saved. And, in some cases, this may be true.
- They believe that the clergy encourage hypocrisy, self-righteousness and greed.
- They believe that the commission given by the Lord to his apostles was permanent and applies to all those he sends to preach. For example, he sent the Twelve and the Seventy without a wage, house or other provisions, but promised he would provide for their needs.

In the early years especially, the group regularly denounced the clergy and Christendom, which they referred to as 'Babylon'. The only genuine servants of the Lord, they insist, are their own itinerant 'preachers' or 'workers' who forsake all possessions in order to preach the apostolic Word. Individuals can be saved only through hearing the gospel preached through their workers; this is called the 'Living Witness' doctrine which developed in the group between 1905 and 1907 and later caused division.

What is their history?

While the group started and developed in Northern Ireland, the story begins with a Scotsman, William Irvine, who in 1893 was converted in Motherwell through the preaching of a Presbyterian minister, John McNeil. Irvine spent two years training in John Anderson's Bible College in Glasgow, before joining the Faith Mission in 1895 as a 'pilgrim' or evangelist. The mission's policy was that each worker should trust God to provide all their needs, and gifts were only distributed to workers as money became available.

A year later Irvine was sent to County Antrim and then to County Clare. A dynamic preacher, he had considerable success in missions with many genuine conversions. Because of their opposition, Irvine became critical of the churches and slowly distanced himself from the Faith Mission. He did not want gifts from them nor did he want to follow mission policy in sending converts back to their own denominations. By 1901 he had severed ties completely with the Faith Mission and gathered a nucleus of converts and 'workers' around himself.

The story now turns to Enniskillen and to Edward Cooney, who was converted in 1884. He was an effective preacher both in churches and in the open air; in Northern Ireland I have met older believers who were impressed and helped by his open-air preaching. Cooney met Irvine in 1897 and they began to preach together from 1901. By 1904 there were 150 'Go-Preachers' associated with the group who held missions in halls, preached in the open air in towns and villages, baptized in rivers and established house churches.

Tensions soon appeared within the group. Irvine was disciplined and withdrew after 1913. His latter years were tragic; and deluded, he died in Jerusalem in 1947. Cooney, too, opposed some of the group's teachings and he was eventually excommunicated in 1928. Others, described as 'the remnant' or 'outcasts', followed Cooney but they were in a minority. Cooney gained new converts and received some support in his native Ulster. He died in 1960.

How big are these two groups?

Cooney's biographer reports that the group Cooney left behind continues, though small, in about six countries: Northern Ireland, Scotland, England, Norway, Australia and the United

States. The larger group from which they separated is also active in many countries. A leader of this group in Ireland informed me that there are only six countries where they do *not* currently operate. Estimates concerning their membership vary from 200,000 to 700,000 worldwide. A former member, Lynn Cooper, estimates the real figure to be between 250-500,000 members. However, the influence of this larger group is considerable, particularly in countries like Ireland; they are also relatively strong and active in England and Scotland, but weaker in Wales.

A warning

I detail some of the group's distinctive beliefs and practices later but here I want to issue a warning. Although the group emphasizes the Bible and the life as well as the death of Jesus Christ, it seriously distorts the free grace of God and modifies biblical teaching concerning the sacrifice of Jesus Christ. For example, they rightly emphasize the perfect obedience of Jesus Christ in his earthly life. However, they then go on to claim we are saved by his life: 'By this complete sacrifice of his life we are reconciled to God.' But that is not what the Bible teaches. Our Lord's whole life was one of suffering but the climax of his sufferings came on the cross where he died for sinners. And without the sacrifice of himself in death there would be no salvation: 'Without the shedding of blood there is no forgiveness' (Hebrews 9:22).

WHAT THEY TEACH

They also wrongly interpret John 17:4 where Jesus says, 'I have ... completed the work...' claiming it relates to his life only. But what *was* 'completed' here? Certainly all his ministry up to that point and more. A contrast is made by Jesus in verses 4 and 5 but not between his life and death. The contrast, rather, is between glorifying the Father on earth, which includes his life, death, resurrection and ascension, then the glory he asks the Father to give him in heaven. Remember, too, that his victorious cry on the cross, 'It is finished' (John 19:30), marks the accomplishment of our salvation.

What is the challenge for us?

In his life Christ obeyed God's perfect law for us. However, that in itself does not save us. He also needed to be 'obedient to death — even death on a cross!' (Philippians 2:8) in order to suffer our punishment. Here is the good news of the gospel. And it is the sinner's *only* hope.

Four things you need to know about this group

If you want to understand the 'Two-by-Two' or Nameless Group, you need to be aware of the following four things.

1. Several divisions have taken place during the approximately one hundred years of their history, which we considered above. One splinter group can be identified as the 'Cooneyites' who followed Edward Cooney when he left the main group in 1928. Among the other groups who left are 'The Message' people. When William Irvine, the original founder of the movement, was excommunicated in 1913, hundreds of people left to follow him. They are called 'The Message' people because of their conviction that Irvine had a special message from the book of Revelation for them.
2. The main group, often called 'The Testimony', claim that they have the only true ministry, because it approximates closely to the ministries of Jesus and his apostles.
3. All the groups distort the gospel and lack a personal testimony to God's saving grace.
4. Many who leave the group speak of legalism, rejection, and emotional as well as psychological abuse. These are serious charges, but they are well documented.

To explain these points, I will ask several questions to clarify their beliefs and practices.

What is the relation between the groups?

The relation between the splinter groups and the main 'Two-by-Two' group is one of suspicion, disagreement and separation. The Cooneyites, for example, have little to do with the main group, but they are small in number.

The 5,000-strong 'Message' people are also extremely critical of the main group. The 'Message' people regard themselves as 'free', and now only meet together socially and not for meetings or Bible studies.

How do the 'Message' people differ from the main group?

Although the main group retained the original teaching of Irvine, the 'Message' people regard Irvine as a prophet, despite the character weaknesses for which he was excommunicated by the main group.

Irvine claimed that he had an 'Alpha message' for God's people. This was probably the message that they should 'sell all and go to preach'. His 'Omega message' concentrated on Jesus judging the earth and divine wrath being visited on those who were not God's people. The 'Message' people criticize the main group for retaining a great deal of Irvine's teaching but then excommunicating him and rejecting his prophet role.

Exaggerated claims are made for Irvine by his followers, including the belief that he was divinely sent to unlock the book of Revelation.

WHAT THEY TEACH

Why does the main group claim the only true ministry?

Basically because of the *location of their meetings in homes*, and also because of their *method of using itinerant preachers* who are unsalaried, homeless, single and work in pairs. Hence the name 'Two-by-Twos'.

How biblical is it for workers to go in pairs?

In evangelism, there are clear advantages for Christians to go out in twos. It provides fellowship, encouragement, protection and possibly a stronger united witness. How biblical is this principle? The Lord Jesus mentions it only twice in the Gospels. He sent the Twelve apostles 'two by two' (Mark 6:7), and likewise the Seventy (Luke 10:1). In the context, the Twelve and the Seventy were sent exclusively to Jews in Israel.

The Seventy were sent to those who lived in regions which the Lord Jesus intended to visit (see Luke 10:1). Their purpose was specific, namely, to prepare for the Lord's ministry in an area. In the Great Commission in Matthew 28:18-20, the Lord does not enforce the principle of going in pairs. When we examine Acts, we see a variation in the numbers of workers serving together. Very often one person went alone as, for example, Philip in Samaria or in the desert, or Peter going to Cornelius. Peter and John were together on occasions, but the 'two-by-two' principle in Acts is only recorded in about eight out of twenty-nine evangelistic and church situations, less than one third of the reported occasions! There is flexibility in the New Testament concerning the method. While one acknowledges that there are situations when it is practical and wise to work in groups of two, the legalism of this group in the matter must be avoided.

Must all workers remain single?

The main group insists on their workers being unmarried. Interestingly, some apostles were married; Peter is an example (Mark 1:30; Matthew 8:14). In 1 Corinthians 9:5 Paul claims the right, like other apostles, to take 'a sister, a wife' as a travelling companion. The two nouns 'sister' and 'wife' are in apposition here, and should be understood to mean a fellow believer (sister) who is married (wife) to the Christian worker. According to Hebrews 13:4 'marriage is honourable' for believers and workers. In fact, the apostle Paul indicates that 'forbidding to marry' is among the 'teachings of demons' (1 Timothy 4:1-3). Beware of legalism!

Should workers be unpaid?

The group does not believe in collecting money in church meetings or paying wages to their

WHAT THEY TEACH

workers. They live in the homes of members and receive gifts from them. They claim that this makes their
ministry unique among Christian churches. But this is
surely not so. Many Christian pastors and missionaries
live entirely by faith. They do not have a guaranteed
wage and live in a house owned or rented by the church.
Their support depends entirely on gifts received from
Christians!

The apostle Paul, on the other hand, teaches that
the preacher has the right to be supported financially
by Christians who benefit from his ministry (see 1 Corinthians 9:7-14 and 2 Corinthians 11:8).

Are Christian homes the only proper location for church meetings?

No, and the words of Acts 7:48 and 17:24 do not condemn church buildings. It is Christians themselves who
are 'God's building' (1 Corinthians 3:9), irrespective of
where they meet. And there is no command to meet only
in homes. The Christians in Acts 2:46 worshipped in the
temple daily. Acts 9:2 may imply that Paul searched for
Christians in the synagogue, not their homes. In Acts
19:9 we are told that Paul proclaimed his message in
'the lecture hall of Tyrannus'.

In 1 Corinthians 11:22 the believers are told to satisfy
their appetite for food and drink in their own houses,
not at the Lord's Supper. This clearly implies that the
Supper was celebrated somewhere other than in their
homes.

WHAT THEY TEACH

What about psychological abuse?

Some former and even current members speak of an unhappy childhood, a sense of rejection, and the long-term effects of membership. These include low self-esteem, depression, anxiety and guilt. They complain of rigid control being exercised by workers over members, including emotional and psychological abuse, even brain-washing. During the 1970s and 1980s no radios were allowed in their homes; TV, videos and make-up are still condemned, as is contact with Christian churches.

Are some group members finding Christ?

Yes, but not in great numbers. One man, after being in the group for nine years, decided to go to a Bible church, where he heard the gospel in 1995. 'I had not trusted in the blood of Jesus, but in the ministry and places/form of assembly but now [I have been] saved through the grace of God alone.' Another man, after fifteen years in the group, testifies, 'I am changed spiritually because of accepting his grace and trusting wholly in the Lord Jesus.' A young lady, who was in the group until her late teens, has a similar testimony: 'I am saved through Christ alone ... believe in eternal security, salvation by the blood of Christ and am trusting in the completed work of Christ on the cross.' And that is the only way to be saved. 'For it is by grace you have been saved, through faith — and this not from yourselves, it is the gift of God — not by works, so that no one can boast' (Ephesians 2:8-9).

RELEVANT COMPARISONS

The Nameless Group	The Bible

CHRIST'S OBEDIENCE

They rightly emphasize the Lord's perfect earthly life but are wrong in saying we are saved by his life, incorrectly using John 17:4 in support.	1. 'Without the shedding of blood there is no forgiveness' (Hebrews 9:22). 2. John 17:4-5 provides a contrast between glorifying the Father on earth, including his life, death, resurrection and ascension, and the glory he asks the Father to give him in heaven. 3. It was on the cross his work was completed: 'It is finished' (John 19:30; see also Philippians 2:8).

TWO BY TWO

From Mark 6:7, Luke 10:1, the Group teaches that their workers should only go out two by two.	1. Our Lord in Matthew 28:18-20 does not confirm that principle. 2. Sometimes the Lord's servants went on their own (Philip in Acts 8, or Peter in Acts 10)

or in larger groups, as with Paul.

CELIBATE WORKERS

This Group insists that their workers must remain single.

Peter was married (Mark 1:30; Matthew 8:14). In 1 Corinthians 9:5 Paul claims the right like other apostles to take 'a sister, a wife' to accompany him on his travels. See also 1 Timothy 4:1-3.

UNSALARIED WORKERS

This is a firm conviction on their part.

According to 1 Corinthians 9:7-14 and 2 Corinthians 11:8, workers have the right to be supported financially by those receiving their ministries.

COMPARISONS

CHAPTER NINE

NEW
APOSTOLIC
CHURCH

A BRIEF HISTORY

I received another request for help. This time it was from a missionary in Africa. Did I know anything about the teachings of the New Apostolic Church (NAC)?

His reason for seeking help was one of concern. Many churches in his part of Africa are being strongly influenced, and confused, by NAC claims and teaching.

Claims

It is not surprising that people in Africa, Europe and elsewhere are confused when they come across NAC teaching. A major reason for the confusion is the claim that the 'NAC is the only congregation which leads to God'.[1] Their claim to exclusivity is emphasized in their writings. The claim is a foolish one. What is more, it is not open to questioning on the part of NAC members.

Consider, for example, the absurdity of their claim. For one thing, it is taught that forgiveness of sins is possible only in the NAC. There are other related claims, such as: 'NAC is the only church in which the genuine doctrine of Jesus and the Apostles is proclaimed'; 'the NAC is the real continuation of the church created by Jesus'; 'All other communities only speak of God, however the NAC speaks God.' They insist that in all other churches, including Pentecostal and Evangelical churches, there is such 'a limited knowledge of God available' that 'it is not enough to be saved'.

These claims are completely unjustified. Consider the claim, for instance, that the NAC is a 'direct continuation' of the early New Testament church. This in turn raises many questions, including that of the apostolicity of the church. Biblically, we must insist that apostolic succession does not consist in the continuing office of apostle or the imaginary unbroken line of descent and blessing from the apostle Peter via bishops and popes. Not at all. We are 'apostolic' as churches and believers only if we embrace and teach the apostles' doctrine which is recorded reliably in the New Testament. That, and that alone, determines whether we are apostolic; in other words, it is a biblical and doctrinal criterion. By this criterion, as we shall see, the NAC is itself condemned.

Without any biblical justification, the NAC also claims that the Christian Church died with the death of the last apostle in the New Testament. This means, according to the NAC, that no one could enter heaven from the end of the first century AD until 1830 when their 'apostle' Johannes appeared!

And that is not all. One of their *special doctrines* teaches that 'humans who did not live at a time of living apostles, did not come into heaven' (*idem*).

Astonishingly, they say this is true of people like Abraham and David; in fact, all who lived before the birth of Jesus.

Again the Bible contradicts this false teaching. Enoch, Hebrews 11:5 tells us, 'did not experience death ... because God had taken him away'. The only possible conclusion is that Enoch was taken to heaven. Moses and Elijah 'appeared in glory' at the transfiguration of the Lord Jesus. These heavenly visitors talked with him about his forthcoming death (the Greek word means exodus/departure) at Jerusalem (Luke 9:31). Romans 4:3-8 also establishes that Old Testament believers, including Abraham and David, were justified by grace through faith, like ourselves.

The NAC states that men of God like Luther, Calvin, Owen and Edwards did not go to heaven when they died! Despite being outstanding students and teachers of the Bible who themselves trusted and obeyed the Lord, the NAC foolishly teaches they were disadvantaged. But why? Because they lacked a 'living' apostle on earth during their life span. Once again they have no biblical support for this irresponsible teaching.

This raises the issue of apostles. Their position in the New Testament church was unique. Ephesians 2:20 states that the Christian Church is 'built on the foundation of the apostles and prophets...' That word 'foundation' in the statement is crucial. A foundation is only laid once.

Afterwards, the rest of the building is erected. Similarly, the role of the apostles was a foundational one, never to be repeated. Their privilege, under the direction of the Holy Spirit, was to teach, preach, establish churches and instruct Christians before, and during, the time the Gospels and Epistles were written. Once the New Testament was complete, their foundational work was ended and apostles would never be needed again in the church.

This fact is confirmed in Hebrews 2:3-4 where readers are warned not to ignore God's 'great salvation'. Several reasons are given for this but a major reason is that this gospel 'was first announced by the Lord' in his public ministry. Another reason is that this gospel of salvation 'was confirmed to us by those who heard him', that is, the apostles. Related to that is the further fact that God also 'testified to it', authenticating the authority of these apostles 'by signs, wonders and various miracles, and gifts of the Holy Spirit...' Now that their unique apostolic ministry is complete, the church no longer needs apostles or revelatory or miraculous gifts. The NAC emphasis then on 'living apostles' must be rejected.

Background

I need to pause and tell you more about this cult in terms of its background, size and influence. The NAC started in Germany as far back as 1836. Interestingly, its roots go back further to Edward Irving who came to encourage the expression of spiritual gifts (1 Corinthians 12:8-10) and apostolic church government. Forced to leave his London church, he established a new church in 1832, which then became a popular centre for advocating his ideas.

Following Irving's death in 1834 as many as twelve men were appointed 'apostles' thus completing the 'apostolic college'. This centre was then organized as the 'Catholic Apostolic Church' (CAC). Their plans were ambitious and international; new churches were established in many countries, largely through the work of these twelve men.

One of the countries where CAC work prospered was Germany. In the period 1860-1862 CAC leaders in that country, wanting an unlimited number of 'apostles', disagreed with the English 'apostles'. 1863 saw the emergence of this breakaway group, the NAC.[2]

Today NAC has about 60,000 congregations worldwide with nearly 300 'apostles'. Its membership is near to sixteen million. Zurich in Switzerland has been the NAC international headquarters since 1980. We need to recognize that the influence of NAC is considerable and worldwide; particularly in Africa, it has been relatively successful.

You may be wondering, however, what this cult says about the gospel and how we can be saved. Apart from emphasizing that salvation is only found in the NAC and through its leaders,

HISTORY

it has very little to say about the Lord Jesus Christ and his unique death for sinners.

Yes, NAC refers to Christ. In fact, Article 2 of their *New Apostolic Creed* describes the Lord Jesus as 'the only begotten Son of God … conceived by the Holy Ghost, born of the Virgin Mary, suffered … crucified, dead and buried … rose again … ascended…' That sounds good but Christ always recedes into the background in their writings in favour of NAC leaders and their own essential mediatorial role. Sadly, nothing is said in these ten articles about the nature and purpose of the Lord's death on the cross.

By contrast, their emphasis is on water baptism being 'part of the rebirth', and Holy Communion which 'establishes our fellowship with Jesus Christ…' Salvation is mediated only through one of their apostles and the sacraments which they alone can administer.

Peter's apostolic message in Acts 4:12 is relevant here and needs to be thundered out to all: 'Salvation is found in no one else, for there is no other name under heaven given to men by which we must be saved.' The salvation purchased by Christ is appropriated only by personal faith in him, and him alone, without any other human mediator or sacrament.

NAC work in England was launched in 1947 by two German detainees in a prisoner of war camp at Langdon Hills, near Laindon in Essex. Their names were Duemke and Quessel. They influenced other German prisoners at this time, as well as two local English families.

Similarly, some Englishmen serving in the Forces in Germany at the end of World War 2 were contacted by

German NAC families. Some of these servicemen became NAC members and continued working actively for the cult on returning to England. Partly for these reasons, NAC work in the UK grew between 1947 and 1965. For example, services were held initially in Laindon, Essex; Camberwell Green, London; and Great Somerford, Wiltshire. But further congregations were then established in Nottingham, Birmingham, Glasgow, Swindon, Bristol, Gloucester, Brynamman (South Wales), Ilfracombe and Tiverton.

Missions were held in many places, some producing settled congregations in places like Dublin, Welling, Cambridge, Chelmsford, Dover, High Wycombe, Leicester, Liverpool, Reading, Meadway and St Albans. The London Central congregation property was bought in 1959 and extended in 1996.

The Bible

First of all, we consider their view of the Bible. In their *Doctrine of the New Apostolic Church* (p. 2), the NAC makes the claim: 'The Bible is the basis of the doctrine of the NAC.'

However, do not be fooled by this statement; it is ambiguous and misleading. Under a section entitled 'The Bible', the NAC makes seven statements concerning the Bible. The statement quoted above is the first of these, but the other six all qualify and contradict this first statement!

The second statement boldly announces: 'The Bible testifies clearly that the NAC is the correct and only church of God.' No evidence is provided for this wild and extraordinary claim.

The Apocrypha

The third statement announces that 'The Apocrypha belongs to the Bible text.' This is disappointing and raises huge questions. The term 'apocrypha' refers partly to thirteen books which were never included in the Hebrew Bible for good reasons. The New Testament writers never quote from any of the apocryphal books. Nor do they attach authority to them in any way.

Remember, too, that Christ acknowledged the same Old Testament as we have when he said to the Jews, 'You diligently study the Scriptures ... These are the Scriptures that testify about me' (John 5:39). The testimony of Christ must be conclusive for us.

There were, in addition, many writings, especially after the New Testament period, which were 'deliberate fabrications and never had any serious claim to canonicity'.[3] Many such documents originated from heretical sects like Gnostics. Some of these writings have been lost while most of the others survive only in fragments or, occasionally, quotations in historical texts which still exist.

One writer makes an accurate observation: 'It is striking how few of the apocryphal books were ever officially excluded, they just never entered the race' for inclusion in the canon of Scripture.[4]

Not sufficient?

NAC's fourth statement claims that trust in the Lord and his Word 'is not sufficient'. What else is needed? 'Without faith in the apostles of the NAC redemption is not attainable.'

This claim will be picked up later, but it is another example of how far removed from the Bible is the NAC in its teachings.

Statements 5, 6 and 7 really make the same point but in different ways. 'The Bible is not the word of God for today' they inform us. And — undermining the trustworthiness, authority, sufficiency and finality of the Bible — the NAC claims that only their apostles can interpret the Bible correctly and make it alive.

Sadly, they stray even further away from God's Word when they insist that NAC apostles 'can announce new obligatory teachings or revelation'. And they have more to tell us: if the Bible disagrees with what their apostles say then it is the latter, not the Bible, that members must accept!

In other words, there must be a blind, unquestioning acceptance by NAC members of all that their leaders say or do, even if it contradicts what God himself says in the Bible.

Now that was not the attitude of the Lord Jesus, for he always submitted and appealed to the authority of the Old Testament Scripture (eg. Matthew 4:4, 6, 7; 22:29, 37-40). And this was also the course followed by the New Testament apostles. Even when the religious leaders of their day gave them clear commands and warnings, the apostles responded: 'We must obey God rather than men!' (Acts 5:29).

Forgiveness

NAC's erroneous view of the Bible leads it into serious error with regard to several other major doctrines. Take forgiveness as one example. *Who* can forgive our sins? The Bible answer is abundantly clear — only God can forgive sins (Mark 2:7). The NAC answer, however, is different: 'Forgiveness of sins is possible only in the NAC';[5] that is, through and from its leaders. Here is a clear contradiction of Bible teaching.

But *how* does God forgive our sins? Once again the Bible's answer is emphatic. God forgives sins only in, and through, his Son, the Lord Jesus Christ: 'In him [that is, Christ] we have redemption through his blood, the forgiveness of sins, in accordance with the riches of God's grace' (Ephesians 1:7).

WHAT THEY TEACH

That Bible statement takes us to the very centre of the gospel message — it tells us that the gospel is about Christ, not about NAC leaders or 'apostles'. And the gospel is about what Christ did, especially in his death on the cross.

Complete and sufficient

In fact, each word in Ephesians 1:7 is important and pregnant with meaning. 'Redemption' is a key term in the Bible — it means release from slavery on payment of a price. And that costly price for Christ was 'his blood', that is, his life given in death as a sacrifice and atonement for our sins.

'Forgiveness of sins' means we are set free by Christ from the guilt, punishment and power of our sins. It is glorious news of a completed and sufficient sacrifice by Jesus Christ. Nothing can or need be contributed by ourselves or others as a basis for our forgiveness and salvation. Salvation is all because of his 'grace' and totally undeserved by us.

Once again the NAC distorts this biblical gospel. 'In the New Apostolic Church', we are told, 'the salvation work started by Jesus is brought to completion by the apostles whom he has sent' (*Q&A 171*). They also insist that the Lord 'has sent ... and still sends' his living apostles 'to teach, to forgive sins...'[6].

Voyage of discovery

For these reasons, I want to appeal to NAC members. My appeal is expressed in the words of a former NAC member, Stephen Langtry, who himself appealed to NAC leaders in January 1999.

Langtry ended his letter with these words:

In 1991, I started a personal voyage of discovery out of the New Apostolic Church… The acknowledgement that I had been wrong and had taught other people those same errors brought with it a wonderful sense of freedom. The words of Jesus, 'and you shall know the truth, and the truth shall make you free' (John 8:32) come to mind … we owe it to ourselves and to those who look to us for guidance to be honest and to act with integrity. A useful starting point for me was to read the Bible anew, to study the history of Christianity and to evaluate NAC doctrines in the light of these … if you do this sincerely it will not leave your life unchanged.

Such a Bible voyage will lead NAC leaders and followers to see the sufficiency and finality of Christ's sacrifice for sin on the cross. No organization or human leader should detract from that sacrifice or add to it.

There are four questions that must be discussed concerning the NAC. These questions enable us to explore further the ethos and fallibility of this group.

Is the NAC cultic?

Our first question is basic — is the NAC cultic? Consider the following evidence. We are informed that 'faithful members of the NAC ask for advice before making all important decisions'.[7] These decisions relate to such major steps as marriage, employment, house relocation and so on.

It is wise to seek advice before making major personal decisions. One suspects, however, that it is permission rather than advice that NAC leaders seek to give. This points to a rigid control of members' lives.

Look at it from another perspective. The 'ideal NAC member', we are informed, 'believes everything' that an NAC leader says, 'unchecked, without understanding ... and without any question'.

Absolute authority

The authority of leaders, therefore, is absolute — blind and total obedience in everything is demanded from members. 'There should be no criticism' of NAC doctrine, we are told, 'either in private or at NAC meetings' (p. 4).

What if an NAC member disagrees with what is taught? The procedure is clear: 'there is no discussion...' (p. 2). 'All decisions', it is stressed, are made centrally. Add to this NAC's claim to exclusivity — no one can know God, receive forgiveness or the Holy Spirit except through the NAC — and we have an alarming picture.

A passive, unquestioning submission to all that is taught or commanded by leaders exposes members to the dangers of mind-control, exploitation and the loss of personal freedom.

The recommendation that members should put photographs of their chief leader in their homes increases one's conviction that NAC is cultic.

Support for Hitler?

A second question relates to NAC's past history: did leaders support Hitler's regime in the 1930s-40s?

The evidence points to an affirmative answer. During the period when over six million Jews were exterminated and many confessing Christians exiled, tortured or murdered by the Nazis, the NAC was actively supporting Hitler's Nationalist Socialist regime. As early as 1932, the NAC Chief Apostle, Johann Bischoff, corresponded personally with Hitler. Messages of support were sent to him, some of which claimed that Hitler was God's specially chosen emissary.

After Hitler came to power in March 1933, Bischoff wrote to all the German congregations denouncing as 'atrocity propaganda' the criticisms being made of Hitler's government.

WHAT THEY TEACH

Learning lessons

Support for Hitler from the NAC appears to have been extensive. At least thirteen German NAC leaders were members of the Nazi Party; opponents of Hitler were excommunicated; NAC young people were encouraged to join the Nazi Party; and finance was raised for the Party.

This is shameful — but has the group learnt its lesson? One wonders. For example, in the former German Democratic Republic (East Germany), NAC youth were directed to give enthusiastic support to the Communist Party's Youth Movement.

Leaders of NAC also gave public support for the Communist government there, despite their ruthless policies of oppression.

Date fixing

My third question asks whether the NAC, contrary to Scripture, has indulged in 'date fixing' concerning the Lord's return.

Yes, and there is a background to NAC predictions. The forerunner of NAC is the Catholic Apostolic Church (CAC), which also gave several dates for Christ's personal return in glory.

The dates given were 1835, 1838, 1842, 1845, 1855, 1866 and 1877. There was disappointment when each date passed without fulfilment of the prophecy.

After division within the church, two new 'apostles', Schwarz and Krebs, taught wrongly that the Lord would return before they themselves died. However, the most famous failed prediction was in the early 1950s.

It was on Christmas Day 1951 that Johann Bischoff, the NAC leader, predicted that Jesus would return during his lifetime.

Over three years later, in July 1954, Bischoff told his supporters at a church service: 'The Lord has let us know that he will come during my lifetime, and thus during your lifetime too. If you cannot make yourself believe in this, if you do not make this final step, you will remain outside.'

His prediction was elevated to the status of official NAC doctrine and became a condition for membership.

Disillusioned

Did Bischoff really believe this prediction? It appears so, for three months later on 12 September 1954 he insisted: 'I am clearly aware that should I die — which will not be the case — then God's work would be destroyed… Should the case really be that I go home, which it will not be, then the work of redemption would be ruined.'

Needless to say, when Bischoff died in 1960 he was exposed as a false prophet and many NAC members became disillusioned. After all, they had sold their homes, resigned from employment, cancelled insurance/pension policies and had suffered ridicule for believing Bischoff.

Yet instead of denouncing Bischoff for his failed prediction, NAC leaders had the temerity to claim that God changed his mind! Why did they not acknowledge that Bischoff was one of the 'many false prophets' whom the Lord Jesus said 'will appear and deceive many people' (Matthew 24:11)?

The Lord's teaching concerning the time of his return is abundantly clear: 'No one knows about that day or hour, not even the angels in heaven, nor the Son, but only the Father' (Matthew 24:36).

Unbiblical

Here is our final question — what does the NAC teach about the 'unsaved' who have died?

Their teaching on this point is weird and unbiblical. Briefly, they insist that people can be saved after death but they must 'still fulfil the same conditions as the living members of the NAC'.[8] These conditions are: belief in NAC apostles, NAC baptism, 'holy sealing' and communion!

A further illustration of NAC's departure from Bible teaching is their official statement that 'From time to time the Chief Apostle unlocks the areas of the dead ones' (p. 4) in order to give salvation to some of them.

They are in error at many points here, including the theory that people can be saved after they die. Listen to what Jesus Christ, the Son of God, says on this subject.

Death seals our destiny

He tells us in Luke 16:19-31 of two men who died. One was poor but a believer, so immediately at death he went to heaven (v. 22). His name was Lazarus and his condition in heaven was an extremely happy one.

The contrast with the other man who died is stark. He was rich and lived on earth in the lap of luxury (vv. 19, 25), but sadly he was not a believer. Our Lord may have used this rich man as a picture of religious leaders in verse 14, who are described as 'lovers of money' rather than lovers of God and his truth.

Death for the rich unbeliever was a tragedy. The Lord Jesus leaves us in no doubt as to what happened to him: 'The rich man also died and was buried. In hell, where he was in torments...' (vv. 22-23). He not only lived on after death but also consciously suffered punishment there.

Nor can anyone leave hell — that is the message of verse 26. Heaven and hell are eternal states with no movement of people from one to the other. Death seals the destiny of each individual.

Contacting the dead

There are other errors in the NAC teaching about unlocking 'the areas of the dead'. The Bible condemns all attempts to contact the dead and no human has authority over the dead or their future. That is the prerogative of Jesus Christ alone. In Revelation 1:17, Christ is 'the First and the Last', eternally existent and omnipotent. He is the life and the origin of all created life (John 1:1-3). And he alone will judge the dead, both small and great (Revelation 20:11-15).

Christ 'was dead' — he tasted death in order to bear the punishment of our sin. Yet he adds amazingly: 'behold I am alive for ever and ever'. Only this victorious one can claim to 'have the keys of Death and Hades'. The 'keys' point to Christ's absolute power. He it is who welcomes believers to heaven and sentences unbelievers to hell.

At his Second Coming, he will reunite body and soul. Then death and Hades will be cast into the lake of fire (Revelation 20:14).

Only Christ is worthy of our trust and obedience.

NAC	The Bible

APOSTLES

Apostles are necessary today, and only NAC have them! Their purpose is to teach, give more revelation, forgive and direct churches.	Ephesians 2:20 makes it clear that the Christian church is 'built on the foundation of the apostles and prophets'. This foundation was laid only once and is never repeated. Once the New Testament was complete and their foundational work ended, apostles would never again be needed in the church.

BIBLE

'The Bible is not the word of God for today', NAC informs us.	'Your Word, O LORD, is eternal; it stands firm in the heavens' (Psalm 119:89). 'Your statutes are my heritage for ever; they are the joy of my heart' (Psalm 119:111).

JESUS CHRIST

While affirming Christ's deity, virgin birth, death, resurrection and ascension, NAC gives greater prominence to their 'apostles' than to Christ.	'He must become greater; I must become less' (John 3:30). 'For we do not preach ourselves, but Jesus Christ as Lord' (2 Corinthians 4:5).

FORGIVENESS

This is only possible in the NAC.	'In him [Christ] we have redemption through his blood, the forgiveness of sins, in accordance with the riches of God's grace' (Ephesians 1:7).

AFTER DEATH

1. Unbelievers can be saved after they die.

2. Believers only went to heaven at times when there were 'apostles' living on earth.

1. Luke 16:19-31.

2. Enoch went to glory (Hebrews 11:5); Moses and Elijah 'appeared in glorious splendour' with Jesus at his transfiguration (Luke 9:31. See also Romans 4:3-8; Revelation 1:18).

CHAPTER TEN

UNIVERSAL PENTECOSTAL CHURCH

A BRIEF HISTORY

Sri Lanka origins

The Universal Pentecostal Church started its work in England as the 'Ceylon Pentecostal Mission', with headquarters in Wimbledon, London. Having changed its name to the Universal Pentecostal Church, in June 1990 they relocated to 20 Acre Lane, Brixton.

Other centres and 'Faith Homes' belonging to the group in the United Kingdom are found at 40 Severn Street, Leicester; 15 Buckingham Road, Edgware, Birmingham; 53 Torquay Gardens, Ilford; and Church Street, Dolerw, Welshpool in mid-Wales.

Successful

Until about 1990, the majority of its members were Sri Lankan, probably as many as ninety-five per cent. The move to Brixton in 1990 was a success, and so many new people began attending the services that they decided to move their monthly Sunday communion service to a Saturday. Several hundred people are now

WHO ARE THEY?

members of this church and its influence in certain areas of England is increasing.

The church is also in association with various other groups: The Pentecostal Mission (India); The New Testament Church (not the commonly-known one) in New York, Toronto and Trinidad; and the Eglise de Pentecote Primitive in Paris. They also have assemblies in Malaysia, Singapore, Australia (Melbourne), Papua New Guinea, Sierra Leone and Switzerland (Zurich).

History

The history of the Universal Pentecostal Church (UPC) is an interesting one. While serving as a missionary in Ceylon (now Sri Lanka), an English woman, Dorothy Brae, came into contact with the Ceylon Pentecostal Mission (CPM). Returning to England, she used her house as a 'Faith Home' according to the practice of CPM. The house was located in Haydon Park Road, Wimbledon, and she lived there with other full-time CPM workers. There is no doubt that Miss Brae gave a considerable impetus to the work of CPM at this time.

As increasing numbers of people arrived in England from Ceylon, her 'Faith Home' was an open house for many of them. Bible studies were held there on Thursday evenings and prayer meetings on Saturday evenings. On occasions, baptisms were conducted in a large tank in the rear garden, while Sunday services were held around the corner in Coronation Hall in Ashcombe Road.

HISTORY

Branches

At this time, an old hospital was bought by CPM in Newark for use as a large Faith Home. Pastor Joseph, who had served in the Indian army, was responsible for this centre and the few members there. In an attempt to increase numbers, he met with a group of West Indian believers in Leicester who had formed their own church. After Joseph had preached for them, they agreed to join the CPM. Interestingly, this West Indian branch still continues in Leicester.

In the early 1970s the Newark branch moved to Nottingham where there was a large Faith Home off Woodborough Road. CPM meetings were held here and also in the Co-op Hall in Nottingham city centre. When Pastor Joseph died in the late 1970s, this Faith Home was closed.

In 1979 the London branch moved a distance of two miles from Wimbledon to Raynes Park with a Faith Home in Oxford Avenue. A hall was bought in Dorien Road for prayer meetings but Sunday services and Bible classes were held in Wimbledon College, a Jesuit school.

Now known as UPC, they purchased their first church building in Acre Lane, Brixton, in June 1990 for £800,000, a property which they obtained from Christian Science. Members contributed sacrificially for this purchase, some selling their own possessions. Today, the building has extensive accommodation facilities for full-time workers and visitors.

Influential people

Another English woman has played a significant role in the work of UPC in England from the beginning. Her name is Pauline Wheeler and her responsibilities have been primarily in the areas of finance and negotiations, especially where new buildings were involved. She has been involved with UPC in different centres and is currently at Brixton.

There is also a white American, Don Spiers, who is extremely influential in the UPC. Earlier in his life he was an architect in the United States, but 'surrendered all to build God's kingdom'.

Rejecting the opportunity to become the 'chief pastor' in UPC, he freelances within the organization visiting different congregations, and travels worldwide. One of his aims is to look for new centres to establish UPC congregations and he attends most annual conventions around the world. This man is an important person within the organization.

Strong character

There is one more person I want to mention here and he is Albert Jebanayagam. From what I can ascertain

he came from Jaffna in Ceylon in the 1960s, but he may have been here earlier. He studied in Bolton and qualified as an accountant, working in a London bank.

A capable instrumentalist and a good singer, Albert was a 'charismatic' figure and able to attract people to the church. He eventually joined the movement's full-time ministry and returned to Sri Lanka to work with UPC or, as it is still known in that country, CPM.

But Albert was a strong character and determined to lead the work in his own way. There was an inevitable rift, with the result that the leadership dismissed him as a CPM full-time worker.

However, that was not the end of the matter. Many of the full-time workers decided to leave CPM with him and Albert established his own 'church' in Sri Lanka, where it is known as the Canaan Fellowship. Albert still travels worldwide, preaching, and is a frequent visitor to England.

Danger signals

Even if one looks only superficially at this organization, there are clear danger signals to be seen. For example, no member is allowed to consult a medical doctor or receive treatment. Sadly, some die as a consequence.

Complete submission to leaders is required and members are expected to share with them the most personal details of their lives. This is only one expression of their heavy shepherding.

Nor are members allowed to mix with other Christians or attend other churches, for they would then become 'unequally yoked'. More seriously, the group emphasizes personal revelations, visions, prophecies and the hearing of 'voices'. Consequently, the Bible is misused and members are enslaved to men reputed to be infallible and supreme.

Pastor Paul

In terms of biographies, the book I now wish to mention is far from being a classic. Nor is it particularly well written. With an unattractive cover and format, this paperback has been produced cheaply in the Third World to make it available to a wide readership in Asia, Africa and Europe. The biographer is anonymous, but is, I suspect, a senior UPC leader. The writer describes his subject in uncritical terms; in many parts it is fanciful and exaggerated. The title of the book is *The Biography of Pastor Paul*.[1]

But why mention this book at all? Well, in order to understand the UPC it is helpful to know about its founder, 'Pastor Paul'. The book throws much light on some of the strange, even mistaken, views and practices of the UPC founder — practices and beliefs that continue today. In the preface, Pastor Paul is compared favourably with the sixteenth-century Protestant Reformers. Referring to 2 Chronicles 16:9, the writer claims that 'The Lord's eyes found such an upright man in Pastor Paul, in the 20th century.'

Converted from Hinduism

Born in South India in 1881 into a Hindu family, the father's intention was that this boy should become a Hindu priest like his grandfather. When he was 14, Paul (his original name was Ramankutty) went to Sri Lanka looking for work. Eventually, a wealthy Christian, Dr Asarappa, who had been converted to Christ from Hinduism through the witness of the Church Missionary Society, gave him work and welcomed him into his home. Paul learnt about the gospel of Christ from this loving family but opposed their Christian teaching.

Four years later, Paul claims to have been deeply affected by a vision of the Lord Jesus. Then, at the age of twenty-one he made an open profession of faith in Christ. The Asarappa family was thrilled and Ramankutty was baptized without delay by a CMS clergyman and given the Christian name 'Paul'.

Returning home, he experienced hostility from his family and, for his personal safety, went back to Sri Lanka where he witnessed freely to the Lord's grace. He was then given two years

HISTORY

training in the CMS Bible Seminary in Kottayam and ordained as an evangelist and catechist. He also married a fine Christian lady.

Private 'revelations'

Nominalism in his church, coupled with a lack of biblical understanding among members, discouraged him greatly. Some Australian missionaries spoke to him of 'Spirit-baptism' and alleged the 'prior necessity' of baptism by immersion. Paul claims to have received Spirit-baptism in 1921 followed later by the ability to speak in tongues. During these months he claims to have come to a much deeper love for the Lord.

However, these experiences were accompanied by a series of visions and hearing 'the voice of God'. He attached major importance to these private 'revelations' and made certain decisions as a result. These included leaving the Anglican Church, forfeiting a regular wage, living wholly 'by faith', and insisting that his full-time leaders and members should literally forsake all in following Christ.

Gradually, Pastor Paul gathered more and more people around him. He established 'Faith Homes' for his full-time workers, all of whom had to be wholly committed to their leader as well as to God.

In 1924 he registered his work in Sri Lanka as the Ceylon Pentecostal Mission. Slowly the work grew, and spread to a number of countries. This numerical growth was due to some extent to the leader's claim to have regular divine revelations and the power to heal and perform miracles. He also maintained tight control over his organization until his death in July 1945.

Concerns?

There were aspects of Pastor Paul's life and teaching which were clearly wrong, but one cannot escape the conclusion that this man was a sincere and earnest Christian. Alongside the mystical and dubious claims of Pastor Paul, there was evidence of grace in his life. Marks of holiness, constant prayerfulness and trust in the Lord, coupled with a zeal for evangelism and a desire to know the Spirit's power upon his preaching, characterized his life.

But what does this church really stand for and how does it compare with Scripture?

Theology

Justification

Concerning justification, we are informed that it is the 'act of God's free grace by which we receive remission of sins'.[2] Although true, this is not an adequate summary of the Bible's teaching on the subject.

Yes, justification is something God alone does in his 'free grace'; as sinners, all we deserve is to be rejected and punished, by God. So why is the UPC statement insufficient, and how does it fail to convey the marvel of the gospel?

The word 'justify' is a legal term; a verdict is given by God the judge regarding our innocence in his sight. When God justifies, he pronounces the believing sinner 'right' and 'not guilty' with regard to his holy law, although the sinner has broken that law repeatedly.

But how can sinners be declared righteous and not guilty? The Bible explains. We are justified through the substitutionary death of Christ, whom 'God presented ... as a sacrifice of atonement, through faith in his blood ... so as to be just and the one who justifies those who have faith in Jesus' (Romans 3:25-26; 8:33). And again, 'Christ Jesus, who has become for us ... our righteousness, holiness and redemption' (1 Corinthians 1:30).

It is the glorious righteousness of Jesus Christ, which is reckoned to my account when I trust in him. Condemnation is no longer a sentence hanging over my head. In fact, all my sins, past, present and future, are all forgiven through Christ. That is fantastic news.

Emphasis

After reading many of their magazines, I am convinced the UPC needs to place much greater emphasis on our Lord's sacrificial death for sinners. After all, that is the heart of the gospel. And it is exceedingly more central

WHAT THEY BELIEVE

than matters like healing, separation, 'entire sanctification', ministry and a 'three-stage Advent', with which they seem to be preoccupied.

To my amazement, they provide no doctrinal statement concerning the nature, purpose, sufficiency and finality of the Lord's death. All they say is that they preach 'his crucifixion'. They refer often to 'the blood' of Christ, but again I have struggled to find references in their publications to the *significance* of our Saviour's death. This is possibly assumed by the UPC, but why not spell it out clearly?

Many testimonies in their magazines refer to 'victory through the blood of Jesus'[3] but such references are usually in the context of occult deliverance, healing or sanctification rather than Christ's penal, substitutionary sacrifice on behalf of sinners, which alone is the ground of our hope and justification. The UPC needs urgently to focus more clearly on 'the Lamb of God, who takes away the sin of the world' (John 1:29).

Distinctive errors

We will now look at some of the distinctive but erroneous teachings of the UPC. These are largely associated with their claim concerning 'private revelations', which is given such great prominence within the UPC.

'Revelations' refers to their claim that important information about, or intimations of, the Lord's particular purpose is being divinely imparted to a leader in the UPC. The word 'private' refers to the mode in which these revelations are supposedly given. Such revelations do not come through the objective, inspired Word of God, namely, the Bible. Instead, they are claimed to come directly from God by means of visions, dreams, a 'voice', a 'presence', tongues-speaking and prophecies.

As we mentioned earlier, illustrations of their claim can be found in the life of Pastor Paul, the founder of UPC. As a young child, for example, it is reported that he heard the Lord Jesus speaking directly to him on several occasions. The voice said 'clearly' to him, 'I am Jesus.'[4] At the age of eighteen, he claimed 'a vision of the Lord Jesus Christ' then, three years later, a further vision in which 'the Lord Jesus spoke to him'.[5] He often felt the Holy Spirit speaking directly to him in a variety of situations.

The UPC founder refers to some 'extraordinary experiences' like 'standing together with the Lord on the top of a very high mountain' in direct conversation.[6] Another weird 'experience' was 'seeing the devil' in answer to his repeated prayers to the Lord.[7]

Authoritarian

Such private revelations are not confined to Pastor Paul. In fact, the 'servants of God' in the UPC are also expected to receive direct messages from heaven. These 'servants of God' are those who have joined the 'full-time ministry'. To do so, they must abandon their jobs, houses, money and, if married, even their wives, and then continue to live apart in order to concentrate on the ministry. The office of 'pastor' is distinguishable from, although related to, that of a 'servant of God'. One crucial difference is that to be a 'pastor' a man must never have been married.

It is these 'servants of God' who lead the UPC, and do so in an extremely authoritarian manner. What they say must be accepted as coming from God. And the reason? Because they are the ones who receive 'revelations', visions and dreams, which enable them to instruct the church. Nor can they be questioned or opposed, since that is viewed as rebellion against God and his servants. Even their reading and teaching of the Bible is deemed to be authoritative, for the same reason.

Sadly, these leaders are believed to give the ultimate interpretation of everything that is allegedly from God. 'As the servants of God', they insist, 'we give the counsel of God.' And this is one reason why the UPC opposes Bible colleges. After all, with their claim of continuous revelation and what appear to be infallible teachers, they do not perceive a need for faithful and responsible Bible teaching from others.

Dreams

How should we respond to this claim regarding private, authoritative revelations? First of all, I question some of the claims concerning private revelations given to the UPC founder and others. A careful reading of the biography of Pastor Paul and the circumstances surrounding these 'revelations' makes me feel extremely sceptical. Was the 'voice' he heard rather a subjective but vivid thought in his mind, which he later externalized as a 'divine voice'? This is probable. One wonders, too, whether what are called 'visions' were in fact dreams, for some of these experiences occurred at night or when Pastor Paul was tired.

It is a scientifically established fact that we all dream and that we dream in sleep about every ninety minutes. On average, an individual has five sessions of dreaming per night of sleep. And some dreams can be very vivid and significant.

I accept the principle that God can sovereignly use a dream to speak to an individual. For example, on my first visit to Asia in 1991 I met a Christian who informed me that God first spoke to her in a dream while she was still a Buddhist. She knew that God was directing her in the dream to go to a nearby Christian church to hear about Jesus Christ. Within a few days of hearing the gospel preached in that church, she had trusted in the Lord Jesus for salvation. One of my questions to her was this: had God used other dreams to speak to her? Her answer in faltering English was emphatic. 'Oh no,

God only speaks to me in the Bible.' As she held tightly to her well-used Bible, she added, 'I do not need dreams.' The woman was right. All we need is the Bible and that is where God speaks to us.

Psychological pressure

Secondly, I have general concerns regarding these private revelations in the UPC. For example, their alleged frequency is disturbing. It leads to high expectations, and even psychological pressure to claim and report extraordinary experiences. The end result is a dependence on these 'revelations'. This serves to boost the status of the leaders and to reassure members that their messages are infallible and from God.

Then there is the tendency to self-importance. For Pastor Paul the reported visions enhanced his own prestige, and gave an impression to people of his greatness. One illustration of this is his claim to have been granted his request to see the devil. The UPC founder felt honoured to have been given this answer to prayer.

His biographer writes, 'Well realising that it lay in God's manifold wisdom not to reveal unsearchable and deep secrets to man, he greatly praised God and glorified Him.'[8] The implication is clear. No other humans had been given this experience.

Prophecy

Thirdly, we need to respond biblically to this UPC emphasis. And they challenge us at this point: 'Even some people of God consider visions, dreams and the voice of God as rare events' (p. 21). Joel 2:28 is then used to support their position: 'Your sons and daughters will prophesy, your old men will dream dreams, your young men will see visions.' This prophecy, quoted in Acts 2:17-18 and fulfilled at Pentecost, needs to be understood correctly. In Acts 2:14-21 Peter explains the significance of what happened on the Day of Pentecost. The outpouring of the Holy Spirit upon the apostles was a fulfilment of Joel's prophecy. It is a unique moment in salvation history. It marked Christ's enthronement in heaven (John 7:39) and was also the inauguration of 'the last days' (from Pentecost to the return of Christ in glory). It inaugurated the new age of the Spirit, who is poured out in abundance on his people.

There are other reasons why Acts 2 is unique. The Christian Church reaches maturity here; it is distinguished from the nation of Israel and becomes international. That is part of the significance of the statement: 'I will pour out my Spirit *on all people.*' That includes Jews and Gentiles, rich and poor, slaves and free, men and women, as well as the young and old.

Unnecessary

What about the prophecies, visions and dreams mentioned in Acts 2:17-18? The background is Numbers

12:6 and it is important. God revealed himself to Old Testament prophets through visions and dreams, but Moses alone was privileged to have direct communication with him (vv. 7-8). Notice, therefore, how in Acts 2:17 the three words, 'prophesy' (also v. 18), 'visions' and 'dreams' are inseparably related, and are possibly 'all one thing' (Luther). 'Prophesy' has 'an umbrella-use' says John Stott.[9]

As John Calvin explains, rather than prediction or giving revelation, the meaning of prophecy here is 'understanding'. Through the gospel of Christ, the Old Testament promise is now fulfilled, namely, that 'they will all know *me...*' (Jeremiah 31:34). Those who know God will also forth-tell ('prophesy') this good news and witness to Christ.

Acts 2:17-18 does not, therefore, encourage visions and dreams. It does something far more glorious; it highlights the fulfilment of rich covenant promises. The most glorious of the promises concerns knowing God. And that is only possible through the Bible.

Doing the 'ministry'

Some years ago a respected pastor in the UPC died. His name was Pastor C. K. Lazarus. Years earlier, as a young man, he informed his UPC leaders that he had decided 'to do the ministry remaining unmarried'.[10] He received a positive response: 'The gospel workers of the Ceylon Pentecostal Mission (the old name of our Mission) are consecrated servants of God; you may join them and do the ministry.' The UPC founder, Pastor Paul, agreed that 'Lazarus is a chosen one for the ministry.' Promptly, Lazarus sold all his possessions and entered the ministry. Soon after, he claimed to have had a dream in which the Lord Jesus laid his hand on him and blessed him.

It was during the UPC Toronto 1998 meetings that another would-be pastor, Menayeto Mankita, says he 'stood up to dedicate [himself] to serve the Lord full-time'[11]. Mankita's family was unhappy with his decision even to join the UPC. One relative thought that 'the pastors at the church were brain-washing' him, while his mother 'thought that this church was a cult'. Persecution from his family continued until he 'was taken for the ministry at the Ohio convention in 1999'. Mankita claims he also received prophecies and dreams during this period.

These two examples illustrate what it means to be a 'minister' or 'servant' of God in the UPC. Both men claimed to have received prophecies and dreams, and the UPC teaches that to such 'servants are revealed the mysteries of the kingdom of God'.[12]

All UPC 'servants' are expected to have private revelations (other members, including children, are also expected to have visions, dreams, speak in tongues and prophesy). But pastors must also remain unmarried and forsake all material possessions. Only such people, we are told, are worthy to preach the gospel.

Pastors Lazarus and Mankita, therefore, met all these requirements.

The UPC is uncompromising in this respect: 'Ministers of the Gospel cannot have any inheritance in the world.'[13] On what bases does the UPC make these demands?

No inheritance

1. 'The Levites had no inheritance, because they bear the ark of the Lord.' The reference is to Deuteronomy 10:8-9. Obviously, the primary application of that verse is to the Old Testament. The Levites were to 'stand before the LORD to minister to him' and assist the priests in their duties at the tabernacle. But the Levitical order, the Aaronic priesthood and all their ceremonial duties have been abolished by the New Covenant in Christ (Hebrews 8).

Forsaking all

2. The Lord Jesus said, 'In the same way, any of you who does not give up everything he has cannot be my disciple' (Luke 14:33). The context here is extremely important.

Three times our Lord repeats the statement, 'he cannot be my disciple' (vv. 26, 27, 33). And there is an important reason for that. In verse 25 we are informed that 'large crowds were travelling with Jesus', and it was to these people, excited about him and interested in following him, that he spoke. He was not speaking, therefore, to prospective 'pastors' or 'servants' but to all kinds of people who expressed an interest in becoming Christians and following Christ. The first principle to learn here is that verses 26-35 apply to everyone who becomes a Christian, not just to a privileged group of 'servants' or 'pastors'.

Priorities

A second major principle is that those considering becoming Christians must recognize the cost involved in following Christ, especially in terms of changed priorities. That is the thrust of verses 26-33.

Four major priorities are mentioned here by the Lord, namely, the priority of Christ over relatives, over one's own personal life (v. 26), and over possessions (v. 33) together with a willingness to suffer for him (v. 27). Just as a builder ensures he has all the materials he needs to complete building a tower, or a king calculates whether he has enough soldiers and weapons to win a war (vv. 28-31) so people should 'count the cost' before professing to follow Christ.

What is emphasized here is the preparedness of heart on the part of each Christian, to put Christ before everything and everyone else. And there are regular situations and relationships where this preparedness needs to be expressed. Here is the challenge to all Christians.

The Lord Jesus himself showed the way. For example, he 'resolutely set out for Jerusalem', where he would die for sinners on the cross (Luke 9:51). This statement is a watershed in Luke's Gospel. That was his mission; his priorities were all related to this one unique task — 'to save' (v. 56). He allowed nothing and no one to hinder him from accomplishing this divine mission. It was a glorious mission for, on the cross, God the Father 'made [Jesus] who had no sin to be sin for us, so that in him we might become the righteousness of God' (2 Corinthians 5:21). Those who, by faith, receive Christ and his salvation must consequently live under Christ's lordship. That is the challenge of Luke 14 and it applies to all believers. There are no exceptions.

Cultic characteristics

Unmarried pastors

But must pastors remain unmarried, as the UPC claims? Not according to the Bible. Many of the Lord's servants in the Old Testament were married. That was also true of the apostles, for example, Peter (Mark 1:30) and evangelists, like Philip (Acts 21:9). Elders, too, who pastor churches and teach and rule by the Word, are to be 'the husband of one wife' (1 Timothy 3:2; Titus

1:6). Some may voluntarily choose singleness (Matthew 19:12; 1 Corinthians 7:7) to be more free to serve the Lord, but that is neither mandatory nor the norm.

The question remains: *what are the cultic characteristics of the UPC?*

Extreme authoritative leadership

One characteristic is their extremely authoritative leadership; to oppose or even question their 'servants' is viewed as opposing God.

Related to this, their leaders claim to be infallible in their teaching. Another cultic feature is the 'heavy shepherding' that takes place within the organization. According to one reliable inside source, 'members are coerced and pressured into revealing every aspect of their lives to leaders. The reason given for this is that, as shepherds, they need to know the state of the flock.'

Everything an individual member does needs a 'covering', that is, permission from the leadership. 'To do something outside of this covering', one member informs me, 'denotes an independent and wrong spirit.'

A further cultic characteristic must be mentioned, namely, their doctrine of separation. This involves 'keeping the unbelieving friend, colleague, neighbour and relative on the other side … the line of partition should be drawn carefully'. Then, in an irresponsible re-interpretation of the terms 'fatherless' and 'widows', they add: 'To visit the fatherless (those who are without God) and widows (those who once had God with them) is important, but to keep oneself unspotted from this world is as important.'[14]

Separation in practice

But what does 'separation' mean for them in practice? UPC members are not allowed to mix with Christians from other Bible-believing churches, not even Pentecostal churches. To attend any church other than the UPC means you have become 'unequally yoked' or 'spiritual gypsies'.

This doctrine of separation, and other doctrines and rules (such as forbidding medical treatment and the wearing of jewellery) are strictly applied to all their members. Nor must members be in touch with 'backsliders' who leave the church.

This feature of withdrawal from (and 'protest' against) society, governments and even families, is cultic. The constant pressure on members to conform leads to a sense of dependence on the group. Consequently, members experience fear as well as feelings of guilt if they leave. These are typical cultic characteristics and express varying degrees of control over members by the leadership.

To conclude, the Bible does teach separation from sin and the world (Romans 12:2; Galatians 1:4; 1 John 2:15-17). Christians should live in obedience to the Word and with radically

WHAT THEY BELIEVE

different priorities, standards and aims, from those of unbelievers. Such holy living requires our engagement in society, not withdrawal from it!

RELEVANT COMPARISONS

The UPC	The Bible

Like the Family of Love, the UPC is orthodox on a number of major doctrines. 'Faith in the Triune God is the backbone of the church,' we are informed[15] and they 'preach Christ, His virgin birth, His works, His teachings, His crucifixion, His resurrection, His ascension, His second coming...'

The new birth is taught too, but identified with conviction of sins, repentance, confession of sins/faith etc. No reference is made to the prior, supernatural work of the Holy Spirit in bringing spiritually dead sinners to life and to Christ (Ephesians 2:1-10; John 3:3-7). This is a serious omission.

JUSTIFICATION

The UPC	The Bible
The 'act of God's free grace by which we received remission of sins'.	The UPC definition is inadequate and covers only one aspect. When God justifies, he pronounces the believing sinner 'right' and 'not guilty' but only on the basis of Christ's substitutionary death for us (Romans 3:25-26; 8:33). The glorious righteousness of Christ is reckoned to my account when I trust in him.

COMPARISONS

POVERTY FOR ALL PASTORS

'Ministers of the gospel cannot have any inheritance in the world.'

Note that:
1. The Levitical order (Deuteronomy 10:8-9), the Aaronic priesthood, and all their ceremonial duties, have been abolished in Christ (Hebrews 8).
2. Luke 14:33 refers to all Christians, not merely a privileged group of 'servants' or 'pastors'; see verses 26,27,33.
3. All those considering becoming Christians must recognize the cost involved in following Christ; read verses 26-33 and reflect on the illustrations used by the Lord in verses 28-31.

CELIBACY FOR PASTORS

Pastors must remain unmarried.

Many of God's servants in the Old and New Testaments were married, including Peter (Mark 1:30), Philip (Acts 21:9), elders/pastors (1 Timothy 3:2; Titus 1:6).

Some may choose freely to be single (Matthew 19:12; 1 Corinthians 7:7) to give themselves more to the Lord but that is not the norm.

CHAPTER ELEVEN

THE UNITED CHURCH OF GOD

WHO ARE THEY?

A BRIEF HISTORY

One important fact to appreciate concerning the United Church of God (UCG) is that it only began in 1996 and then as a breakaway group from the Worldwide Church of God (WCG). While the latter was endeavouring to become more biblical and trinitarian, the UCG was formed by a group of WCG members who wanted to pursue some Old Testament practices. These practices could, in effect, undermine the gospel of grace.

It is estimated that the UCG has 200 members in the UK served by eight ministers. 160 members are located in England in eight churches.

Widespread

The second thing to note about the UCG is that it has a well-organized group of churches spread over thirty-six countries. An interesting break-down of these countries reveals that the church is located in twelve African countries, eight South American countries, six Western European countries (including the United Kingdom, France, Italy and Switzerland), and four Australasian countries. The church is weakest in Eastern Europe, where it has a presence only in Estonia. The UK centre is in Milton Keynes.

Website

A third observation about the UCG is that it makes effective use of an internet website. The church is upfront in describing itself, its aims and resources. Its openness in this respect is welcome.

Mission statement

Fourthly, this church appears well intentioned in terms of evangelism and offering counsel to people. For example, its Mission Statement declares that 'The mission of the UCG is to preach the gospel of Jesus Christ and the Kingdom of God in all the world, make disciples in all nations and care for those disciples.'

The statement itself appears satisfactory on the surface but we will need to examine the terminology more carefully to see what it really means. But make no mistake about it, the UCG is eager to help and counsel people: 'We desire', they say, 'to share God's way of life with those who earnestly seek to worship and follow our Saviour, Jesus Christ. Our ministers are available to counsel, answer questions and explain the Bible.'

Leadership

Fifthly, the overall leadership of this church is in the hands of a Council of Elders. At a General Conference of Elders in Cincinnati, Ohio (3-5 December 1995), twelve elders were elected to function as 'the first permanent Council of Elders for the United Church of God — *an international association*'.

As many as nine of these twelve elders represent the United States and the remaining three are denoted 'international' in representing Canada, Europe and Spanish-speaking countries. Since 1995, the council members are chosen from nominated elders at the General Conference, 'and serve staggered terms'. Notice that the church is centrally led and is predominantly American in terms of both leadership and membership.

Fundamental beliefs

But what do they believe? Their website identifies their 'Fundamental Beliefs' and there are twenty of them. In a preamble, however, we are warned that this 'is not intended to be a comprehensive statement' of their beliefs. Clearly theological development is taking place within this church, and we are informed that matters relating to belief 'will be addressed by a process adopted by the Council of Elders'. The church's doctrinal position appears fluid and vulnerable, as well as questionable in some areas.

Commendable features

There are commendable features included in these Fundamental Beliefs, such as a high view of Scripture; the reality of Satan; the fact and significance of human sin; the physical resurrection of Christ; followed by his ascension and session at the right hand of God; and an emphasis on personal faith in Jesus Christ as Saviour, for forgiveness and justification.

RELEVANT COMPARISONS

The UCG	The Bible

GOD

Consider, for example, their doctrine of God, which is lengthy but ambiguous.

There is no reference to the divine attribute of holiness, and statements concerning the person of Christ and the Holy Spirit are inadequate. They describe the Holy Spirit as 'the Spirit of God and of Christ Jesus ... the power of God and the Spirit of life eternal'. This fails to affirm the distinct personality of the Holy Spirit and the co-equality of the Holy Spirit within the Godhead. At best, these statements point to a binitarian not trinitarian position; at worst, they express a non-trinitarian, or 'oneness' doctrine.

CHRIST'S DEATH

The statement concerning Christ's death is useful, in that it brings out our Lord's

COMPARISONS

real humanity, sinlessness, active obedience, as well as the sacrificial nature of his death 'for the sins of humanity ... sufficient to pay the penalty for every human being's sins'.

What it does not do is to highlight the substitutionary nature of this death, its glorious accomplishment, and successful application.

One also suspects that behind their statement regarding the Lord's sacrifice is a hint of the earlier Worldwide Church of God doctrine, namely, that his death only saves us from the death penalty, freeing us to go on to give obedience to the law. I hope this is not so.

NO DISTINCTION BETWEEN PRIMARY AND SECONDARY DOCTRINES

There is no distinction drawn between primary and secondary doctrines. For example, they regard matters like seventh-day Sabbath observance, tithing, millennialism, as primary beliefs as important as their teaching on Christ and salvation. The same primary

As a response, I limit myself to two points.

1. Colossians 2:16-17 is extremely relevant: 'Therefore do not let anyone judge you by what you eat or drink, or with regard to a religious festival, a New Moon celebration or a Sabbath day.'

This passage clearly

significance is attached to strict observance of the seven Old Testament Holy Days and the observing of the New Testament Passover on the night of the 14th of Abib, 'the anniversary of the death of our Saviour'.

In addition, they stipulate that all meats designated 'unclean' in Leviticus 11 and Deuteronomy 14 'are not to be eaten' by Christians. This requirement, again, is put on a par with the major doctrines of God and Scripture.

Some of these Old Testament practices, which the UCG perpetuates, raise major questions concerning discontinuity and continuity between the Old and New Testaments and threaten the gospel of grace by imposing legalism on Christians.

teaches that no one has the right to demand that Christians should observe regulations about ceremonially 'unclean' meats or special days. The reason given in verse 17 is that a Christian has been freed from bondage to such requirements: 'These are a shadow of the things that were to come; the reality, however, is found in Christ.' This is a major truth with far-reaching implications.

The Old Testament ordinances which the UCG seeks to perpetuate are no longer binding since they were only a 'shadow' of 'the reality' which is in Christ. The UCG provides extensive information on observing 'holy days' including a calendar, dates and a 'sunrise/sunset table generator', which all serve to focus on the 'shadow' rather than the reality in Christ. Now that Christ has come, the shadows (which in earlier times served as pointers to him) have disappeared, being gloriously fulfilled in the reality of the gospel.

2. The question of 'unclean' foods was a problem in the early church. Our Lord abolished the distinction between 'clean' and 'unclean' in Mark 7:19 (cf. John

4:9) and this was impressed on Peter in Acts 10:11-16, 28 (see also Acts 15). In 1 Corinthians 10:26-33 Christians are told they should refrain from certain foods. However this is not because they are 'unclean' but because of love in not wanting to offend other Christians (cf. Romans 14:15).

The United Church of God must face up to this New Testament teaching, and major exclusively on the reality of Christ rather than retaining shadows.

CHAPTER TWELVE

HORST
SCHAFFRANEK

WHO IS HE?

A BRIEF HISTORY

A Christian was walking through a city shopping centre recently. Unexpectedly, a stranger offered him five booklets, which seemed Bible-based. All of them had been written (or transcribed from addresses) by Horst Schaffranek.

The Christian felt uncomfortable. The stranger was harsh and intolerant as he talked about Christians and the multiplicity of churches in each town. Anyway, the Christian had never heard of Schaffranek.

He bid goodbye to the stranger and put the booklets in his pocket.

Background

Later the Christian approached me. His question was: 'Who is Horst Schaffranek?' I confessed my ignorance. He showed me the booklets and I agreed to make enquiries.

The Internet has been a considerable help in my search for information. My judgement is that Christians should be aware of Schaffranek's influence as well as the errors he teaches.

Born in 1923 in Schlesien, Germany, to Roman Catholic parents, Horst Schaffranek appears to have professed faith in Christ as a young man. He eventually became a Free Church minister in Stuttgart in 1954, and until the mid-1970s he was known in German evangelical circles.

Married with seven children, Schaffranek began to major on his distinctive views from the early 1970s. He developed the 'Schaffranek community' for his followers, together with some centres scattered around the country. The literature from this group informs us that Schaffranek has been active for over fifty years as an evangelist, counsellor and teacher in many denominations in Germany — as well as in many other countries like the USA, Canada, Latin America, Europe, Africa, the Middle East and the Far East.

Claims

The claim is that he 'brings to light the standards of the New Testament that God's people have abandoned and thus challenges them to consequent obedience'. We vigorously dispute this claim.

Schaffranek is still alive and his home is in Rickenbach, Germany. He and his followers are well known to the Evangelical Alliance in Germany — but for the wrong reasons! They have a reputation for disturbing Christian meetings, using aggressive methods and insulting language. Two examples can be given.

In 1996, an aged German minister, Paul Deitenbeck, was insulted and intimidated by a group of Schaffranek's followers during and after a theology lecture he gave in Krelingen. Their technique is at first to give people the impression of being gracious and friendly. Then, unexpectedly, during or after a meeting, these same people become aggressive and abusive. Frequently, they have to be forcibly removed from meetings by police.

Another occasion was the German Evangelical Churches Conference held in Stuttgart in 1999. The concluding service in Gottlieb Damlier Stadium was marred by Schaffranek's disciples demonstrating in the service in an appalling manner.

Questions

In Germany over recent years, in regional and national gatherings of churches and their leaders, such behaviour has continued unabated. On one occasion, Schaffranek's followers claimed that the conference president had agreed that they should disturb the meetings! This was, of course, totally untrue.

Two questions must be raised at this point. The first concerns the reasons for such behaviour in opposing church leaders and disturbing

meetings. A second question concerns Horst Schaffranek himself. What kind of influence does he have
on his followers? Is he a cultic figure?

Concerning the latter, former disciples of Schaffranek, and church leaders who have suffered disturbances, agree in their concern for his followers. One
former member, for example, is convinced that Schaffranek's messages can be likened to a 'brain laundry'
— all his followers think in exactly the same way, with
no deviation at all. They appear to be indoctrinated and
give little evidence of thinking for themselves.

A number of people who had been associated with
this movement state that Schaffranek himself will not
tolerate personal criticism. Nor will members allow
anyone else to criticize their leader. As one person
observed, there 'prevails a certain papacy' in the movement; an infallibility is attached to Schaffranek which
is neither healthy nor scriptural.

Confused theology

Equally disturbing are reports of individuals being
pressurized and pursued by telephone calls and visits
to their homes — even for years after leaving the Schaffranek community. Young people who join them are not
encouraged to have contact with their families. The
overall impression, therefore, is of a cultic-type leader
who exercises immense control over the thinking and
behaviour of his followers.

But why does Schaffranek insist that his people protest in meetings? There is a theology that prompts this type of behaviour, but it is confused and lacks biblical balance and warrant. I need to explain.

Despite using the Bible, Schaffranek is heretical with regard to some major doctrines, specifically the doctrines of God and Scripture. According to one website, he teaches that all humans can obtain 'realizations' in 'becoming like God... You can become God on this earth.'

Here is a blatant denial of Bible teaching: 'I am God, and there is no other; I am God, and there is none like me' (Isaiah 46:9; 45:18-22). Even in heaven — where believers will be conformed to the likeness of Christ — we will remain *created beings*.

In terms of purity we will be like Christ. However, we will continue to be *unlike* Christ in terms of his essential glory as God the Son, a glory he shares exclusively with the Father and the Holy Spirit.

Revelation

Schaffranek's view of the Bible and revelation must also be condemned. Ruether, a German church leader, reports that Schaffranek has 'left the soil' of Holy Scripture. How? Because

WHAT HE TEACHES

he regards the Bible as being a 'second class' level of revelation.

According to Schaffranek, the superior 'first class' level of revelation consists of private, direct revelations and guidance allegedly given him by God. This is a fundamental and tragic error.

He has abandoned the Bible as his supreme authority in matters of faith and conduct. It is on the basis of his false claim to receive direct revelations from God that Schaffranek also offers distinctive teaching concerning the church.

'The Lord is leading His people back to 1 Corinthians 1:10, "...that all of you agree..." that is *one* body in *one* locality...'[1] This is central for Schaffranek. And, he insists, 'only the church in one locality is a sufficient protection against attacks'.[2]

For Schaffranek, a multiplicity of churches in a locality is sinful, demonic and a major hindrance to the growth and reviving of Christ's church. It also incurs the judgement of God. Such divisions, he argues, are 'always a result of a lack of light, of God's presence...'[3]

Peace and trouble

On the basis of 1 Corinthians 11:19 ('No doubt there have to be differences among you'), Schaffranek justifies his aggressive policy of protesting at such divisions by disturbing and wrecking denominational and inter-denominational meetings.

WHAT HE TEACHES

However, the context of this verse is the Lord's Supper, particularly the 'divisions' (v. 18) in the local church arising out of selfish, thoughtless attitudes. In verse 19 Paul adds that such divisions are graciously overruled by God, who enables us to distinguish — between those who are divinely 'approved' in their behaviour and attitudes, and those who are not.

Yes, Schaffranek misunderstands the text. He is wrong in saying that God wants us to purify the church by creating and perpetuating disturbances. Do I need to attack my brothers in the Lord? Schaffranek's answer is: 'If you want to have peace, you will first have to have trouble',[4] and 'wrong ideas will have to be destroyed'.[5]

Sadly, Schaffranek ignores important aspects of the Bible teaching. Truth is important and heresies must be opposed. Bible-believing churches need to express more visibly their unity in the gospel. But Christians must also 'love each other' (John 15:17; 1 John 3:14), 'speaking the truth in love' (Ephesians 4:15). In fact, 'the Lord's servant must not quarrel; instead, he must be kind to everyone ... not resentful ... gently instruct...' (2 Timothy 2:24-25).

Our prayers are needed for this man and his followers — especially that God 'will grant them repentance leading them to a knowledge of the truth, and that they will come to their senses and escape from the trap of the devil...' (2 Timothy 2:25-26).

RELEVANT COMPARISONS

Schaffranek	The Bible

GOD

Any human person can obtain 'realizations' in 'becoming like God ... You can become God on this earth'.

Schaffranek's teaching is a clear denial of what the Bible says about this crucial doctrine of God. Note especially:

1. There is only one God. 'I am God, and there is no other; I am God, and there is none like me' (Isaiah 46:9; 45:18-22).

2. a. Christians are being slowly conformed in their earthly lives to the likeness of Christ (Romans 8:29) in the sense of moral purity.

   b. Christians will also 'see him as he is' and be 'like him' (1 John 3:2) in terms of moral character.

   c. Even in heaven, Christians will remain created beings; they will never share his essential glory as God the Son. That glory, Christ shares only with the Father and Holy Spirit in the Holy Trinity of divine persons.

BIBLE

Abandoning the supreme authority and sufficiency of the Bible, Schaffranek regards the Bible only as a 'second class'

Note, for example:
1. Our Lord's appeal was always to the written, revealed Word of God: Matthew 4:4, 7 and 10;

level of revelation. The 'first class' level of revelation, he teaches, consists of his own private, direct revelations from God.

19:4-6; Luke 24:44, 46.

2. The apostolic church regarded the Scripture as being final and sufficient for bringing people to Christ and to spiritual maturity. No other revelation is required: 2 Timothy 3:15-17.

THE LOCAL CHURCH

God, it is alleged, revealed to him that there should only be 'one body in one locality' rather than a multiplicity of churches belonging to various denominations. He uses 1 Corinthians 1:10 in support.

1. Christians are one in Christ and in the truths of the gospel of Christ: Galatians 3:26-29; 1 Corinthians 12:12-27.

2. There is an urgent challenge for Christians to express more visibly and locally their unity in Christ: John 17:20-24; Ephesians 4:12-16; 1 Corinthians 1:10-13.

3. Differences among Christians in this life are inevitable (e.g. Acts 15:36-41; Galatians 2:11). However, these differences must be handled sensitively, lovingly and with biblical balance and priorities.

4. 1 Corinthians 1:10. Christians need to face the challenge of these words. The 'schisms' mentioned here had not yet developed but the apostle is eager to avoid a major separation of

the believers into two or more churches. Today, believers have a responsibility to maintain and promote the unity of the Spirit in local churches. However, the violence and rude behaviour of Schaffranek's followers will never contribute to church unity.

AGGRESSION AND DISTURBANCE OF MEETINGS

Schaffranek misinterprets 1 Corinthians 11:19 ('For there must be factions among you'), claiming its support for wrecking meetings held by other Christians.

Note:

1. The context of 1 Corinthians 11:19 is the Lord's Supper, especially the 'divisions' (v. 18) in the local church arising out of selfishness.

2. In verse 19 Paul adds that these divisions are wisely overruled by God to reveal those who are 'approved' by God in their behaviour and those who are not.

3. Christians must 'love each other' (John 15:17; 1 John 3:14), 'speaking the truth in love' (Ephesians 4:15). God's servants 'must not quarrel; instead, [they] must be kind to everyone ... not resentful ... gently instruct...' (2 Timothy 2:24-25).

CHAPTER THIRTEEN

WILLIAM BRANHAM

WHO IS HE?

A BRIEF HISTORY

William Branham is important for three reasons.

1. Branham's disciples are contacting increasing numbers of evangelical pastors and churches. Some pastors are confused as to whether or not his teaching is biblical. They are asking for help.

2. Branham's books, cassettes, tracts and videos are available in many languages. They are pouring into countries like Argentina, Bolivia, Brazil, Chile, Columbia, Venezuela, Ecuador, Honduras, Mexico and Paraguay. They are also penetrating effectively into other areas of the world like England, the Netherlands, France, Germany, Spain, Hungary, Romania, Lithuania, Russia, the Philippines and South Africa.

    This is not an exhaustive list. It is probable that you will soon come into contact with someone who has received Branham's books or cassettes.

3. People make foolish claims concerning him. For example, Branham is regarded as 'the twentieth-century prophet'; 'a man sent from

God'; and 'a prophet to the Gentiles' whose ministry 'has been unparalleled since the days of our Lord Jesus Christ'.

When did he live?

William Marrion Branham (1909-1965) was born in Kentucky, USA. Following a personal healing as a young man, he felt a call to preach and became an independent Baptist pastor. The ministry of William Branham spanned a thirty-two-year period from 1933 to 1965.

In his itinerant work, he emphasized healing, deliverance and prosperity. In his book *All Things are Possible*,[1] the historian D. E. Harrell reports that many participants in the 'healing revival' that 'erupted' in 1947 in the USA regarded Branham as its 'initiator'.

His simple messages, and reports of many alleged healings, made him extremely popular worldwide.

Why is he considered a special person?

Firstly, because of what is known as 'the pillar of fire' photograph. In January 1950 a photograph of Branham was developed in which the negative appeared to show a light above his head 'in a halo-like form'. Rather than seeking a technical explanation, his supporters regard the phenomenon as supernatural. They say the light is a supernatural entity and claim that this is 'the only supernatural Being ever photographed'!

When Branham himself was informed about the photograph, he expressed no surprise. He said that before the photo was taken, he 'heard the Pillar of Fire descend into the building with a sound of rushing wind'. Astonishingly, people believed him.

Branham claimed that 'the same Being' photo-graphed in 1950 had appeared to him earlier in 1933 with the message: 'As John the Baptist fore-ran the first coming of Christ, you will forerun the Second Coming.'

Secondly, Branham is considered to be 'spe-cial' because it is stated that he could read the hearts and minds of others, at least during heal-ing meetings. The claim is that 'the hearts of the people were revealed — the past, the present and the future'.

That is not all. They add: 'and not one time did it fail ... God was doing through this ministry exactly as he had done in the ministry of our Lord Jesus Christ 2000 years ago'.

What happened? Branham told 'the people of their past life ... sins would be called out, secrets of their hearts revealed...' Even Walter J. Hollenweger, who interpreted for Branham in Zurich, was 'not aware of any case in which he was mistaken in the often detailed statements he made'.[2]

Foolishly, many followers accepted his claims. In fact, when he died in 1965, many 'expected him to be resurrected, some believing him to be God, others believing him to be virgin-born'.[3]

Should we reject these claims?

1. Yes, of course. After all, only God is omniscient. No human is able to reveal the thoughts and secrets of individuals. That is God's prerogative alone.
2. To claim that the 'light' that appeared in the photo was a 'Supernatural Being', and by implication God, is absurd. There are plausible explanations of this phenomenon, such as glare or reflections, accidental film exposure, or deliberate 'touching-up'.
3. Furthermore, now we have the complete Bible, God does not 'reveal' himself physically to anyone, and certainly not in photographs! Apart from God's glory stamped on creation (Romans 1:19-20), all that we 'see' of God here and now is found only in the Bible.
4. We must reject the claim that Branham had achieved 'exactly' what our Lord's ministry achieved 2000 years ago.

   Christ's miracles were unique, functioning as 'signs' verifying his deity and confirming his claims. For example, to answer John the Baptist's doubts as to whether he was the promised Messiah, Jesus referred to his own mighty miracles as evidence of the fact (Luke 7:22). No comparison can be drawn between the Lord's ministry and that of Branham.

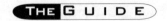

Is there an occult explanation?

There is evidence for such an explanation. For example, he claimed esoteric, mysterious experiences from his childhood. According to Branham, he experienced 'supernatural visitations' even at the ages of three and seven. Throughout his life, he claimed, he was guided by an angel. It was in a secret cave in 1946 that an angel supposedly first 'appeared' to Branham. On this occasion, he reports, he was given the power to discern people's illnesses and thoughts.

Are these encounters associated with the occult? That was the opinion of Rev. W. E. Best, pastor of Houston Tabernacle Baptist Church, at the time.

In 1950 Best, a godly Reformed pastor, challenged Branham's colleague, Rev. F. F. Bosworth, to a debate over this healing ministry. The debate was attended by 8,000 people and Best argued his case well, despite many interruptions. After insisting on the uniqueness of our Lord's earthly miracles, Best proceeded to emphasize the unique authority given to the apostles.

He rightly argued that this authority, including gifts of healing, was confined to the foundational period of the New Testament Church in the apostolic era. While God in his sovereignty can heal whenever he pleases, 'no man has the power to heal', insisted W. E. Best.

Was it the work of God?

Amidst uproar in the meeting, Best claimed there were those 'who used sorcery to bewitch people, so that people are sincerely misled and say it's the power of God'.

Another person suggested that Branham 'hypnotizes his audience'. The use of hypnotism and his own psychic powers may have contributed to Branham's reputation as a healer and a 'revealer' of people's secrets. Best, however, may be on the right path in suggesting a more sinister force as an explanation of Branham's experiences and healings.

A 'healing' is not necessarily the work of God. This point needs to be stressed. For example, the devil and his hosts can also work in extraordinary ways. In Egypt, Pharaoh's servants performed miracles (Exodus 7:11, 22; 8:7), while in Samaria Simon the sorcerer astonished people with his 'wonders' (Acts 8:9-11). In Philippi, Paul delivered a young woman possessed by a spirit of divination; she clearly had unusual abilities which attracted the attention of many people (Acts 16:16).

According to 2 Thessalonians 2:9-10, the man of sin will be revealed 'with all kinds of counterfeit miracles, signs and wonders...' (cf. Revelation 13:11-14). Tentatively, I suggest there may have been a mix of psychic and occult factors contributing to Branham's success.

Was Branham clear about the gospel?

Yes and no! His sermons point to the way of salvation through Christ alone. He underlined texts like Acts 4:12: 'Salvation is found in no one else, for there is no other name under heaven given to men, by which we must be saved.'

Branham declared: 'It is Christ or perish ... salvation is *not* Jesus *plus*. It is Jesus *alone...*' [italics original]. The Lord Jesus, he added, shed his 'innocent blood to atone for our sins and rose again, to redeem...'

I must warn, however, that his presentation of the gospel came (and still comes) in a package which is unbiblical.

What else do Branham's followers claim?

People 'watched with astonishment', it is claimed, as Branham's 'prophetic ministry unfolded before them'. They also tell us that people are 'still being challenged by the legacy of his ministry'.

Branham's 1964-65 English sermons are now available in printed form. There is excitement, too, on the part of his followers because twenty-four recently discovered messages have been made available on cassette.

There is more being claimed by this group. It is stated that in the 1940s, 1950s and 1960s

Branham's ministry was superior to that of other 'evangelists' and 'revivalists' operating in the United States.

How? Other men, they say, 'left only memories of signs and wonders' after their death. By contrast, the ministry of William Branham is supposed to have 'left the legacy of *A Message*'. And that Message, they inform us, is 'cherished' by thousands of believers around the world.

The claim expands. Branham left a Message which challenges 'traditional Christianity' and 'our traditional way of thinking about practically everything that is called Christian'. They see their website as 'a serious challenge' to our faith. We are challenged, 'not only to believe that God has sent a prophet to this Last Age, but also to believe the Message he brought to *restore, correct and set the bridge of Jesus Christ* in order for the rapture'.

No wonder some pastors and congregations, especially in Eastern Europe, Africa and South America, are confused over Branham's claims and message.

Why are these claims confusing?

Their confusion is aggravated in two ways:

1. Branham claimed that he had enjoyed 'constant communication with God and Angels' and, as a result, received a divinely given message for people in the end-times.

Such a claim must be rejected as being illusory and occult.

2. Confusion is deepened by the group's insistence that through the ages, God's people have 'always followed a man' and a man of God's choosing.[4]

The logic of their argument is clear. Paul urged believers to be 'followers of me' (1 Corinthians 4:16; 11:1). Then they argue that God does not use stars or angels to reveal his Word to people. No, 'He chooses a man like Moses, Elijah and the prophets.'

We agree wholeheartedly. John Calvin, for example, is one of many Reformed writers who uphold this principle. In his commentary on Acts 10 Calvin illustrates the principle in action. God did not send an angel to preach to Cornelius in Caesarea. Rather, the angel was sent to tell Cornelius to bring Peter from Joppa, as he would preach the Word to him.

Yes, God is sovereign but chooses to use men and human preaching to bring the elect to faith in Christ. This is important.

Is there a contradiction?

However, Branham and his followers assume that because God revealed himself in Bible times

WHAT HE TEACHES

through visions or angels, he continues to speak to chosen individuals today in the same way. But he is wrong. Rather than using angels or visions, as in the Old and New Testament periods, God now speaks through the Word and by men expounding that Word faithfully.

Furthermore, as their argument develops, it self-destructs. They point out that most people in Christendom are 'following someone', whether it is a pastor, bishop, pope or evangelist. That is fair enough on one level, though a true Christian is, above all, a follower of Christ, not men.

But they then contradict the very principle they have stated by insisting that we should follow a *single* uniquely and divinely gifted man! He alone, they claim, is able to bring the Word or 'present Truth' to the contemporary world just prior to the Lord's return.

This claim is obviously without foundation in Scripture. When Paul urged his readers to follow him as he followed Christ, he clearly did not mean they should follow him to the *exclusion* of, say, Peter or John. Indeed, he condemns a factional spirit in 1 Corinthians 1:10-17.

However, the claim that Branham's ministry is unique unfortunately appeals to some who lack good Bible teaching.

Check all things

However, there are some points where we can agree with this group.

1. 'Check all things' by the Word, they insist, and 'not by emotion or sensations…' Correct, but remember that they themselves are mishandling the Word.
2. Their criticism of the 'charismatic church world today' is also perceptive. They regard many charismatic speakers as 'entertainers and not preachers … the excessive joking and laughing which accompany much of their preaching is unbecoming to the Gospel'. I can only agree with this.
3. They state that some use 'mass, fervent religious hype and psychology to influence and deceive the people'. Sadly, it is a fact.
4. They reject 'decisionism'. Branham rightly underlines the necessity of repentance and faith, followed by perseverance in the Word and obedience as evidences of saving faith. This needs to be emphasized today.

But what is Branham's distinctive 'message' relating to becoming a Christian?

After reading the available material, I have concluded that two crucial points lie at the heart of this 'message'.

1. His strong note of protest at ways in which his contemporaries cheapened the gospel of grace

and tolerated sin. The protest was reasonable, but he became unbiblical in the way he expressed it.

2. More significantly, despite his emphasis on 'salvation', 'grace' and 'faith', his teaching on the crucial matter of becoming a Christian is confused and unbiblical.

His exposition of key terms like 'grace' and 'salvation' is woefully inadequate and always coloured by a strong protest against a type of sin-indulging decisionism. He spells out his understanding of these terms in his three 'steps to salvation'.

What are the three 'steps to salvation'?

Justification

For Branham, the first step to salvation is justification, which he mistakenly describes as 'God's first work of grace in you'.[5] In reply, we must insist that justification is not an experience but a legal declaration by God that the sinner who trusts in Christ is righteous before him.

To be justified is the opposite of being condemned. And, according to the Bible, it is the action and decision of God our judge: 'Who will bring any charge against those whom God has chosen? It is God who justifies' (Romans 8:33). But how can God declare us righteous when, in fact, we are sinners? Only because Jesus Christ fully bore our sin and punishment, once-for-all, when he died as our substitute on the cross. And, in his

glorious grace, God imputes Christ's righteousness to each believer.

To put it differently, God credits Christ's
righteousness to my account when I trust in
the Lord Jesus. In fact, God regards this divine
righteousness as now belonging to me as a
believer (Romans 4:5).

Branham, therefore, is wrong in his teaching
about justification. As a result, all his other teaching is out of line with the Bible. You have been
warned!

Sanctification

The second step to salvation for Branham is sanctification. Although he quotes 1 Thessalonians
4:3-4 and 2 Thessalonians 2:13, his teaching is
misleading and superficial in the extreme.

He views sanctification as 'an absolutely
wonderful experience' in which the individual
'feels swept, clean, fresh...' It is further described
as 'cleaning the vessel of all evil works and the
dominion of sin ... creating in us the desire to
always live a holy and sanctified life...' (p. 11).

Branham's view is a dreadful mishmash of
ideas from within 'holiness', 'faith' and 'charismatic' circles. It is a view that is imposed upon, and
distorts, the biblical teaching on the subject.

The Bible views sanctification in two main
ways. It is initially God's definitive act in setting

aside the sinner for his glory and freeing him from the power of sin (1 Corinthians 1:2; 6:11; Romans 6:18).

In addition, sanctification is a life-long process of conforming us to Christ's likeness. The believer is active in this process but dependent on the Holy Spirit (Romans 8:13-14; 1 Thessalonians 5:23).

Holy Spirit baptism

The third step to salvation for Branham is 'Holy Spirit baptism'. This is described as 'experiencing salvation' (p. 25), a spiritual 'resurrection' producing 'a new birth, a new life...' (p. 28).

Branham confuses the initial supernatural work of the Holy Spirit in regeneration with the conscious and experiential reception of the Spirit by 'the hearing of faith' (see Galatians 3:2). Although these two events may coincide in time, they are distinct. We cannot receive the Spirit by faith until we have first been *given* faith in regeneration.

Conversion is only possible as a consequence of the initial, supernatural work of the Spirit in new birth. All sinners are spiritually dead; they must first be made alive to God before they can believe and repent (John 3:3-7; Ephesians 2:1-5).

To conclude, Branham's 'three steps' could well confuse sinners rather than lead them to salvation. This is the tragedy of his teaching.

RELEVANT COMPARISONS

Branham	The Bible

BRANHAM'S UNIQUE MINISTRY

It is claimed that only Branham is able to bring 'present Truth' to the contemporary world prior to the return of Christ. Therefore, we need to follow 'someone' and that 'someone' should be Branham!

Paul urged Christians to be 'followers of me' (1 Corinthians 4:16, 11:1). But this Pauline exhortation: (a) meant they should follow Paul in the way that he followed Christ; and (b), did not mean that Paul should be followed to the exclusion of Peter or John. Paul also (c) condemns a factional spirit in 1 Corinthians 1:10-17 where there is exclusive preoccupation with one human leader.

JUSTIFICATION

Branham wrongly describes justification as 'the first step' to salvation which he then describes as 'God's first work of grace in you'.

Justification is not an experience but a legal, objective declaration by God that the sinner who trusts in Christ is righteous before him. It is the opposite of being condemned. And, in the Bible, justification is the action and decision of God as judge: 'Who will bring any charge against those whom God has chosen? It is God who justifies' (Romans 8:33).

COMPARISONS

SANCTIFICATION

Branham's teaching is superficial and misleading. He views it as 'an absolutely wonderful experience' in which the person 'feels clean...'

Sanctification is:

a. initially God's definitive act in setting aside the sinner for his glory and freeing the person from sin's power (1 Corinthians 1:2; 6:11; Romans 6:18);

b. a life-long process and fight of conforming us to Christ's likeness; we are active in this process but dependent on the Holy Spirit (Romans 8:13-14; 1 Thessalonians 5:23).

REGENERATION

Branham confuses the initial supernatural work of the Holy Spirit in new birth with the conscious acceptance of the Spirit by faith and also Spirit-baptism.

It is not possible to receive the Spirit by faith until we have first been given faith in regeneration: John 3:3-7; Ephesians 2:1-5.

THE GUIDE

CHAPTER FOURTEEN

MORAL
RE-ARMAMENT

WHAT IS IT?

The superintendent of a hospice in Philadelphia, U.S.A., found himself at variance with his committee, who felt he was being extravagant in the quality and amount of food he gave to the destitute boys in his care. Appointed to this post in 1904 by the Lutheran Church of Pennsylvania, Frank Buchman had used most of his $600 a year salary to furnish the hospice more adequately but now, three years later, a crisis had arisen. Buchman was now ordered to give his boys less food. In October 1907 he wrote, 'They refused to let us have good butter. What they provided was rancid. The fish was not fresh. You can't run a Christian institution that way...'

There was no alternative for the superintendent but to leave the hospice and, feeling extremely bitter towards the committee and exhausted, he was advised by his doctor to go on a Mediterranean cruise. The cruise, although enjoyable, did not meet his deep personal need and in the summer of 1908 this dejected and embittered young man arrived in the Lake District in time for the Keswick Convention.

He derived no help at all from the main convention meetings but, while walking alone on the

Sunday, he noticed a small chapel where a service was in progress. Buchman joined the small congregation and heard a woman preacher, Mrs Penn-Lewis — who was a close friend of the Welsh revivalist Evan Roberts — preaching about the death of Christ. God spoke to him through the message. 'A doctrine which I knew as a boy,' he remarked later, 'which my church believed, which I had always been taught, that day became a reality for me. I had entered the little church with a divided will, nursing pride, selfishness, ill-will. The woman's simple talk personalized the cross for me that day, and suddenly I had a poignant vision of the Cruci-fied. With this deep experience of the love of God in Christ ... I wrote to the six committee men in America against whom I had nursed the ill-will and told them of my experience, and how at the foot of the cross I could only think of my own sin. At the top of each letter I wrote this verse:

> When I survey the wondrous cross
> On which the Prince of Glory died,
> My richest gain I count but loss
> And pour contempt on all my pride.

'It wasn't difficult to write the first three lines of that hymn, but to write the fourth line was like writing in my own blood.'

Buchman was now determined to share his faith with others and generally to help people. Returning to America, he accepted the post of YMCA secretary in Pennsylvania State College and it was here, through

HISTORY

the visit of F. B. Meyer, that Buchman was again challenged.

Observing him hard at work, Dr Meyer told him that he should listen more to God than to telephones and make personal interviews more important than the organizing of meetings. He immediately acted on the advice. 'It was then,' Buchman writes, 'I decided to devote an hour, from 5 a.m. to 6 a.m. every morning before the telephones would begin to ring, to listen to the Voice of the living God, in a daily time of quiet. Everything is so different when the Holy Spirit is a daily reality.' This practice of silence or a Quiet Time in which he listened to the inner voice of God is one of the distinctive features of Moral Re-Armament.

The movement spreads further afield

Evangelistic work in India, China and Japan, then a new appointment in Hartford Theologic- al Seminary, provided Buchman with numer- ous opportunities for helping people. While in Hartford, he travelled regularly to Yale to hear Professor Henry Wright lecture on the relevance of Christianity and it was from Wright that Buch- man learned to use the four moral standards of honesty, purity, unselfishness and love, as well as the triangle — God, myself, my neighbour.

In Cambridge in 1921 the thought suddenly came to him: 'I will use you to remake the world,' and for the next ten years his centre of operations was Oxford, where he gathered over 100 students together under the name of the Oxford Group. Slowly other groups were established in South Africa (1928), Canada and the U.S.A. (1932), Switzerland (1935), Holland (1937) and Scandinavia in 1938.

He was troubled in the spring of 1938 by the recurring thought: 'Moral and spiritual re-armament. The next great movement in the world will be a movement of moral re-armament for all nations.' This thought gripped Buchman and his followers. After being known by such names as the Oxford Group, Buchmanism, the New Groupers and the First Century Christian Fellowship, it was now decided to rename the movement as Moral Re-Armament (MRA) to mark their leader's sixtieth birthday.

There followed seven busy years in the United States for Buchman before he left in 1946 with 150 helpers to work in post-war Europe. One of the most important developments was the purchase of a mountain hotel in the fashionable Swiss village of Caux. During the Second World War the hotel sheltered Jewish and Italian refugees as well as British and American escaped prisoners of war. Renamed 'Mountain House', the hotel has become the MRA international centre for conferences and reconciliation work, providing 'a common ground for people of all faiths, and people of no faith, to work together to build a new world'. When Buchman died in 1961 at the age of eighty-three, the work of MRA was both influential and international.

The movement today

There is no formal membership of the movement but people from different church denominations, as well as those without any faith, are involved in the MRA. In Great Britain there are full-time workers who are active in industry, education, inner-city and multi-racial communities. In addition, they have an English conference centre in Tarporley, Cheshire, and considerable use is made of plays and films as a means of communicating the message of moral and spiritual renewal. The Westminster Theatre in London, for example, is owned by the MRA.

It is generally assumed, especially in the light of Buchman's passionate and fearless love of Christ and the movement's high moral and spiritual aims, that Moral Re-Armament is unquestionably Christian and biblical. That there are Christians within its ranks and positive Christian elements in its work, I readily concede. Much of this is work which Christian churches should have been doing. However, when we assess MRA teaching, although it has no official creed, we find that some of its beliefs are at variance with the Bible and, sadly, I must draw attention to these differences here.

RELEVANT COMPARISONS

Moral Re-Armament	The Bible

MANKIND

Buchman saw the line of division in the world lying not between Christians and non-Christians, or between the world religions, but between men whose allegiance is to God and spiritual values (whatever their religion) and those who are dedicated to their destruction. Embracing people of all religions, MRA is not specifically Christian.

The Bible divides mankind into two basic categories only: those who trust in Christ and enjoy eternal life, and those who are without Christ and without hope (cf. John 3:15-18, 36; 10:9; Galatians 2:16; Ephesians 2:11-13).

CONVERSION

A basic conviction of MRA is that the revolution we most need is the change in human character itself. 'Human nature can change. When men are freed from the control of forces like self-interest, hatred, pride, fear or lust, a passion gets liberated in their hearts which issues in social, economic and national change.'

How do people change? It involves five stages:

Conviction: awareness of personal sins;
Contrition: being sorry for sin;

While Buchman and others have known genuine conversion to Christ, 'change' for the MRA is not specifically Christian conversion.

1. It wrongly stresses man's ability to change himself (cf. John 3:3-8; Romans 7:18; Ephesians 2:8-10).

2. It wrongly suggests that deep spiritual change can take place apart from Christ and faith in him (cf. John 6:44; 2 Corinthians 5:17; Galatians 4:4-7).

3. While there is a strong pietistic strand in MRA writings, the work of the triune God in our

Confession: telling God and people we are sorry;

Conversion: living differently and better, then trying to keep the four absolutes of honesty, purity, unselfishness and love;

Continuance: persevering in this new life of obedience and love.

CHRISTIAN LIFE

An individual must express his change of life in a striving to keep the four absolutes — absolute honesty, absolute purity, absolute unselfishness, absolute love. These absolutes can be attained by means of four principles:

- Sharing in the confession of sin and temptation;
- Surrender of one's whole life to God;
- Restitution to people who have been wronged;
- Guidance in listening to and obeying God's 'inner' voice.

salvation is minimized (cf. Titus 3:4-7; 1 Peter 1:2).

Buchman borrowed the four absolutes from Robert Speer's book *The Principles of Jesus* (1902), in which the author claimed that these absolutes were the standard of the Sermon on the Mount. Buchman also heard these same absolutes from Professor Wright in Yale.

Three observations must be made here:

1. The four absolutes are a hopelessly inadequate summary and statement of the Sermon on the Mount.

2. It is not the four absolutes but the whole revealed will of God in the Bible which is the standard of life for believers (cf. 2 Timothy 3:16).

3. Not even the four absolutes can be kept perfectly (cf. 1 John 1:8, 10).

GUIDANCE

'When man listens, God speaks. When man obeys, God acts,' wrote Buchman. But how does God make known his will? 'Through friends, the Scriptures and the teachings of your faith, even through circumstances.' Such guidance may come as a compelling thought or insistent conviction or whisper, but if heeded the consequences may be far-reaching. For this reason a 'quiet time' each morning when one is able to meditate, listen, pray and read is invaluable. 'Inner guidance', wrote his biographer Theophil Spoeri, 'became the determining force in Buchman's life.'

It is true that the Bible teaches the fact of God's guidance and providence (Psalm 32:8; Isaiah 58:11; Daniel 4:34-35; Matthew 6:26-33), the importance of praying to God (Jeremiah 33:3; Luke 11:2-13; 1 Thessalonians 5:17), and reading and then obeying the Scriptures (Psalm 119:97; Colossians 3:16; James 1:21-25), but the MRA account of guidance is excessively subjective and lacks the objectivity and supremacy of the Bible. Guidance comes from God through the Bible ultimately and not from within oneself.

CHAPTER FIFTEEN

FAITH
MOVEMENT

WHO ARE THEY?

A BRIEF HISTORY

It was a desperate plea for help from a Christian. And the writer came to the point immediately. Were the views she had heard in sermons over recent months really biblical?

Are Christians really 'little gods'? Is it true that 'the cross has no salvation in it … a place of failure and defeat'? Was Jesus 'the first person ever to be born again'? These were just a few of the questions that troubled this Christian as she listened to the sermons. 'Please help me — quickly' was the plea. Unwittingly, she had been drawn into the Faith Movement. Many of the church members were excited about these new ideas but she was dubious and even distressed about them. Sadly, this is not an isolated example.

My task in this chapter is to place these 'strange', unbiblical ideas in context by providing a brief outline of the history and origins of the Faith Movement.

Where do we begin? Perhaps by mentioning some of the big names involved in teaching these unbiblical ideas. They include Kenneth Copeland, Benny Hinn, Morris Cerullo, Oral Roberts, Fredrick Price, Marilyn Hickey, Jeremy Savelle and many others. Are you surprised by some of these names? All I can say is that the Faith Movement has been extending its influence into mainstream Pentecostal and Charismatic church life through popular preachers like Hinn, Cerullo and Copeland to such a degree that many now regard them as being orthodox.

How did this Faith Movement begin? Providing an exact date is difficult but we can trace its origins with confidence. Two of the important early names to note are E. W. Kenyon and Kenneth E. Hagin.

Essek William Kenyon (1867-1948) was an evangelist, pastor, broadcaster and author. At the age of nineteen he started preaching, then pastored several churches in New England and established Dudley Bible Institute in Massachusetts, USA. Interestingly, this college was financed from his evangelistic work where many thousands of people were reported to have been saved and also healed. The college was later relocated to Rhode Island.

In Los Angeles Kenyon planted a Baptist church and pioneered radio evangelism with his daily programme from 1931, *Kenyon's Church of the Air*.

He wrote sixteen books. While not a Pentecostal, he influenced many Pentecostals and Charismatics. Individuals in very different movements were influenced by Kenyon such as 'Ern' Baxter, T. L. Osborn and Jimmy Swaggart. His writings were also important for Hagin, Copeland and others in the Word of Faith movement (WOF).

What did he believe? Well, the four distinctive teachings prominent among WOF teachers can be traced back to Kenyon, such as guaranteed health through Christ's

HISTORY

death, wealth/prosperity, the spiritual death of Christ and the theory that Christians are 'little gods'.

Many of Kenyon's statements are distressingly heretical. Consider the following. 'The believer is as much an Incarnation as was Jesus of Nazareth';[1] '... the cross has no salvation in it...';[2] 'Sin was not set to His account. He became sin';[3] 'His body did not become mortal until the Father laid our sin nature upon Him when He hung on the cross ... Satan took possession of His spirit...'[4]

What about Kenneth E. Hagin? Ill health and the alleged sight of hell with its penetrating darkness led to his professed conversion in April 1933 as a sixteen-year-old. Claiming physical healing then Spirit-baptism in 1937, he began to preach and entered the Pentecostal ministry as an itinerant Bible teacher and evangelist. In 1974 he founded the Rhema Bible Training Centre and within a fourteen-year period 100,000 students had graduated there. A daily radio programme on 180 stations to thirty-nine states, another eighty countries reached by short wave and millions of published copies of the eighty-five books he authored only illustrate the extent of his influence and popularity.

There is a dark side to Hagin. Although regarded as 'dad' of the WOF movement, scholars believe he plagiarized Kenyon's teaching (e.g. Hank Hanegraaff, *Christianity in Crisis*), and without giving credit. Hagin also claims many visions, out-of-body experiences, direct revelations, even eight personal visits from Jesus and alleged visits to both hell and heaven. Sadly, almost all the important WOF teachers have been influenced by Hagin, including Kenneth Copeland.

And Hagin's views? They are almost identical to those of Kenyon. Here is a small sample of his heretical beliefs: 'Adam was created on terms of equality with God...';[5] 'You are as much the incarnation of God as Jesus Christ was';[6] for Jesus 'spiritual death also means having Satan's nature...';[7] '...no believer should ever be sick...'[8]

Where did these unbiblical ideas come from? Many of Kenyon's ideas, recycled by Hagin, stem from the cults. To be more precise, the ideas originate from some cults in nineteenth-century America, which are often grouped together under the umbrella term of New Thought or New Metaphysic. Some of these cults, including Christian Science, deny the reality of sickness and death, re-affirm the 'power of mind', emphasize positive confession of 'faith' and teach a form of pantheism.

Can this link between Kenyon and the cults be proved? Yes, it can. For example, Kenyon attended Emerson College of Oratory in Boston after the New Thought ideas came to dominate the college. Again, Phineas P. Quimby (1802-66), the New Thought originator, taught that humans are a part of God and therefore all are 'gods'. That is exactly what Kenyon and Hagin taught, although Kenneth Copeland puts it more strongly: '... you do not have a God in you. You are one.'

WHAT THEY TEACH

Or listen to Morris Cerullo: 'You're not looking at Morris Cerullo; you're looking at God.'[9]

The New Thought cults and the Faith Movement then both proclaim man's divinity yet the latter reserves worship for three — God the Father, Jesus Christ and the Holy Spirit. Hanegraaff calls this 'henotheistic' rather than polytheistic (p. 111). But whatever we call it, it is heresy. Humans do not possess God's divine nature; God is unique, distinct from creation, eternal and independent.

Here then are the origins of the Faith Movement. Today Kenneth Copeland is regarded as their major teacher. A tele-evangelist, author and 'healer', he came under the influence of Kenyon's teaching and especially that of Hagin's. In his early ministry, he actually memorized Hagin's messages. 'Satan conquered Jesus on the cross,' Copeland proclaims. And, in hell, Christ was an 'emaciated, poured out, little, wormy spirit'.[10]

These ideas strike at the heart of the Christian gospel. But it was on the cross, not in hell, Jesus Christ made atonement for our sin once and for all. That is what the Bible teaches. 'Since we have now been justified by his blood, how much more shall we be saved from God's wrath through him! ... when we were God's enemies, we were reconciled to him through the death of his Son...' (Romans 5:9-10).

What Copeland and others do is to remove Christ's accomplished redemptive work from the cross to devilish experiences and encounters in hell. That is a distortion of the biblical gospel. Sadly, other Faith Movement teachers like Benny Hinn and Jeremy Savelle not only support Copeland, they recycle his detestable errors.

There are other distinctive and disturbing teachings propagated by the Faith Movement. One is what they call 'Positive Confession'. Created in God's image, the claim is that we have the ability to create what we need. The 'spiritual law' is that we say it, do it, receive it and tell it. Another distinctive is that God does not will sickness for his people although, inconsistently, Oral Roberts created a medical school in his university! Financial prosperity is another distinctive and we have the right to be rich especially if we give to the movement's teachers.

These errors, however, pale into insignificance in the light of their bizarre view of man's divinity and their tragic re-interpretation of Christ's sacrificial death. Our response must be that of the apostle Paul: 'If anyone is preaching to you a gospel other than what you accepted, let him be eternally condemned!' (Galatians 1:9).

RELEVANT COMPARISONS

The Faith Movement	The Bible
GOD	
Humans, as a part of God, are all 'gods'.	'I am the LORD, and there is no other; apart from me there is no God' (Isaiah 45:5).

COMPARISONS

PERSON OF CHRIST

'You are as much the incarnation of God as Jesus Christ was.'[11]

Christ's uniqueness in terms of his deity, pre-existence, co-equality and intimacy with the Father is constantly emphasized in the New Testament. See, for example:
John 3:16: '...his one and only Son...'
John 8:57: '...before Abraham was born, I am!'

CHRIST'S SINLESSNESS

'Sin was not set to His account. He became sin.'[12]

'...he committed no sin, and no deceit was found in his mouth' (1 Peter 2:22; Isaiah 53:9).

Without being made a sinner, nevertheless our sin was reckoned to his account as he died in our place and for our sin: 'He himself bore our sins in his body on the tree...' (1 Peter 2:24).

CHRIST'S DEATH

'... the cross has no salvation in it...' [13]

'For the message of the cross is foolishness to those who are perishing, but to us ... it is the power of God' (1 Corinthians 1:18).

'...we preach Christ crucified...' (v. 23).

'Satan conquered Jesus on the cross' (Copeland).

'Now is the time for judgement on this world; now the prince of this world will be driven out' (John 12:31).

Section B:

Unitarian churches and movements

CHAPTER SIXTEEN

UNITARIAN
CHURCHES

WHO ARE THEY?

A BRIEF HISTORY

While all Unitarian churches are autonomous, they are linked together by means of a General Assembly, which was established in 1928 to give encouragement and cohesion to the work. The first avowedly Unitarian Church, which was opened in London in 1774 by Theophilus Lindsey, is now the site of the assembly's headquarters.

Historically, Unitarianism has its roots in anti-trinitarian views in the seventeenth century expressed by some Anabaptists and other groups in certain European countries before entering England. In the early eighteenth century, anti-trinitarian sympathy deepened and won most support especially amongst Presbyterians and General Baptists in England. From 1774, in England, some people who rejected Trinitarian theology began to organize official Unitarian churches.

Unitarian teaching has always tended to be intellectual and committed to rejecting miracles, an infallible Bible and the need for personal salvation from sin. For Unitarians, man is essentially good.[1]

In the United States of America, it was in the eastern area of Massachusetts and under leaders like Charles Chauncy (1705-1787) and Jonathan Mayhew (1720-1766), both from Boston, that a liberalizing theological movement began which developed into Unitarianism in the early nineteenth century. The American Unitarian Association was formed in 1825 and some of its members were distinguished individuals. The Divinity School of Harvard University was opened in this early period under Unitarian auspices.

In Britain and the Commonwealth countries of Australia, New Zealand and South Africa there are an estimated 15,000 Unitarians, whereas there are about 150,000 in the United States and Canada. Romania (where organized Unitarianism began under the Unitarian Prince Sigismund in 1568 at the Diet of Torda), Hungary, Czechoslovakia, Western Germany and the Khasi Hills of Assam, India, all have Unitarian churches, with an approximate total membership of 20,000. Although not calling themselves Unitarian, there are many who agree doctrinally with Unitarians yet who may be in Protestant denominations or movements like the Watchtower.

The religious affiliations of the Unitarian General Assembly in Britain are both revealing and disturbing. For example, it is an associate member of the British Council of Churches and also of the World Congress of Faiths. In one of its official publications the assembly defines Unitarianism as 'a liberal religious movement arising out of Christianity, expressing itself largely but not wholly in Christian forms and terms, and in the spirit of the man Jesus. It is liberal in rejecting the idea of a unique and final revelation of truth and in trusting men to discover and believe as much as they can for themselves; it is a religious movement inasmuch as it has churches and a ministry and ways of worship... It is glad to remain Christian where it can but glad also to discover other truth and beauty and goodness in other faiths and other lives. Unitarians know of no better man in religion than Jesus of Nazareth but they believe that there have been others like him in the past, and that there will be others like him again.'[2]

The main factor in checking the progress of Unitarianism in the United Kingdom and America especially during the nineteenth and early twentieth centuries was the vigorous and fruitful preaching of the gospel under the power of the Holy Spirit. There were numerous outpourings of the Holy Spirit upon churches, communities and counties or states at regular intervals, with the result that large numbers of people were converted and the truth of God's Word was vindicated.

This is a salutary lesson for us in our contemporary situation, namely, that despite our evangelism, apologetics and social involvement, nothing but the outpouring of the Holy Spirit upon the church will radically alter our situation and cause the truth to prevail in our land.

RELEVANT COMPARISONS

Unitarians	The Bible

GOD

They deny the Trinity, affirming that in God there is only one personality, namely, God the Father. Even when referring to God as Father they feel human language is inadequate to define what is beyond definition. For this reason some find it more helpful not to use the word 'God' at all.

They usually reject miracles, believing that the natural order of the universe is never broken or superseded.

'God said, "Let us make man in our image"' (Genesis 1:26; cf. 11:7).

'... in the name [the one name, yet including three persons] of the Father and of the Son and of the Holy Spirit' (Matthew 28:19).

BIBLE

In contemporary Unitarianism the individual conscience, guided by human reason, is the source of what is believed. While the Bible is respected as a 'helpful guide' containing religious insights, it is rejected as the Word of God. God continues to reveal himself in life, in the order and beauty of nature, in moral standards, spiritual desires, human aspirations and in the love of what is pure and good. Thus they teach 'universal inspiration'.

'To the law and to the testimony: if they speak not according to this word, it is because there is no light in them' (Isaiah 8:20, AV).

'Your word is truth' (John 17:17).

'All Scripture is given by inspiration of God, and is profitable for doctrine, for reproof, for correction, for instruction in righteousness, that the man of God may be complete, thoroughly equipped for every good work' (2 Timothy 3:16-17, AV).

COMPARISONS

PERSON OF CHRIST

Jesus was only a man and as such should not be worshipped. He was an example and has shown us what man's life can be like when he obeys God's will and co-operates with the Spirit. Jesus is one of the many great spiritual leaders of the world.

'You are the Christ, the Son of the living God' (Matthew 16:16).

'For this reason the Jews tried all the harder to kill him; not only was he breaking the Sabbath, but he was even calling God his own Father, making himself equal with God' (John 5:18).

'I and the Father are one' (John 10:30).

'I am the way and the truth and the life. No one comes to the Father except through me' (John 14:6).

'For in Christ all the fulness of the Deity lives in bodily form' (Colossians 2:9).

DEATH OF CHRIST

Modern Unitarians do not believe that men and women need a mediator to approach God. Therefore Christ's death was not sacrificial or substitutionary.

Not all Unitarian churches observe the communion; those who do regard it as a mere remembrance of the life, works and teachings of Jesus Christ.

'Therefore no one will be declared righteous in his sight by observing the law' (Romans 3:20).

'But now in Christ Jesus you who once were far away have been brought near through the blood of Christ' (Ephesians 2:13).

'For through him we both have access to the Father by one Spirit' (Ephesians 2:18).

'For Christ died for sins once for all, the righteous for the unrighteous, to bring you to God' (1 Peter 3:18).

RESURRECTION OF CHRIST

Most Unitarians interpret our Lord's resurrection as his deeds and thoughts living on in the lives of others in history. There was no physical or spiritual resurrection of the Lord.

'Why do you look for the living among the dead? He is not here; he has risen!' (Luke 24:5-6).

'He was buried ... he was raised on the third day according to the Scriptures' (1 Corinthians 15:4).

HOLY SPIRIT

The Holy Spirit is regarded in several ways: for example, as the influence of Christ's teaching on people; as God's way of revealing himself in the whole of life; or as the 'Power' beyond us.

He is not regarded as a person in the Godhead co-equal with the Father and since man is basically good there is no need for his regenerating and sanctifying work in people.

The Holy Spirit is a person with a mind (Romans 8:6), knowledge (1 Corinthians 2:11) and a will by which he acts (1 Corinthians 12:11). He also speaks (Acts 13:2), teaches (Luke 12:12; John 14:26) and can be grieved (Ephesians 4:30).

'If I go, I will send him to you' (John 16:7).

'How is it that Satan has so filled your heart that you have lied to the Holy Spirit? ... You have not lied to men but to God' (Acts 5:3-4).

'Because you are sons, God sent the Spirit of his Son into our hearts ... who calls out, "Abba, Father!"' (Galatians 4:6).

MAN AND SIN

Unitarians assert their belief in man and his essential goodness. Although people are capable of great cruelty, this is regarded as a falling away from their essential goodness, which is best displayed in babies.

'Surely I was sinful at birth, sinful from the time my mother conceived me' (Psalm 51:5).

'For out of the heart come evil thoughts, murder, adultery, sexual immorality, theft, false testimony, slander' (Matthew 15:19).

'There is no one righteous, not even one' (Romans 3:10).

'For all have sinned and fall short of the glory of God' (Romans 3:23).

SALVATION

All religions are regarded as equally valid schemes of salvation and Jesus belongs to the class of the great saviours of mankind. No mediator is needed to approach God and no special requirement is needed on man's part to attain salvation.

'I am the gate; whoever enters through me will be saved' (John 10:9).

'Salvation is found in no one else, for there is no other name under heaven given to men by which we must be saved' (Acts 4:12).

'Believe in the Lord Jesus, and you will be saved' (Acts 16:31).

FUTURE STATE

They believe that the process of dying is one of the processes of life and their aim is to approach

'I know that my Redeemer lives, and that in the end he will stand upon the earth. And after my skin has been

it without fear. There are three general Unitarian positions here:

1. Those who believe in personal immortality;
2. Those who believe their deeds and thoughts survive only in the memory of other people;
3. Those who don't know.

destroyed, yet in my flesh I will see God' (Job 19:25-26).

'Then they will go away to eternal punishment, but the righteous to eternal life' (Matthew 25:46).

'For a time is coming when all who are in their graves will hear his voice and come out — those who have done good will rise to live, and those who have done evil will rise to be condemned' (John 5:28-29).

'Just as man is destined to die once, and after that to face judgement' (Hebrews 9:27).

PRAYER

True prayer aims at effecting a change in ourselves so that, by our example, we may change others. For many Unitarians private prayer has been equated with honest work rather than with the devotional life, and there is a general dislike of petitionary prayer. Believing that man has direct access to God in prayer, they do not pray 'through Jesus Christ'.

'"For I know the plans I have for you," declares the Lord, "plans to prosper you and not to harm you, plans to give you hope and a future."' While God's purpose was clear, prayer was one of the means he decreed through which he would accomplish his purpose, so he continues, 'Then you will call upon me and come and pray to me, and I will listen to you' (Jeremiah 29:11-12).

'My Father will give whatever you ask in my name' (John 16:23).

'Pray continually' (1 Thessalonians 5:17).

'If we ask anything according to his will, he hears us' (1 John 5:14).

CHAPTER SEVENTEEN

THE WAY
INTERNATIONAL

WHO ARE THEY?

A BRIEF HISTORY

Victor Paul Wierwille established 'The Way International' in 1958 and for well over twenty years led the work from his headquarters in New Knoxville, Ohio, U.S.A. After his retirement the leadership of the movement was entrusted to Rev. Craig Martindale.

Having completed studies at Chicago University and Princeton Seminary, Wierwille was ordained to the Christian ministry. For several years he pastored an evangelical, reformed church in Van Wert, Ohio, but his teaching soon became suspect. A denominational church committee was eventually appointed to assess the orthodoxy of Wierwille's views and to recommend appropriate disciplinary measures.

However, in May 1958 Wierwille resigned from his pastorate before the committee's work was completed. Almost immediately, he formed The Way International and significant numbers of people joined the new cult.

By 1987 there were an estimated 100,000 members in Europe and the United States. In 1995 there were 725 members in Britain but about forty-eight congregations.

How it began

For at least five or six years before his resignation, Wierwille had begun to develop and popularize his own unbiblical ideas. One important factor in this early period was the decision to burn his 3,000 theology books and commentaries. The reason he gave for this drastic action was that he had 'set out on an independent path for discovering the meaning of Scripture'. He added, 'I have read every commentary in existence; I consign every one of them to Gehenna.'

Another significant factor which contributed to Wierwille's unorthodoxy was his claim that God had spoken audibly to him one day as he prayed. God is supposed to have said to him, 'I will teach you the Word as it has not been known since the first century and you will teach it to others.' Wierwille consequently redefined an apostle as 'one who brings new light to his generation' and was convinced that he had a crucial apostolic role to fulfil. He had no hesitation in claiming that he was the only preacher who taught the original doctrine of the apostles!

In 1953, his study course entitled *Power for Abundant Living* (PFAL) was published. This course became a popular and influential method of disseminating his teaching and still remains an integral part of The Way's initial teaching programme. However, many of Wierwille's ideas in this and other works can be traced to the writings of E. W. Bullinger. 'Even more serious,' affirms Joel A. MacCollam, 'Wierwille lifted numerous and substantial direct quotations from Bullinger's *The Giver of his Gifts* and *How to enjoy your Bible* without giving any credit to the original author. In much of Wierwille's work there is no "new light" to this generation, only a reflection of another's efforts.'

How The Way works

Nearly all the recruits to this cult are contacted initially through the 'friendship' and personal witness of members. Recruits are mostly in their late teens or early twenties and have usually been impressed by the friendliness and concern of Way members. The work of personal friendship is then supplemented by fellowship in the home. Individuals are gradually pressurized and brainwashed into thinking that only Wierwille's statements and interpretation of the Bible are infallible.

Each Way member is called a 'leaf', while the local group is known as a 'twig' and the regional work as a 'branch'. The analogy is continued at all levels with the directors, for example, being known as the root and the headquarters in Ohio as the trunk. In the United States, Way members have infiltrated some evangelical churches and Bible colleges with the specific aim of recruiting young believers. A person's 'faith' and commitment to The Way is evidenced when he enters upon and completes the expensive *PFAL* course of instruction.

Despite its emphasis on friendship and the Bible, The Way is a dangerous, heretical cult.

RELEVANT COMPARISONS

The Way	The Bible

BIBLE

The Way	The Bible
The Old Testament and the four Gospels are unnecessary and not part of the Word of God. 'The Bible as a whole', asserts Wierwille, 'is not relevant to all people of all times.'	'Your word is truth (John 17:17). 'All Scripture is God-breathed and is useful for teaching, rebuking, correcting and training in righteousness' (2 Timothy 3:16).

TRINITY

The Way	The Bible
A false doctrine not found in the Bible. 'Trinitarian dogma ... degrades God from his elevated, unparalleled position...'	See other chapters, and especially chapter 25 on the Holy Trinity for a detailed biblical answer.

JESUS CHRIST

The Way	The Bible
'Jesus Christ's existence began when he was conceived by God's creating the soul-life of Jesus in Mary.' Christ was a human being only and created specially by God.	'I tell you the truth, before Abraham was born, I am!' (John 8:58). 'I came from the Father and entered the world' (John 16:28). 'Who, being in very nature God, did not consider equality with God something to be grasped, but made himself nothing, taking the very nature of a servant, being made in human

Jesus had no direct fellowship or contact with God before his baptism.

likeness' (Philippians 2:6-7).

'No man has seen God at any time; the only begotten Son, which is in the bosom of the Father, he has declared him' (John 1:18, AV).

'Did you not know that I must be about my Father's business?' (Luke 2:49, NKJV).

DEATH OF CHRIST

Wierwille denies that Christ died sacrificially on behalf of other people.

'I lay down my life for the sheep' (John 10:15).

'Christ loved us and gave himself up for us as a fragrant offering and sacrifice to God' (Ephesians 5:2).

HOLY SPIRIT

The Spirit of God is regarded as an impersonal force or ability; his distinct personality and deity are denied.

'Do not grieve the Holy Spirit of God, with whom you were sealed for the day of redemption' (Ephesians 4:30).

'All these are the work of one and the same Spirit, and he gives them to each one, just as he determines' (1 Corinthians 12:11).

SALVATION

If we 'only believe' we shall:

'Believe in the Lord Jesus, and you will be saved' (Acts 16:31).

1. 'be saved'

'For my Father's will is

that everyone who looks to the Son and believes in him shall have eternal life' (John 6:40).

2. enjoy a legal right to victory over all sin;

'For sin shall not be your master, because you are not under law, but under grace' (Romans 6:14).

'If we claim to be without sin, we deceive ourselves and the truth is not in us' (1 John 1:8).

3. realize God's will for us, which 'is success in everything', including freedom from illness. For example, if we have a headache we can say, 'Look here, headache, you have no power over me. You were defeated over 1900 years ago. It says so in the Word and I believe the Word: therefore, be gone from me.'

'Three times I pleaded with the Lord to take it [thorn in the flesh] away from me. But he said to me, "My grace is sufficient for you, for my power is made perfect in weakness." Therefore I will boast all the more gladly about my weaknesses, so that Christ's power may rest on me' (2 Corinthians 12:8-9).

EVIDENCES OF PERSONAL SALVATION

There are two infallible signs of the new birth:

1. Speaking with tongues. 'Open your mouth wide and breathe in,' exhorts Wierwille, 'You are now going to manifest the Spirit's presence ... Move your lips, your throat, your tongue. Speak forth, the external manifestation is your proof

'Not everyone who says to me, "Lord, Lord," will enter the kingdom of heaven, but only he who does the will of my Father who is in heaven' (Matthew 7:21-23).

'But the fruit of the Spirit is love, joy, peace, patience, kindness, goodness, faithfulness,

COMPARISONS

in the sense world that you have Christ within.'

2. Willingness to pay a 'donation' (quite large) in order to receive Wierwille's twelve lessons entitled *Power for Abundant Living* (PFAL).

gentleness and self-control...' (Galatians 5:22-23).

Passages like Acts 8:14-17; 9:18-22 do not support the view that all believers spoke with tongues at their conversion.

Wierwille appears to teach for material gain and is condemned by biblical passages such as 2 Peter 2:3: 'In their greed these teachers will exploit you with stories they have made up. Their condemnation has long been hanging over them, and their destruction has not been sleeping' (cf. 1 Timothy 6:3-5; Titus 1:10-11).

CHAPTER EIGHTEEN

'JESUS ONLY': THE APOSTOLIC ONENESS MOVEMENT

A BRIEF HISTORY

What's
Wrong
With the
Name
JESUS
?

These were the words on the front page of a leaflet circulated to houses in my home area some time ago. The leaflet was published and distributed by the First United Pentecostal Church. After reading the leaflet, people began to ask questions such as, 'Who are these people?' 'What do they believe?' No one seemed to know very much about the group but the leaflet was clearly misleading and heretical.

It was at this point that a friend asked me to investigate the First United Pentecostal Church. I soon discovered that the group was not Pentecostal at all but one of a number of groups which denied the doctrine of the Holy Trinity. Their 'Jesus only' teaching is popular today; in some reasonably 'live' Bible churches one hears talk of being baptized in the name of 'Jesus only'. Clearly these Christians and churches are often

unaware of the historical background to this teaching
and its theological implications, not only for baptism
but also for the doctrine of the Holy Trinity. This chapter may help to clarify the issues for Bible-believing
Christians.

The historical background

During the second decade of its history, American
Pentecostalism was plunged into a major doctrinal
controversy concerning baptism in the name of Jesus.
It began in 1913 at a worldwide Pentecostal meeting
at Arrayo Seco, Los Angeles, when R. E. McAlister
preached from Acts 2:38 on 'baptism in Jesus' name',
in which he claimed that all baptized believers in the
apostolic age were baptized in the name of Jesus Christ
alone, rather than in the name of the Father, Son and
Holy Spirit.

There was opposition to McAlister's message, but
men like Frank J. Ewart and John C. Scheppe were
won over to his side. Within a short time, Ewart was
confirmed in this view, especially when he felt that
answers to prayer resulted from his praying in the name
of Jesus. Verses like Matthew 17:8; John 10:30; 14:13;
Philippians 2:9-11 and Colossians 3:17 were wrongly
used by Scheppe and others to support a 'modalist'[1]
theory of the Trinity. While the much earlier heresy
of Sabellius had taught that the Father alone was God
and that he had manifested himself as the Son and then
as the Holy Spirit, these 'Pentecostal' leaders regarded

Jesus, not the Father, as the only one God. For them, Jesus manifested himself in the 'form' or 'office' of Father, Son and Holy Spirit at different times.

Along with evangelist Glenn A. Cook, Ewart led this new movement, assisted by some prominent leaders of the Assemblies of God like G. T. Haywood, E. N. Bell and H. A. Goss, who all played a key role in propagating the new teaching. A magazine was published and edited by Ewart under the title of *Meat in due season*, which had the dubious distinction of being the first 'oneness' periodical.[2]

As members of the Assemblies of God were the most vocal in advocating the new theology, they were disciplined by their denominational General Council meeting at St Louis in 1916. The council strengthened its trinitarian theology and thereby expelled many of its assemblies and as many as 146 ministers.

Those expelled from the Assemblies of God gradually organized themselves into 'oneness' churches of various shades, but they held in common certain distinctives such as a 'modal' view of the Trinity, the insistence that baptism by immersion was essential to salvation and that such baptism should be carried out only in the name of Jesus. They also retained a 'Pentecostal' position concerning the gifts and Spirit-baptism.

Some of the 'oneness' Pentecostal churches active today include the Apostolic Church of Jesus,[3]

Apostolic Faith (Hawaii),[4] Associated Brotherhood of Christians,[5] Assemblies of the Lord Jesus Christ,[6] Pentecostal Assemblies of the World,[7] Jesus Church,[8] Apostolic Overcoming Holy Church of God,[9] Church of Our Lord Jesus Christ of the Apostolic Faith,[10] Bible Way Church of Our Lord Jesus Christ World Wide, Inc.,[11] New Bethel Church of God in Christ (Pentecostal),[12] the Apostolic Gospel Church of Jesus Christ,[13] and the larger United Pentecostal Church.[14]Altogether there are well over seventeen such denominations which share in common the 'Jesus only' teaching.[15]

I now want to pinpoint the main errors of this teaching:

1. The 'Jesus only' teaching denies the biblical doctrine of the Holy Trinity.
2. Baptism in the name of Jesus is normally an expression of non-trinitarian theology.
3. The movement has an unbiblical doctrine of salvation.

RELEVANT COMPARISONS

The 'Jesus Only' movement	The Bible
HOLY TRINITY	
The Father, Son and Holy Spirit are only different expressions or 'manifestations' of the one true God, who is Jesus. A United Pentecostal Church radio speaker confirms this error: 'I want	1. The Father is not the Son (John 12:49-50; 14:23, 28-31); the Son is not the Spirit (John 16:7-14), and the Spirit is not the same as the Father (John 14:16-17).

to tell you what the great truth is. We do not believe in three separate personalities in the Godhead, but we believe in three offices which are filled by one person.'[16]

2. Passages like Matthew 3:17; 17:5; 26:39; John 14:26; 16:7, 13-14; 17:4; Luke 23:34, 46 are meaningless if Jesus alone is God. For example, how do you explain the Father's voice at our Lord's baptism? Was the Lord Jesus praying to himself when he prayed? Did the Lord really submit to the Father's will in Gethsemane or was it play-acting?

3. The Bible teaches that there are three distinguishable but co-existent, co-equal and co-eternal persons designated God (see, for example, 1 Corinthians 8:6; John 1:1; Acts 5:3-4) and in the unity of the Godhead they constitute the 'one God' (1 Timothy 2:5). In the words of Jim Beverly of Atlantic Baptist College, 'These three are Persons and yet the "one God". Only this position does justice to the teaching of the New Testament.'[17]

BAPTISM

'Oneness' Pentecostals insist that all believers must be baptized in the name

1. The trinitarian formula of baptism given by the Lord Jesus Christ in Matthew

of Jesus only. In support of this view they use texts such as Acts 2:38; 8:16; 10:48 and 19:5. Furthermore, they argue that 'the name' of Matthew 28:19 is the same as 'the name of Jesus Christ' in Acts 2:38; their conclusion is that Jesus is the Father, the Son and the Holy Spirit!

28:19 must govern our theology of Christian baptism.

2. The phrase, 'in the name of Jesus Christ', may have the primary meaning of baptisms being carried out under the authority and command of Jesus Christ, the head of the church. In Acts 2:38, for example, Peter would have been conscious of complying with the Great Commission recorded in Matthew 28:19-20.

3. Significantly, the phrase 'in the name of Jesus' in relation to baptism is used only sparingly in Acts and then only at strategic moments to mark the extension of the church amongst the Jews (2:38), the Samaritans (8:16) and the Gentiles (10:48).

4. Calvin maintains that the words of Acts 2:38, 'in the name of Jesus Christ', are not a formula to be used in baptism but rather a declaration that all the efficacy of baptism is found in Christ alone. 'Christ is the mark and end whereunto baptism directs us,' stresses Calvin, 'wherefore, everyone profits in baptism as he learns to look to Christ ... for we are both made clean by his blood, and also

we enter into a new life by the benefit of his death and resurrection.'[18] This is part of the significance of the same phrase used in Acts 19:5.

The use of these New Testament texts by 'oneness Pentecostals' is therefore both irresponsible and unbiblical.

SALVATION

Baptism by immersion in the name of Jesus alone is essential for salvation. Some groups, like the United Pentecostal Church, also believe that 'speaking in tongues' is necessary for salvation.

While baptism is commanded by Christ and richly significant, it is not essential to salvation (see Luke 23:42-43; John 3:14-17; Acts 16:31; Ephesians 2:8-9).

Concerning speaking in tongues, we are not told anywhere in the New Testament that all Christians spoke in tongues; rather Paul's question in 1 Corinthians 12:30 shows clearly that this was not the case.

CHAPTER NINETEEN

WHERE ARE TODAY'S ARIANS?

WHO ARE THEY?

Everywhere! That is a brief but somewhat exaggerated answer to this important question. However, this brief answer needs to be amplified in order to identify correctly some of today's Arians. But let me distinguish between Unitarians and Arians. Like Arians, Unitarians reject the Trinity, Christ's deity and other major doctrines. On the other hand, Arians are not as sceptical as Unitarians as they have a higher view of the Bible and do not eliminate the miraculous elements from Bible history. They also acknowledge Jesus to be an angel rather than a mere man.

Explanation

The term 'Arians' requires explanation. The term dates back to Arius who died in AD 336. Arius was a presbyter as well as a theologian and an influential church leader in northern Egypt. Trained in theology in the famous Antioch centre, Arius began to question the doctrine of the Trinity.

The basic facts are these. Arius refused to accept that Jesus Christ, the Son of God, was co-equal with the Father as God. According to Arius, the Lord Jesus was inferior to the Father and only a 'creature', yet still very important. Only God the Father, he argued, is uncreated and without beginning. To quote Arius, 'there was when he [the Son] was not' and he argued this — albeit wrongly — from Bible verses like Colossians 1:15. The Father then, in the view of Arius, called the Son into existence by his sovereign will. Arians, therefore, were those who followed the teaching of Arius.

Heresy

Under the influence partly of Athanasius (AD 328-373), Arius's teaching was rejected as being unbiblical. In church councils like Nicea (AD 325) and Constantinople (AD 381) it was condemned as heresy.

But where do we find Arians today? My answer is only introductory and concentrates on one group in the West that shares Arius's teaching, namely the Watchtower Society.

The more commonly used name for the Watchtower is Jehovah's Witnesses (JWs). They claim a direct descent from Arius and are proud of it, too. For them the historical link is supposed to be Jesus, Paul, Arius, Wycliff and Luther, then directly to their original founder in the nineteenth century, Charles Taze Russell.

This claim by the JWs is an obviously absurd one. Their only doctrinal affinity is with Arius; that is not in dispute. But they have no historical, theological affinity

WHAT THEY TEACH

with the others and certainly not with the Lord Jesus whose teaching they distort.

What do the JWs teach concerning Jesus Christ? Like Arius, they claim that Jesus Christ had a beginning, that is, he was created. In this sense, he is only 'a' god but not God.

When was Jesus created? The JW answer is emphatic. Jehovah created all that exists and, JWs claim, Jesus was the very first one to be created. Their theory is that Jesus was created as an angel, in fact as the archangel Michael. Jesus, as an angel, was mighty but privileged to be a 'working partner' with Jehovah in creating the rest of creation. However, they insist that Jesus was not Jehovah, although he was 'a god'. This is a recycling of Arius's teaching and the similarity is striking.

Christadelphians

Before we look at the way in which they misinter-pret some important Bible statements, we can identify another contemporary group as possibly being Arian in theology. This group is known as Christadelphians and predate the JWs by nearly thirty years. There is evidence that Russell was influenced in the early stages by ideas taught by the Christadelphian leader, John Thomas, an Englishman. Rejecting the Holy Trinity, Christadelphians then disagreed with the eternal sonship of Christ. For them, Jesus was created. At this point, they disagree with Arius, insisting the Jesus did not exist at all prior to his birth by Mary. An identical view is held by The Way International and was first articulated by their founder, Victor Paul Wierwille.

Warning

How can we answer Arians, especially JWs? Obviously we must turn to the Bible for our answers. Our duty is to believe and practise only what is clearly taught in this unique Word of God. However, a word of warning is necessary here. JWs impose their views on the Bible instead of allowing the Bible text to speak to them. They tend to twist the text to fit their own views and also insert words in their translation that are not in the original text.

Colossians 1:15

One Bible verse misunderstood both by Arius and JWs is Colossians 1:15 and especially the statement with regard to Christ, 'the firstborn over [JWs translate as 'of'] all creation'. Here, three observations are necessary in order to understand the statement correctly. Firstly, the JW translation wrongly introduces the word 'other', which was not in the original Greek, into their translation of verses 15-17 in order to deprive Christ of his glory as God. This is dishonest.

WHAT THEY TEACH

Secondly, the Greek word translated 'firstborn' means priority and sovereignty over all. If Paul had wanted to say that Jesus was the first to be created then he would have used another but similar Greek word, *protoktistos*.

Thirdly, understood against the Hebraic background to the New Testament, this title 'firstborn' in Colossians 1:15 has a dominant redemptive reference. In Exodus 12:1-28, the firstborn was appointed by the Lord to represent the family. The Passover lamb represented the firstborn and died in his place and, therefore, for the whole family. Similarly, 'Christ is our Passover' (1 Corinthians 5:7); he is both the firstborn who represents the elect family of God and also 'the Lamb of God' (John 1:29) who takes away our sin, saving us from divine wrath. The statement, therefore, has been misunderstood both by Arians and JWs.

Revelation 3:14

Many other texts could be cited. For example, the JW translation of Revelation 3:14 ('the beginning of the creation *by* God' *[italics mine]*) substitutes 'of' for 'by' thus mistranslating the Greek word. Furthermore, rather than support their theory that Christ is created, the Greek word translated 'beginning' means the source, origin and active cause of what exists. This makes an enormous difference to understanding the statement. For instead of being viewed as the first of those created, Jesus is rather the agent and originating source of creation. He is the creator, not a created one!

Evidence

The Bible evidence for Christ's deity is overwhelming. He forgives sins. Some Jews objected: 'Who can forgive sins but God alone?' (Mark 2:7). But Jesus healed the crippled man so that they should 'know that the Son of Man has authority on earth to forgive sins'. The implication is clear: only God can forgive sins and here Christ underlines his own deity by forgiving sins himself.

He claimed equality with God too: 'I and my Father are one' (John 10:30). More than oneness of purpose is intended here for the Jews were ready to kill Jesus for blasphemy (v. 33). And there is a lot more evidence. For example, the description of Jehovah in Psalm 102:25-27 is applied to Christ in Hebrews 1:10-12. Isaiah also saw the glory of Christ (Isaiah 6:1; John 12:41) while in Zechariah 2:9-11 two distinguishable persons are described as Jehovah. Then in the opening verses of Zechariah 3 these two persons called Jehovah speak to each other! Or think of God's unique claim in Isaiah 48:12 which Jesus applies to himself in Revelation 1:8 and 22:13.

CHALLENGE

Yes, Jesus was fully God but also man. He needed to be the God-man in order to fulfil his unique mission. And that is the wonder of his earthly life and death for our sin. Only God could achieve salvation for us.

Challenge

A final challenge to Christian readers. Do not be intimidated by Arians, whether they be JWs or members of other groups. Tell them of the Triune God and of the eternal Son of God who died for sin. At the same time, pray for such people. They desperately need Christ. And praise God that some JWs are regularly coming to Christ from the darkness and errors of Arianism.

CHAPTER TWENTY

JEHOVAH'S WITNESSES

A BRIEF HISTORY

It is claimed there are '6,000,000 persons' in 'over 230 lands' who are Jehovah's Witnesses. I cannot verify these statistics but two observations are pertinent.

Firstly, growth in the number of Jehovah's Witnesses has fluctuated in recent years. For example, between 1993 and 2001 their growth in the United Kingdom has slowed down.

Secondly, Watchtower yearbooks reveal that there are twice as many baptisms as there are active Witnesses. This points to a high dropout rate. There are now many more ex-Jehovah's Witnesses than active ones!

Disillusioned

To meet this situation, an annual National Convention of ex-Jehovah's Witnesses was established in America a few years ago. What happens to those who leave this organization, known as the Watchtower Bible and Tract Society?

Some are disillusioned, despairing of ever finding the truth. A number have been converted to Christ and have joined Bible-teaching churches.

Quite a few testimonies of former Witnesses have been published in book form or articles over the years.

Other former members have gone into Judaism or cults like the Mormons or one of the several Witnesses' breakaway groups like the Dawn Bible Students. The Watchtower is certainly not the united, solid organization it claims to be.

Governing Body

Raymond Franz illustrates the extensive disillusionment among former Jehovah's Witnesses. He was excommunicated from the Watchtower Society in 1981. The reason? Because he disagreed with decisions made by its Governing Body.

In 1983 Franz published *Crisis of Conscience* in which he detailed many of the arbitrary, unbiblical decisions made by the Governing Body. He spoke with authority as he himself spent nine years as an active member of this elite, ruling body. For example, the prohibition then placed on lifesaving organ transplant surgery, and the continuing prohibition of blood transfusions, were only two of the decisions that disturbed Franz.

Another prohibition imposed by the Governing Body was that Witnesses in Malawi should not comply with the government law that all citizens should have a 'party card'. Yet, at the same time, says Franz, the Governing Body approved the policy of Witnesses in Mexico bribing officials to obtain certification that they were members of the 'reserves' who have served a year of military service!

Such double standards, alongside other dubious and unbiblical decisions by the Governing Body, disillusioned Franz. It raised for him a 'crisis of conscience' as this small group of men attached infallibility to their own opinions and prejudices.

Silent lambs

The Lord's words in verses 6 and 9 of Matthew 15, insisted Franz, were applicable to the Watchtower's Governing Body: 'Thus you nullify the word of God for the sake of your tradition … their teachings are but rules made by man.'

But further problems have come to light since Franz wrote his helpful book twenty years ago. These problems within the Watchtower organization are disturbing.

Think, for example, of the 'silent lambs'. The term refers to people who have been discouraged by Watchtower leaders (at local and national levels) from getting help when they have been molested or abused.

Bill Bowen is only one of the local leaders who relinquished his position as congregation elder to challenge the Jehovah's Witnesses practice of refusing to report known paedophiles (and others engaged in criminal activity) to secular law enforcement authorities.

One reason given in the past for this reluctance to report such crimes was that it would 'bring reproach upon Jehovah's Name'. As a result, it is claimed by both current and former members of the Watchtower, 'a significant number of child abusers have been shielded from prosecution and the lives of many children have been tragically affected'. Reliable sources say that 'now many are coming forward with their stories, and are seeking justice'.

Real problem

At the time of writing, in the USA, a popular TV programme, *Dateline NBC,* is filming some of the victims' stories. They intend to broadcast a programme on the subject of paedophilia among Jehovah's Witnesses towards the end of 2004. No one is suggesting that such abuse is rampant among Jehovah's Witnesses in general, or that it is not found among other religious groups, but it is a real problem for the Jehovah's Witness movement and more widespread than was first thought.

One of the related problems concerns individuals who are excommunicated for speaking out against abuse. This happened to Barbara and Carl Pandelo of Belmar, New Jersey, who criticized the organization's handling of their daughter's allegations of sexual abuse by another member.

The problem of paedophilia among the Witnesses extends beyond America to other countries, including the United Kingdom. For example, at Alloa Sheriff Court in Scotland, a Jehovah's Witness called Thomas Maxwell was found guilty of a string of sexual attacks and cruelty to girls which dated back over thirty years. In June 2000 he was placed on probation because of his voluntary exile to Leverburgh in the south of the island of Harris, but when further offences were discovered, he was sent to prison.

Sadly, there are many accounts of sexual abuse among Witnesses provided on the 'silentlambs' website.

Moral inconsistencies

I have highlighted the paedophilia problem within the Watchtower movement partly in order to encourage Christians to witness even more boldly to them.

Another reason for drawing attention to this problem is that Jehovah's Witnesses have greatly criticized Christendom, including Evangelical churches, for inconsistent behaviour and hypocrisy. They have regularly dismissed churches as 'synagogues of Satan'.

Some of their criticisms are valid, and apply not only to apostate churches but also, sadly, to a few Bible-teaching churches. Repentance, issuing in radical transformation of personal and corporate church life, is urgently required in such cases. However, Jehovah's Witnesses need to look critically at their own organization and recognize the glaring moral inconsistencies which exist there.

Cults

A helpful sermon was preached by the late Dr Martyn Lloyd-Jones on cults, recorded in his exposition of Ephesians 6:10-13.[1] He underlines 'the wiles of the devil'[2] and 'the subtle foe'[3] before illustrating these subtle wiles in three related areas — heresies, cults and counterfeits. I want to summarize what he says about cults.

First of all, Lloyd-Jones identifies some common characteristics of cults. For example, they 'sound like Christianity', they offer 'very great blessings' and their devotees are 'always sincere'.[4]

Next, he suggests some tests that can be applied to cults. One test concerns their origin. Do they claim a direct revelation or a 'very important' founder? Again, cults 'always recognize, and are governed by, an authority additional to the Bible'.[5]

Lloyd-Jones is correct, but with regard to Jehovah's Witnesses it is more subtle. Witnesses only read the Bible using official 'explanations' of the text provided by local leaders or Watchtower literature.

Glorious gospel

Thirdly, cults go astray 'with respect to certain essential doctrines'[6], such as Scripture, Christology, the Holy Spirit, the Holy Trinity, creation, sin, salvation and prayer.[7]

Jehovah's Witnesses fail most of these tests. For example, they deny the Trinity then dismiss the Holy Spirit as a mere power. They relegate Jesus Christ to the status of an angel, and salvation is a combination of good deeds and faith.

In their view, our Lord's 'ransom sacrifice' only removes Adam's sin. His death is not a completed work but merely the basis on which we strive to achieve our personal salvation.

By contrast, listen to what the Bible really says: 'He himself bore *our* sins in his body on the tree...' (1 Peter 2:24; cf. 2 Corinthians 5:21). Here is the glorious gospel of God, 'that the Son of God was made a sin-offering, that God laid our iniquities upon Him'.[8]

All we must do to be saved is 'Believe in the Lord Jesus Christ' (Acts 16:31). Any other message is the devil's counterfeit.

Early history

How did the Watchtower cult emerge and develop? The story begins with Charles Taze Russell (1852-1916). His parents were Calvinists in theology and members of a Congregational church in Pittsburgh, Pennsylvania, where the Bible was taught faithfully.

Russell accepted the God-centred theology of the church and of his parents until, at the age of sixteen, he was ridiculed by a friend for believing in such an 'unreasonable' doctrine as hell. Within weeks, Russell began his search for a more acceptable creed and rejected the orthodox Christian faith.

Own group

At an Adventist meeting two years later, Russell was delighted to hear the speaker advocating the annihilation of unbelievers, and scorning the doctrine of eternal punishment. From these earlier Adventists, Russell also learned of an unsuccessful attempt by one of their leaders to propose a date (like 1843) for Christ's return. Consequently, prophesying the end of the world and Christ's return has been a regular feature of Witness teaching.

Russell might have joined this group, but differences soon emerged and he decided to lead his own group. Further disagreement with a colleague led Russell to launch his own magazine, and this enabled him to establish over thirty Bible study groups in the following months. He then registered 'Zion's Watch Tower Tract Society' as a legal entity in 1884. Only in 1956 did the movement adopt its present name — the Watch Tower Bible and Tract Society.

Russell wrote a number of books (now known as *Studies in the Scriptures*) together with a weekly sermon, which, between 1904 and 1914, was sent to about 3,000 newspapers in North America and Europe.

Scandal

Despite his growing popularity, Russell's last years were characterized by scandal and deceit. He was involved in several court cases and, to put it mildly, his character did not emerge unscathed.

His wife left him in 1897 and later sued him for divorce on the grounds of his 'conceit, egotism, domination and improper conduct in relation to other women'.

One of the legal advisers to the group, Joseph Franklin Rutherford, succeeded Russell but only after ignoring Russell's explicit wishes and using his legal training to seize control of the organization. In protest, many leaders from Russell's era promptly left and formed breakaway groups upholding Russell's teachings.

Rutherford launched a magazine, later named *Awake*, and reorganized the system, placing greater emphasis on witnessing and literature distribution. Those who opposed his decisions were expelled.

This led to the formation of several additional sep-aratist groups during the early years of his leadership, including the Dawn Bible Students' Association and the Laymen's Home Missionary Movement. By now, it is thought that approximately twenty groups had broken away from the Watchtower.

Unreliable translation

Before he died in 1942, Rutherford nominated Nathan Homer Knorr to succeed him as the third president. The latter's strengths lay in his administrative and intellectual gifts. He insisted, for example, on a more thorough training of members, and encouraged the New World Translation of the Holy Scriptures, which was completed in 1960.

This translation is most unreliable; there are numer-ous examples of misleading translations of original words, as well as insertions not present in the original Greek texts.

The last president was Frederick Franz. After his death, leadership of the cult was vested in the Gov-erning Body.

New light?

Have the views of this cult remained the same during its history? The answer is both 'yes' and 'no'. Their position

WHAT THEY TEACH

remains unchanged on major subjects such as the Holy Trinity; the deity, death and physical resurrection of Christ; the Holy Spirit; new birth, conversion and justification by faith; and eschatology. These orthodox biblical doctrines have been rejected consistently and vehemently by its leaders.

On the other hand, details concerning these views and the interpretation of Scripture have changed significantly over the years. This raises another contemporary issue with regard to this cult, namely, their 'New Light' doctrine.

What is this doctrine? It is the principle that 'the light keeps getting brighter and brighter'. This is based, wrongly, on Proverbs 4:18: 'The path of the righteous is like the first gleam of dawn, shining ever brighter till the full light of day.'

This verse does not, as they imply, refer to prophecy or direct revelation from God. The context establishes the point. Proverbs 4:10-18 embodies a contrast between two ways of living, namely, the ways of wisdom and of wickedness. The term 'way' points to a structured, purposeful movement in a single direction, whether wickedness or wisdom.

In verses 18-19 the metaphors of light and darkness are used helpfully. 'Light' signifies happiness, security and life, whereas 'darkness' points to misery, ignorance, failure and death.

Rather than referring to direct revelation as claimed by Witnesses, verse 18 assures us that believing, godly persons have the light of God's wisdom to guide them throughout their lives.

At the beginning of their Christian experience, it is like commencing a journey at dawn with welcome but limited light from the Word. However, there is increasing light and warmth given to believers through the Word as they continue their journey to heaven. Such light enables and sustains believers in honouring God, as they become more mature in age and experience.

Revised teaching

The Watchtower interpretation of Proverbs 4:18 is clearly wrong. But the cult does believe that in 1918 it was appointed as God's channel of information to the human race.

When they deem it appropriate, the leadership issues modifications or 'reversals' in teaching even though the revisions contradict earlier instruction. They argue that even though they have made corrections to their teaching yet, over the last century, they have been moving closer to the truth.

There is need to pause here and question this 'New Light' principle in the context of some different examples of revised teaching. For example, until 1995 Witnesses taught that their own preaching work is a 'separating work'. By this they mean that those who join their movement are 'sheep' who will inherit the kingdom, but those who refuse are 'goats' to be annihilated at Armageddon.

From 1995 a change was made in the teaching. They now claim that it is not their preaching, but Jesus himself who will undertake this separating work at Armageddon.

Rape and blood

Another incredible example is their teaching on rape, which, incredibly, has changed about twelve times over the past thirty years. Until 1993, for example, if a woman was raped at knifepoint or gunpoint and did not scream, the Watchtower considered it fornication, not rape. From 1993, this has changed. 'Rape', they now agree, 'is an act of violence. It is not sex.'

Another example is their ban on blood transfusion. This prohibition has resulted in the unnecessary deaths of some Witnesses, as well as much conflict and suffering.

Gary Busselman, a former Witness whose wife died as a result of the blood transfusion and organ transplant issues, researches the Watchtower's changing positions regarding blood. Now, he affirms, 'there are two ... blood treatment procedures acceptable to Jehovah's Witnesses ... *both procedures* are for the benefit of "sustaining life", a use for blood *distinctly ruled out* by the Watchtower as an acceptable use for blood!'[9]

Additionally, both procedures utilize 'ingesting blood through injections into the veins', another procedure that was previously ruled out completely.[10]

Summarizing, he says, 'The *Watchtower* for 15 June 2000 represents an historic shift in the Watchtower Society's blood policy.'

Appeal

Other examples of changing their teaching can be multiplied, such as their many proposed dates for the end of the world, ranging from 1874, 1910-1912 and, more recently, to 1975 and 'this generation'.

In conclusion, I appeal to those involved in, or attracted to, this cult. The changing, contradictory views of Watchtower leaders illustrate their fallibility. They are false prophets, so do not listen to them.

Again, God does not give new revelations — he has already made his final revelation in Christ (Hebrews 1:2-3). Rather than heeding the fallible views of men, read the Bible for yourself, without their literature. At the same time, listen to the Son of God: 'You must be born again'; 'He who comes to me will never go hungry, and he who believes in me will never be thirsty' (John 3:7; 6:35). The Lord's people hear and obey Christ's voice, not the voices of fallible men (John 10:27).

RELEVANT COMPARISONS

Jehovah's Witnesses　　**The Bible**

PERSON OF CHRIST

COMPARISONS

Christ was the created archangel Michael and although he was 'a god' and a mighty one, yet he was not Jehovah.

Despite a virgin birth, Jesus was no more than a perfect, mortal man while on earth.

Two things happened at the baptism of Jesus — he was 'born again' and became 'the Christ' or Messiah.

'For to which of the angels did God ever say, "You are my Son..."? ... But about the Son he says, "Your throne, O God, will last for ever and ever..."' (Hebrews 1:5, 8).

Also in Hebrews 1:10-12 the description of Jehovah in Psalm 102:25-27 is applied to Christ.

In his human nature, Jesus was filled with the Spirit (Matthew 3:16; Luke 4:1) not born again at his baptism. He was 'the Christ' at his birth according to Luke 2:11.

'In the beginning was the Word, and the Word was with God, and the Word was God' (John 1:1).

'I and the Father are one' (John 10:30; cf. vv. 31, 33).

'Anyone who has seen me has seen the Father' (John 14:9).

'For in Christ all the fulness of the Deity lives in bodily form' (Colossians 2:9).

See also the section below on creation and chapter 25 on the Holy Trinity.

DEATH OF CHRIST

Jesus atoned only for the sin of Adam and not for our personal sins. His death provided an exact payment for what Adam lost, namely, perfect human life in Eden. This 'ransom sacrifice' was not a finished work, but rather the basis from which individuals work to provide their own salvation.

'Since we have now been justified by his blood, how much more shall we be saved from God's wrath through him! For if, when we were God's enemies, we were reconciled to him through the death of his Son, how much more, having been reconciled, shall we be saved through his life!' (Romans 5:9-10).

'Their sins and lawless acts I will remember no more' (Hebrews 10:17).

'The blood of Jesus, his Son, purifies us from all sin' (1 John 1:7).

RESURRECTION OF CHRIST

There was no bodily resurrection of Christ. He was raised only as a spirit-creature. No one knows what happened to his body. The post-resurrection appearances of Christ were materializations in different bodies; it was only because Thomas refused to believe that Jesus appeared in a body similar to that in which he died.

'Look at my hands and my feet. It is I myself! Touch me and see; a ghost does not have flesh and bones, as you see I have ... he showed them his hands and feet' (Luke 24:39-40).

'"Destroy this temple, and I will raise it again in three days"... But the temple he had spoken of was his body' (John 2:19-21).

SECOND COMING OF CHRIST

Jesus was crowned as king on 1 October 1914 and returned secretly and invisibly; in 1918 he cleansed Jehovah's spiritual temple and raised certain believers to reign with him in heaven.

1. 'Exalted to the right hand of God' (Acts 2:33).

'After he had provided purification for sins, he sat down at the right hand of the Majesty in heaven' (Hebrews 1:3).

2. It is wrong to set dates for the Second Coming: 'No one knows about that day or hour, not even the angels in heaven, nor the Son, but only the Father' (Matthew 24:36).

'Therefore keep watch, because you do not know on what day your Lord will come' (Matthew 24:42).

'So you must also be ready, because the Son of Man will come at an hour when you do not expect him' (Matthew 24:44).

'Therefore keep watch, because you do not know the day or the hour' (Matthew 25:13).

3. He will return visibly and gloriously: 'Look, he is coming with the clouds, and every eye will see him' (Revelation 1:7; cf. Zechariah 12:10; Hebrews 9:28; 1 John 3:2).

HOLY SPIRIT

The Holy Spirit is not a person but the invisible, impersonal force of God which moves people to do God's will.

'... how is it that Satan has so filled your heart that you have lied to the Holy Spirit? ... You have not lied to men but to God' (Acts 5:3-4).

'The Spirit told Philip...' (Acts 8:29; cf. 13:2; 16:7).

'All these are the work of one and the same Spirit, and he gives them to each one, just as he determines' (1 Corinthians 12:11).

CREATION

All that exists was created by Jehovah; Jesus was the first to be created, then God used Jesus as his 'working partner' to create the rest of creation.

The universe was created at least four and a half billion years ago and each creative 'day' in Genesis 1 is 7,000 years in length.

Several important verses are twisted by the Watchtower to prove that Jesus was created. Note especially the following:

1. *Colossians 1:15* in their *New World Translation* is 'firstborn of all creation'. The Greek word translated 'firstborn' is *prototokos*, which does not mean 'created' but rather sovereignty and priority over all. The NIV accurately translates it as: 'the firstborn over all creation'. *Prototokos* occurs eight times in the New Testament and nowhere means creation. If Paul had wanted to say Christ was created, he would have used a different Greek word, *protoktistos*.

Sadly, the NWT introduces the word 'other' which is not in the Greek, in their translation of verses 15-17 in order to change the true meaning of the passage.

2. *Revelation 3:14*: their translation, 'the beginning of the creation by God', is wrong because:

a. The phrase 'by God' is not a translation of the Greek which is the genitive *tou theou*, meaning 'of God' not 'by God';

b. The Greek *arche* (beginning) means the origin or active cause of what exists. Helpfully, the NASV includes the footnote, 'origin or source'. Jesus is not, then, the first of those created, but the originating source or agent of creation. While he is the Creator (John 1:3), he himself is uncreated.

SATAN AND ANGELS

Through rebellion Lucifer became Satan, who in turn corrupted other angels. Satan and his host were cast out of heaven in 1914 and their influence and activity confined to the

'I saw Satan fall like lightning from heaven' (Luke 10:18 — long before 1914! cf. 2 Peter 2:4; Jude 6).

'They will be tormented day and night for ever and ever' (Revelation 20:10).

earth. Complete annihilation will be their doom after the millennium.

MAN

Man was created perfect in the image of God but, having no soul, he is not immortal.

The distinction between soul and body in man is seen in the following verses:

Matthew 10:28: 'Do not be afraid of those who kill the body but cannot kill the soul. Rather, be afraid of the one who can destroy both soul and body in hell.'

Philippians 1:23-24: 'I am torn between the two: I desire to depart and be with Christ, which is better by far; but it is more necessary for you that I remain in the body.'

Hebrews 12:23, especially the words 'the spirits of righteous men made perfect', refers to believers still awaiting a resurrection body but who continue to enjoy fellowship with God. Between death and the general resurrection there is a conscious, spiritual existence (cf. Isaiah 14:4-17; Ezekiel 32:21).

In *Revelation 6:9-11* it is not the blood of the martyrs (as Jehovah's Witnesses teach) but their souls that 'called out in a loud voice', and the white robes given to them stress that those mentioned in verses 9-10 exist personally.

In *Revelation 20:4:* John saw the souls of the martyrs.

HELL

Hell is only a symbol of annihilation; there is no eternal punishment.

There are four different words translated 'hell' in the AV. The Hebrew word *'Sheol'* and the Greek word *'Hades'* usually refer to the place of the departed. *'Tartarus'* is used only in 2 Peter 2:4 to describe the place where the fallen angels are detained. *'Gehenna'* in the New Testament refers, not to annihilation, but to the eternal punishment of the wicked.

'Then they will go away to eternal punishment...' (Matthew 25:46). The New World Translation's 'cutting-off' is incorrect. The Greek word *'Kolasin'* is used four times in the New Testament and in each case the idea is of punishment.

'They will be tormented day and night for ever and ever' (Revelation 20:10). The Greek *'Basanizo'*, translated 'tormented' in the NWT of Revelation 11:10, still means the same thing in Revelation 20:10! It is deceitful to give it the meaning of annihilation here.

For further study see Eryl Davies, *The Wrath of God* (Evangelical Movement of Wales) and *Condemned for Ever!* (Evangelical Press).

BLOOD TRANSFUSION

Receiving a blood transfusion violates the law of God and puts the guilty person's hope of eternal life in jeopardy. (Most of the groups, however, who seceded from the Watchtower disagree strongly with them on this point.)

Genesis 9:4: 'But you must not eat meat that has its lifeblood still in it.' This text does not forbid blood transfusions for the following reasons:

1. It is a divine command against eating or drinking the blood of animals.
2. Unlike the drinking of animal blood, blood transfusions do not involve the death of the donors; they actually preserve life.
3. There is no similarity between drinking blood through the digestive organs and transfusing a donor's blood directly into the patient's bloodstream.

Leviticus 17:10-11
1. The phrase 'any blood' does

not include human blood for no human blood was offered on the altars by Jews.

2. The reason for the prohibition is given in verse 11, namely, in order to provide atonement for sin, God appointed the blood of animals; such blood was to be used exclusively for this purpose and not used as food.

3. The blood of animals was also important because it pointed to — and found fulfilment in — the shedding of Christ's blood on the cross.

Acts 15:20, 29

1. Gentile converts were advised not to eat animal blood to avoid unnecessary offence to Jewish Christians who still preferred to abstain from blood (see v. 21). To maintain the closest possible fellowship between the two groups, this decree was issued to the Gentile churches.

2. There is no mention in the passage of the possibility of losing eternal life if

the advice is ignored. On the contrary, verses 9-11 show that salvation is by grace through faith and not through the keeping of rules. It was not the subject of personal salvation that was under consideration here but rather church fellowship between Jews and Gentiles.

SALVATION

Through Jesus' ransom, which removed our sin inherited from Adam, we have a second chance to start afresh from where our first parents began. The perfect life which Jesus lived gives us the chance to earn our salvation, especially through visitation, the sale of Watchtower literature and attending meetings and conventions.

Believers are divided into two classes: the 'anointed class' — the 144,000 who must believe, be baptized by immersion, preach and live 'worthily' until death; and the 'other sheep' who must also believe, be baptized as a symbol of dedication, do 'field work', like selling literature, but do not need justification, the new birth nor sanctification.

Titles such as 'Study of

1. Christ's death is the only ground of our salvation:

'We implore you on Christ's behalf: Be reconciled to God' (2 Corinthians 5:20).
'But now he has appeared once for all at the end of the ages to do away with sin by the sacrifice of himself' (Hebrews 9:26; cf. vv. 13-25; Romans 4:25; 8:3-4).

2. Salvation cannot be earned:

'For the wages of sin is death, but the gift of God is eternal life in Christ Jesus our Lord' (Romans 6:23).
'...who has saved us and called us to a holy life — not because of anything we have done but because of his own

Scriptures necessary for salvation' and 'Growth to salvation necessary' in their book *Make sure of all things* reveal their unbiblical doctrine of salvation.

purpose and grace' (2 Timothy 1:9).

'...he saved us, not because of righteous things we had done, but because of his mercy' (Titus 3:5).

3. We receive salvation through faith alone:

'For God so loved the world that he gave his one and only Son, that whoever believes in him shall not perish but have eternal life' (John 3:16).

'He who believes has everlasting life' (John 6:47; cf. 20:31).

'For we maintain that a man is justified by faith apart from observing the law' (Romans 3:28).

NEW BIRTH

It is only Christ and his 144,000 'body-members' who are born again, that is, spirit-begotten with the hope of heaven. This number was completed in 1931 and there are only about 7,000 of them still alive.

Faithful men of God

There is no distinction in the Bible between 'born again' and unregenerate believers and up until 1935 the Jehovah's Witnesses themselves denied this distinction.

'By this he meant the Spirit, whom those who

like Abraham, Isaac and Jacob and the prophets are not in the kingdom of God but they will be representatives of God on the earth.

believed in him were later to receive' (John 7:39).

'Repent, and be baptized, every one of you, in the name of Jesus Christ for the forgiveness of your sins. And you will receive the gift of the Holy Spirit. The promise is for you and your children and for all who are far off — for all whom the Lord our God will call' (Acts 2:38-39).

'If anyone does not have the Spirit of Christ, he does not belong to Christ' (Romans 8:9).

'Everyone who believes that Jesus is the Christ is born of God' (1 John 5:1; cf. John 3:3, 5; Galatians 3:13-14).

'...many will come from the east and the west, and will take their places at the feast with Abraham, Isaac and Jacob in the kingdom of heaven' (Matthew 8:11-12).

'There will be weeping there, and gnashing of teeth, when you see Abraham, Isaac and Jacob and all the prophets in the kingdom of God, but you yourselves thrown out' (Luke 13:28-29).

SECOND CHANCE

COMPARISONS

They allege that John 5:29 and Hebrews 9:27 teach that some will have a second chance after death. For example, they claim that 'the resurrection of judgement' in John 5:29 is for people who, when on earth, wanted to do right but lacked the knowledge. Such people, they say, will be brought back into the paradise earth and, after being taught the truth, will be judged on the basis of their response to it and rewarded accordingly — either with life or annihilation.

According to Romans 1:18 and 3:23 all people are sinful, without excuse and guilty before God. Those who have not heard the Word will be judged according to the light of conscience (see Romans 2:12).

In John 5:29 note that their destinies are already decided. The past tense, 'did the good deeds' and 'committed the evil deeds', makes this clear.

John 3:18-21, and especially verse 18, shows that our destiny is settled before we die and is dependent on our acceptance or rejection of Christ.

CHAPTER
TWENTY-ONE

CHRISTADELPHIANS

A BRIEF HISTORY

A small group

The next group we will examine is small in number and active, but relatively unknown. The membership is falling and now stands at under 17,000 in the UK. There are only about 300 'ecclesias' in Britain, with a further 100 or so smaller fellowships.

I am referring to Christadelphians. You may not have heard about them as they tend to be overshadowed by Jehovah's Witnesses who are much more aggressive in their outreach and recruitment.

Bible emphasis

Like Jehovah's Witnesses, Christadelphians place a strong emphasis on the Bible. In the past, members claimed to read the Bible daily although, apart from their lay teachers, most members now read the Bible only three or four times a week. And they are knowledgeable on many Bible subjects.

Despite their study of the Bible, they reject many major Bible doctrines such as the Holy Trinity, and the deity and sinlessness of Christ.

They also reject Christ's substitutionary, penal sacrifice on the cross, his physical resurrection and salvation by grace through faith alone.

Concerning justification, their view is that faith, baptism and works are all part of our response, with each aspect being necessary and contributory to salvation.

Christadelphians have always denied that the Holy Spirit is the third person in the Holy Trinity but their explanations are varied and conflicting. Some have even interpreted references to the Holy Spirit in terms of an angel.

Divisions

Divisions have taken place within this movement. For example, there is the 'Berean Fellowship', which is small and located mainly in America. Another group, with about 1,000 members worldwide, is named the 'Dawn Fellowship'.

There are other small and medium-sized groups such as 'Old Paths', 'Advocate' and 'Servants of Christ'. The main group worldwide is called the 'Central Fellowship' with approximately 40,000 members.

These divisions within Christadelphianism have arisen because of theological differences over subjects like the inspiration of the Bible, the atonement, eschatology, church discipline, and practical matters relating to daily life in the world.

The social, corporate life of members is very similar to that of the strict and separatist stance of other Exclusive Brethren groups.

Unorthodox

Although originating in America during the mid-nineteenth century, this cult was founded by an Englishman, John Thomas (1805-1871), whose father was a Congregational Church minister in London. After qualifying as a medical doctor at St Thomas's Hospital, London, he obtained his MRCS before sailing to America, intending to develop his medical career.

Surviving a shipwreck *en route* to America, he felt he should devote himself to God's service. While practising medicine for some years in America, Thomas engaged himself in an intense study of the Bible.

He was soon fascinated by the last book in the Bible, Revelation, as well as some of the more difficult parts of the major and minor prophets in the Old Testament.

His views became increasingly unorthodox and intolerant; for example, he insisted that salvation was conditional on the acceptance of his own interpretation of the Bible.

Milestone

1848 was a significant milestone in Thomas's life. That year, in addition to receiving the American medical degree of MD, he visited England in order to propagate his views.

He travelled and preached extensively throughout the country for two years. In 1862, when he returned to England, he discovered numerous small groups called Thomasites meeting in various towns and cities.

Initially, these groups met in their own homes for the breaking of bread. Soon the Birmingham group emerged as the most influential, providing guidance and speakers for the network of groups.

On his second visit to England, Thomas wrote a large commentary on the book of Revelation, entitled *Eureka*, in which he claimed to have solved all the problems of interpretation!

Expansion

The growth of the movement was slow. In 1865 they only had about 1,000 adherents worldwide and most of these were from Britain.

It was an early recruit of Thomas's, Robert Roberts, who led the British branch of the movement and he published a magazine entitled *The Ambassador of the Coming Age*. On his last visit to England in 1871, Thomas renamed the magazine *The Christadelphian* (from the Greek for 'Christian brothers'). Roberts assumed leadership of the cult when Thomas died.

One of the cult's main textbooks, *Christendom Astray,* was written by Roberts with the purpose of criticizing orthodox Christian doctrines and vindicating Christadelphian views.

Today, Christadelphianism remains one of the smaller cults and continues to receive more support from Britain than from any other country. It does not believe in ordained ministers, and the administration of the local *ecclesia* is the responsibility of all male members.

Deceiving themselves

As with all cults (as well as churches), what is at issue is nothing less than the revealed gospel of Christ. No question is more important. Can sinners be saved? If so, how?

The answer to that crucial question needs to be an accurate one, because wrong answers — and there are many of them at present — deceive people, leave them unsaved and in danger of hell itself.

Sadly, despite their emphasis on the Bible, Christadelphians distort the real gospel of Christ and deceive both themselves and others in the process.

How do I substantiate my claim that they are distorting the gospel? I quote directly from their website and a document there called *Our Faiths and Beliefs*.

Heretical

Despite saying that they 'believe that salvation is attained through faith in Christ' (paragraph 6), almost immediately, they tell us that faith is tied in with water baptism and that without the latter there can be no salvation. The next paragraph is just as alarming. 'Doctrinally', they inform us, 'the Christadelphians are unique in Christendom in our understanding of the nature of Christ and the way in which we are redeemed by his death.'

In fact, they are not 'unique' in this respect. But they are certainly heretical in teaching that the Lord Jesus was only a man who needed salvation himself because he had a sinful nature. This teaching contradicts what the Lord says, for example, in John 1:1, 14; 8:58 (cf. Exodus 3:14) and Colossians 2:9. Jesus was the exact representation of the nature of God (Hebrews 1:3) and was without sin (1 Peter 2:22).

The next question to ask Christadelphians concerns the death of Jesus Christ. How are we redeemed?

Once again their answer is distressing. 'We reject … that Christ could die as a replacement sacrifice for us, thus covering all our sins forever with that one act. Certainly it is through his sacrifice that we may be forgiven,

but *only if* we walk the path of self-denial that he marked out for us' (Italics mine; para. 7, *Our Faith and Beliefs*).

Christ our Substitute

In order to underline the gospel of Christ as revealed in the Bible, I want to reply in three ways.

Firstly, the Bible clearly teaches that the Lord Jesus died as a substitute for our sins on the cross. 'He himself bore our sins in his body on the tree', writes Peter in his first epistle (2:24).

This language of 'bearing' sin belongs to the Old Testament sacrificial system in which an innocent animal, without blemish, was sacrificed in place of the worshipper. The transfer of guilt and punishment was indicated when the worshipper identified himself with the victim by placing his hands on the head of the animal.

Substitution is also implied in Peter's later statement: 'For Christ died for sins once for all, the righteous for the unrighteous, to bring you to God' (3:18; see also 2 Corinthians 5:21).

Christ is sufficient

Secondly, the Bible emphasizes that Christ's once-for-all sacrifice was sufficient to cover *all*

WHAT WE BELIEVE

our sins: 'For Christ died for sins once for all...'; 'For Christ was sacrificed *once* to take away the sins of many' (1 Peter 3:18; Hebrews 9:28; see also Hebrews 10:11-14).

Thirdly, we are saved wholly by what Christ did for us on the cross; there is no contribution at all that we can make to our salvation. Not even baptism is needed to supplement Christ's work for us.

Listen to the glorious words of the gospel: 'For it is by grace you have been saved, through faith — and this not from yourselves, it is the gift of God — not by works, so that no one can boast' (Ephesians 2:8-9).

RELEVANT COMPARISONS

Christadelphians   **The Bible**

GOD

The orthodox Bible teaching concerning God is rejected. There is no Trinity of persons in the Godhead and Christadelphians accuse Christians of believing in three gods. (This is a failure to understand the Trinity for we do not teach there are three gods but rather that the one God eternally exists in three persons.) They regard the Son and Spirit as creations of the Father and believe only God the Father existed before the man Christ Jesus.

'Therefore go and make disciples of all nations, baptizing them in the name of the Father and of the Son and of the Holy Spirit' (Matthew 28:19).

See also Isaiah 63:8-10 and 'Before Abraham was born, I am' (John 8:58; cf. John 17:5).

For a fuller treatment of this subject see chapter 25.

BIBLE

They profess to believe the whole Bible as the Word of God and sometimes refer to themselves as 'Berean Bible Students'. Great emphasis is placed upon the study of the Old and New Testaments but their diligence and zeal in Bible study have led them into error. There are several reasons for this, such as the emphasis on certain scriptures to the neglect of others, wrong principles of interpretation, but particularly the absence of the Holy Spirit's illumination of the Word.

'Nor does his word dwell in you, for you do not believe the one he sent. You diligently study the Scriptures, because you think that by them you possess eternal life. These are the Scriptures that testify about me, yet you refuse to come to me to have life' (John 5:38-40).

'...but God has revealed it to us by his Spirit' (1 Corinthians 2:10; cf. Psalm 119:18).

PERSON OF CHRIST

For Christadelphians, Jesus was not the eternal Son of God, nor did he exist at all prior to his birth by Mary. Jesus was not perfect nor was his birth miraculous. He is regarded as a mere expression of God the Father in human form and is not to be worshipped on the same level as the Father.

'No one has ever seen God, but God the One and Only, who is at the Father's side, has made him known' (John 1:18).

'All may honour the Son just as they honour the Father. He who does not honour the Son does not honour the Father, who sent him' (John 5:23).

'Before Abraham was born, I am' (John 8:58)'

'He committed no sin,

and no deceit was found in his mouth' (1 Peter 2:22).

WORK OF CHRIST

There was no atoning purpose nor value in the Lord's death. He died to express his Father's love and not to remove the wrath of God from sinners.

'But he was pierced for our transgressions, he was crushed for our iniquities...' (Isaiah 53:5).

'The Son of Man did not come to be served, but to serve, and to give his life as a ransom for many' (Matthew 20:28).

'Since we have now been justified by his blood, how much more shall we be saved from God's wrath through him!' (Romans 5:9).

DEVIL

No personal devil exists. The devil is explained away as the sin which is committed in the flesh and the name 'devil' is simply a personification of sin.

'Resist the devil, and he will flee from you' (James 4:7).

'He [the devil] was a murderer from the beginning, not holding to the truth, for there is no truth in him. When he lies, he speaks his native language, for he is a liar and the father of lies' (John 8:44; cf. Job 1:6-12; Matthew 4:1-11; Acts 5:3; Revelation 20:1-3).

HOLY SPIRIT

They deny that the Holy Spirit is a divine person but regard him as some kind of invisible power

'And I will ask the Father, and he will give you another Counsellor to be with you for ever — the

or energy proceeding from the Father. Believers are not indwelt by the Spirit.

Spirit of truth. The world cannot accept him, because it neither sees nor knows him. But you know him, for he lives with you and will be in you' (John 14:16-17).

'But the Counsellor, the Holy Spirit, whom the Father will send in my name, will teach you all things...' (John 14:26; cf. John 15:26; 16:7-13).

'All these are the work of one and the same Spirit, and he gives them to each one, just as he determines' (1 Corinthians 12:11).

SALVATION

They deny the biblical doctrine of salvation by grace. In their view salvation is achieved by baptism (by immersion, administered by their own leaders) plus obedience to Christ's commandments. There is no guarantee of salvation but after baptism the person begins a life of probation and his ultimate destiny depends on his character and performance after baptism.

'For God so loved the world that he gave his one and only Son, that whoever believes in him shall not perish but have eternal life' (John 3:16).

'For it is by grace you have been saved, through faith — and this not from yourselves, it is the gift of God — not by works, so that no one can boast' (Ephesians 2:8-9).

FUTURE STATE

Extinction at death, not eternal punishment in hell, is God's punishment of sinners, while believers have their sphere of glory on earth alone (not heaven) after the general resurrection. Between physical death and the resurrection of the dead, even believers are in an unconscious state but their eternal life is experienced as a result of the resurrection and then enjoyed on the earth.

All the Jews will return to Canaan. The ancient kingdom of Israel will be restored and Jesus will return and reign on the earth. After a new temple is built then the offering of sacrifices will be resumed. Christadelphians will be raised and given immortality while the wicked will be annihilated.

Hell. 'Do not be afraid of those who kill the body but cannot kill the soul. Rather, be afraid of the one who can destroy both soul and body in hell' (Matthew 10:28; cf. Luke 12:4-5).

'Then they will go away to eternal punishment' (Matthew 25:46; cf. Luke 16:19-31; Revelation 20:10-15).

Heaven. '...today you will be with me in paradise' (Luke 23:43).

'...to be away from the body and at home with the Lord' (2 Corinthians 5:8; cf. Philippians 1:21-23).

'After that, we who are still alive and are left will be caught up together with them in the clouds to meet the Lord in the air. And so we will be with the Lord for ever' (1 Thessalonians 4:17).

The priesthood as well as the sacrifices and temple of the Old Testament have been fulfilled in Christ and will never be reinstated (Hebrews 9:12; 10:12). In the New Covenant all believers are priests and enjoy direct access to God (1 Peter 2:9; Revelation 1:6).

SECTION C:

PERSONAL AND PASTORAL CHALLENGES

CHAPTER
TWENTY-TWO

PERSONAL AND PASTORAL CHALLENGES

First encounter

For my first encounter with cult activity, I must go back to my university student days. Two ladies in their early twenties called at the house where I lodged at the time. I opened the door to find that they were Jehovah Witnesses.

Sad story

They were sincere, articulate, earnest and well-drilled in presenting the organization's message. We discussed key Scripture texts for an hour or so and I then gave my testimony (I had only recently been converted).

One of the ladies seemed interested. I sensed that giving one's own testimony, in the context of reading and expounding key biblical texts, can be effective on such occasions.

I wanted to find out why they had joined the Watchtower, so I asked them for details. They responded to my request. Their story was a sad one and left a deep impression on me.

I discovered that they had grown up together in the Midlands and attended a local Anglican church. In their late teens they were eager to know more about the Bible. But rather than provide them with regular Bible studies, the vicar urged them to involve themselves in the social life of the church, particularly in preparations for the Christmas pantomime! They were disappointed but continued to read and discuss the Bible together.

Three questions

Three questions troubled them more than others. I was intrigued. What were they? The first concerned the Holy Trinity of divine persons. How could God be both one and three? A second question concerned the person of Jesus Christ. Was he equally God with the Father? And their third question was 'What is a Christian?' Yes, they were key questions.

Tragically, they found no one who could give them Bible answers. As you might expect, they were extremely critical of the clergyman for refusing to help them with their questions.

A few weeks later a Jehovah's Witness called at one of their houses and they were drawn into Bible studies and into the organization. 'These were the first and only people', they told me, referring to the Watchtower, 'who answered our questions about Jesus and the Trinity.'

But they were trapped. Their words have lingered with me over the years.

PERSONAL CHALLENGE

Spiritual needs

Reflecting on that first encounter with the cults was painful but fruitful. It was a spur for me to engage in more vigorous, extensive evangelism. I was determined to attempt to reach unbelievers before the cults contacted and deceived them.

Apart from seeing the importance of regular, faithful Bible teaching in local churches, I now became more aware of the spiritual needs and darkness of those who enter the cults. Who will tell them the true gospel of Christ? And who will pray for their conversion?

These reflections and convictions stayed with me during my experience in two contrasting pastoral situations. In the context of ongoing systematic house-to-house visitation, we identified and witnessed to scores of people belonging to various cults, especially JWs and Mormons.

Our aim, of course, was much wider than reaching cult members. However, having made an initial contact, we felt a burden to ensure that we had shared the gospel with them. How could we proceed?

Starting point — prayer

Prayer was the obvious starting point. There were unexpected, even immediate, results too. One young housewife, for example, felt an increasing burden for the conversion of Jehovah's Witnesses and gave herself to prayer as well as intensive Bible study.

There were also opportunities at times for prolonged Bible discussions with individual Witnesses and their leaders. But it was not easy, and the responses were often rude and angry. Nevertheless some of them were hearing the gospel and engaging with the biblical text.

Yes, prayers were being answered. And in the Lord's sovereign grace, over the following year and a half, one Jehovah's Witness was converted in a remarkable way and another professed faith.

Aggressive

My second pastorate was a young city church where regular house-to-house visitation was maintained for several years. Such visitation may not be right or even possible for some churches. In my experience, however, it provided the opportunity to meet many people, establish some good relationships and, of course, share the gospel with individuals. But contact with cult members was more difficult.

Adherents of cults like the Watchtower, Scientology, Spiritism and the Baha'i were aggressive towards us and entrenched in their beliefs. Local Mormon recruits were more friendly and willing to listen. Their understanding of the Mormon creed was poor but they spoke highly of

monetary assistance and caring support received from the cult.

One breakthrough among the JWs, however, had little to do with us. Sovereignly, the Lord was at work. Prayers were being answered.

Buying books

Unknown to us, one of the local Jehovah's Witness leaders came to see that the organization's teaching on blood transfusion was unbiblical. This led him to question other Witness teachings. He now determined to read the Bible without the aid of Watchtower books.

His purpose was to find out what the Bible was really teaching. Along with friends, he visited our local Christian bookshop regularly. They bought books, usually one-volume commentaries on the Bible.

Slowly, they began to talk about their study of the apostle Paul's letter to the Romans. A few of them came to understand that salvation was by grace alone, appropriated only by faith.

It was Romans chapters three, four and five that had challenged them initially. That is not surprising, for in the history of the church many have been converted through reading Romans, including some of the church's most significant leaders.

PERSONAL CHALLENGE

Romans

Augustine is one example. The Lord dealt with him savingly as he read Romans, particularly the verses towards the end of chapter 13.

Martin Luther, too, came to faith and gospel liberty through reading Romans. He grappled with chapter one and the meaning of verse 17: 'For in the gospel a righteousness from God is revealed, a righteousness that is by faith from first to last, just as it is written: "The just will live by faith".' The light of the gospel shone into his heart and mind. He saw clearly that the only way to be right with God was through the one sacrifice of the Lord Jesus for sin. And he saw, also, that this divine righteousness is imputed, or reckoned, to sinners only when they trust in Jesus Christ. Justification is by 'faith alone'.

John Bunyan was led to Christ through reading Luther's exposition of Romans. John Wesley found his heart 'strangely warmed' as he heard Luther's *Preface to Romans* being read in a meeting.

So it was for this small group of Jehovah's Witnesses in my area. They seemed excited with the message of Romans. Their unease with the Watchtower was evident, but they refused to come to our church.

The key to outreach

I do not know the end of the story. Were they converted? Again, I cannot answer the question with any certainty.

PERSONAL CHALLENGE

They stopped visiting the bookshop and refused contact with us.

On reflection, three points stand out for me.

1. *The power of the Word.* It 'is living and active...' (Hebrews 4:12) and all our evangelism must be Word-based. Remember to keep the Bible central when you are witnessing to unbelievers.

2. *Prayer is essential.* If it is the Lord alone who prospers and applies the Word then prayer must be high on our list of priorities.

3. *Cult members are in desperate need of the gospel* and should not be ignored in our outreach. Perhaps it is more difficult and time-consuming to share the gospel with such people, but they must be included in our local evangelism.

Neglected

Our gospel outreach witness should at least include sharing the gospel with members of various cults. Too often, we have ignored or neglected these people for a variety of reasons. But they really need the gospel.

Occasionally I hear former cult members complain that no one had shared the gospel with them for years while they were in the cult, even though they had probably met many born-again

Christians on their door-to-door visitation or street canvassing as active cult members. Are you guilty of being silent when you should be pointing such individuals to the Lord Jesus Christ?

I now want to refer to some important pastoral challenges we need to face if we are to receive cult or former cult members into our churches. Make no mistake about it: there are pastoral challenges here for our fellowships.

Pastoral challenges: Welcome

The first pastoral challenge is a basic one and it concerns *the welcome we extend to people*. Without this, our outreach work and attempts at nurturing these individuals will be seriously undermined.

Perhaps these are much bigger and deeper problems than churches realize, but I will confine my attention to those with cult associations. For example, what if a Jehovah's Witness known in your locality for his or her zeal turns up unexpectedly at one of your Sunday services? You may be shocked. And, possibly, your suspicions are aroused. Why has he come?

Or it may be a former member of a nearby church who converted to the Mormon faith seven years earlier. Now she walks into your church and seems eager to be in the worship service. Is she really welcomed?

The challenge may be even more demanding. Imagine two young men in their twenties walking into your church. They are polite and eager to hear the Bible expounded. But as they enter the church, most of the congregation turn and stare at them.

Some are shocked and whisper to those sitting nearby. The reason? These two men are Hare Krishna followers and they are confused. They want to know more about Jesus Christ. A few days earlier they had been given a tract explaining the gospel. They were intrigued and wished to know more about a loving God who gave his Son to die bearing the punishment of sinners.

Yes, here they were in church for the very first time. But they were conscious of people looking at them, some with disdain and suspicion. Admittedly, their faces were marked with paint, their heads were shaved except for a small pigtail and their clothes were colourful. Church members felt distinctly uncomfortable at seeing them and, after the service, unsure whether to ignore them or not.

It was one of the church elders who took the initiative after the service ended. He shook their hands warmly in welcoming them. Next he introduced them to some believers of their own age and sex then invited them home for a meal and discussion.

The welcome was warm and sincere. What is more, some of the believers in the church felt convicted by the example of their church elder.

Is it an extreme or uncommon example? It may be in terms of Hare Krishna disciples who come to our churches seeking the Lord. But what of strangers who visit our churches, possibly searching for the Truth? Are they made to feel welcome?

I hear of 'visitors' to some evangelical churches who have found congregations unwelcoming and indifferent; some of these visitors have been ex-cult members. Here is a pastoral challenge churches must face up to.

Understanding

Another pastoral challenge is for believers, especially church leaders, *to understand the needs of ex-cult-members who come to our churches.* Allow me to illustrate this challenge in four ways.

1. Sometimes, those who have been in a cult feel extremely *guilty* for leaving the cult. Perhaps it is a feeling of guilt for having been drawn into and deceived by them. This feeling of guilt and shame can be crippling. Or it may be a sense of guilt for having 'let down' their friends and leaders in that cult.

2. Others have a paralyzing *fear.* Some ex-Jehovah's Witnesses or former Exclusive Brethren or Cooneyites, for example, may be frightened because they were 'disfellowshipped' by their group.

This may have involved rejection and exclusion by their families and close friends. Their own future consequently appears dark and lonely.

Sometimes an ex-cult-member may fear that it was a mistake to leave the cult. Perhaps the exclusivist claims

PASTORAL CHALLENGE

of the cult still ring in his ears: 'Churches are synagogues of Satan and only the Watchtower has the truth.' Cultic leaders have even told members that they will go to hell if they forsake the cult. It is a real fear, especially for those who want to be right with God and have assurance of their salvation. We need to understand their fears.

3. Another example of the need for understanding is their *rejection* by friends and relatives. There may be loneliness and a desperate need to 'belong' to a fellowship. Some Christian families have been brilliant in this respect and welcomed such people into their home for an unlimited period. Their love and understanding have expressed the Lord's love in helpful ways.

4. A final example where understanding is needed concerns the continuing, *strong influence of the cult* on an individual, even months after they have forsaken the cult and been converted to Christ.

In my pastoral experience, this was particularly true in relation to ex-JWs. For many months, even after their conversion, the ideas and practices of that cult lingered with individuals.

They needed understanding as well as practical teaching concerning their new-found freedom in Christ. Were a fixed weekly number of hours for 'ministry', such as door-to-door visitation, still required? Should they act on medical advice and receive blood transfusions? Are they really free to vote in local/government elections?

Such people need to be listened to, understood and helped to understand what the Word teaches.

Seriousness

A further pastoral challenge is that *we need to be more serious in our churches about our faith and our walk with the Lord.* That is what many ex-cult-members expect. After all, they are serious themselves.

In fact, their following of Christ is often costly; they are hungry to know God, to understand his Word correctly and to please the Lord in their lives. Entertainment, endless singing or mere socializing are not priorities for them. In this respect, we can learn from them.

Teaching

One final pastoral challenge will suffice. And this concerns *the lack of Bible knowledge and theology on the part of many Christians in our churches.* Far too often, Christians are unable to answer basic questions from ex-cultists and others concerning major Bible doctrines. This is tragic, and I appeal to church leaders to address this challenge as a matter of urgency.

There are many ways of responding to this pastoral challenge but here is one way I found helpful and enriching in my church situation.

PASTORAL CHALLENGE

I invited all the church members to embark on a basic Christian reading course and to meet me monthly after a weeknight meeting to share their findings. The agreed syllabus was basic.

My aim was three-fold. Firstly, I wanted Christians to dig more deeply in the Word and become more familiar with the Bible text. We began with John's Gospel, using Hendriksen's commentary. This certainly stretched the people!

The second aim was to introduce them to church history. We started with Ryle's *Five English Reformers* then his *Five Christian Leaders*. Only one chapter a month was read but their accounts of what they had learnt and how they felt challenged were thrilling and edifying to us all. To see biblical doctrines illustrated and influential in these historical situations was helpful.

The third aim was to engage with systematic theology. Because it was easy to read, I started them with Pink's *Sovereignty of God*. It worked, too! Monthly discussions on the book were animated and instructive.

Overall, I felt that a significant number of believers were growing in their understanding of the Bible and theology. They began to share this understanding more with others. How are you responding to this pastoral challenge in your church?

Postscript

Summary of
major Bible doctrines

CHAPTER
TWENTY-THREE

THE BIBLE

WHY IS IT UNIQUE?

Who is right? Which teaching should I accept? How can I know what is true or false? These are important questions which people are continually asking in our contemporary, confused situation. Where should we turn for reliable answers to these questions? The claim made in this book is that the Bible alone provides truthful and, therefore, dependable answers to our questions concerning God, salvation and life after death, etc.

Can we trust the Bible? Why is the Bible so special? Here are some reasons why you should turn to the Bible and accept its teaching.

The Bible is divine

One major reason why the Bible is unique is that it is God's book; it comes from God and is God's self-revelation of himself and his purposes. Writing to Timothy, the apostle Paul declares, 'All Scripture is inspired by God...' (2 Timothy 3:16, NASB). 'Inspired' here means 'breathed out' from God: the Scripture is not a record of man's search for God and his ideas, but rather truth which originates with God and which he communicates through the Bible. Peter tells us, 'For prophecy never had its origin in the will of man, but men spoke from God as they were carried along by the Holy Spirit' (2 Peter 1:21). The Bible is no ordinary book; in fact, it is described as 'the word of God' (1 Thessalonians 2:13) or 'your word' (John 17:17). This is the only book which we can safely trust and use.

The Bible is dominant

Because the Bible is divine, it should dominate both our thinking and behaviour. Our Lord Jesus is an example to us in this respect. When resisting the devil in the wilderness, he appealed to the authority of God's Word by telling his enemy three times, 'It is written' (Matthew 4:4, 7, 10). Altogether, the Lord used the phrase, 'It is written' on another fifteen occasions, particularly when answering people's questions. For the Lord Jesus Christ, the words and teaching of Scripture settled all these questions. Similarly, God's Word alone should determine what we believe and how we live.

The Bible is dependable

Despite the cynical claims of the critics, there is compelling evidence for the dependability and trust-worthiness of Scripture. For example, consider its origin: 'All Scripture is inspired [i.e. breathed-out] by God'

WHY BELIEVE IT?

(2 Timothy 3:16). Can you really believe that 'the God who cannot lie' (Titus 1:2; Hebrews 6:18, NASB) breathed out mistakes and discrepancies in this self-revelation through the prophets and apostles?

Remember also that the Old Testament prophets recognized that they were under the authority and leading of the Holy Spirit (Micah 3:8; 2 Samuel 23:2; Zechariah 7:12, etc). They were unable to change, or detract from, or add to the words God had given them (Numbers 24:13; Amos 3:8). In addition, the New Testament apostles and writers were also led by the Holy Spirit in their preaching and writing (2 Peter 1:21; 1 Thessalonians 4:2; 1 Corinthians 14:37; Galatians 1:6-12).

What is important to notice here is that the inspiration of the apostles was a fulfilment of Christ's promise that he would send the Holy Spirit to them, to 'teach you all things and … remind you of everything I have said to you' (John 14:26); 'He will guide you into all truth … and he will tell you what is yet to come' (John 16:13).

One of the most convincing arguments for the trustworthiness of Scripture is the attitude of the Lord Jesus Christ himself. He believed in the historicity of creation, including Adam and Eve (Matthew 19:4-5) and the universal flood in the days of Noah (Matthew 24:37-39), as well as

Jonah's experience of being in the belly of a large fish for three days (Matthew 12:40). Christ saw the Old Testament as pointing to, and finding fulfilment in, himself (Luke 4:16-21; 24:25-27, 44-47; John 5:39-47). Like our Saviour, we can safely depend upon the Bible as being completely trustworthy.

The Bible is diverse

Because the Bible is such a remarkable book, it is rich and diverse. For example, in the writing of the Bible, God used about forty human authors over a period of approximately 1,500 years to write sixty-six books.

The style and content vary, too: Hebrew is the dominant language of the Old Testament, and Greek is the main language of the New Testament. There is a progressive revelation by God of himself and his purposes, until the climax is reached with the ministry of the Son of God (Hebrews 1:1-2).

But we must be careful how we interpret the Bible. We need to ask questions such as: 'Is the chapter or book historical, poetical or prophetical? What is the background and the meaning intended by the writer? Do I understand the meaning of the words and am I able to study the passage in the light of the whole of Scripture?'

In this way, we can avoid the errors and absurd interpretations of those who have twisted the meaning of the biblical text (2 Peter 3:16).

WHY BELIEVE IT?

The Bible is durable

The Bible is 'the living and enduring word of God' (1 Peter 1:23). Quoting Isaiah 40:7-8, Peter tells us: 'All men are like grass, and all their glory is like the flowers of the field; the grass withers and the flowers fall, but the word of the Lord stands for ever.' The Bible never changes and will always remain the only true and relevant Word of God.

The Bible is directing

Like a signpost, the Bible points to, and unveils, the glories of the triune God and his salvation in Christ. In particular, the Bible points to Christ as the only mediator between God and man (1 Timothy 2:5), and Christ himself affirmed, 'These are the Scriptures that testify about me' (John 5:39).

The Bible is dynamite

God uses the Bible, in preaching, personal reading and witness, in powerful ways to save sinners and edify and sanctify saints (Romans 1:16; 1 Thessalonians 2:13; Romans 10:17; John 17:17).

CHAPTER
TWENTY-FOUR

WHAT GOD
IS LIKE

WHAT IS HE LIKE?

What is God really like? The same question can be expressed differently: how does the Bible describe the nature and character of God? The following paragraphs give some of the answers the Bible gives to these questions.

God is spirit

This truth was emphasized by the Lord Jesus Christ in John 4:24; it means that God does not have a physical body, nor can we identify him with anything material. God's nature is spiritual and, therefore, he is invisible (1 Timothy 1:17; 6:15-16). This was why the Lord Jesus told the woman of Samaria to be more concerned about how, rather than where, she worshipped God. True worship does not depend upon external things like a beautiful building, music or colourful vestments. Because 'God is spirit', he wants us to worship him 'in spirit and truth'. In other words, we must worship God in a spiritual, inward and believing manner.

Although God is spirit, he has all the characteristics of personality, that is, understanding, will and affection (Ephesians 1:3-6, 9, 11), which enable us to know and have fellowship with him.

God is independent

No human being can live independently of other people. We depend on other people to provide food and work or prepare medicines and houses for us. Nor is it possible for us to live independently of God: God sends the sunshine and the rain and enables the seeds to grow (Psalm 104:13-15; Matthew 5:45); indeed, our breath is in his hands and he decides what we do with our lives (Daniel 5:23). If God did not support and preserve us, we should die quickly.

By contrast, God is completely independent. No one brought God into existence or contributes to his welfare. No, for God is completely self-sufficient. He has no need of anything from outside either to support or to enrich himself. While God creates and preserves all his creation, he himself is complete and independent (Isaiah 40:12-28).

God is unlimited

As humans, we have many limitations. No human being, no matter how clever, can know everything. There is also a limit to our strength. For example, there are some weights which are too heavy for us to carry and there are bacteria and germs which our bodies cannot resist. Nor can we be in more than one place at a time and this is a real limitation upon us. There is also a limit to our physical lives on earth. God does not have any of these limitations.

God has unlimited knowledge (Psalm 139:1-6; Romans 11:33-36; 1 Samuel 2:3) and power (Genesis 18:14; Exodus 15:3-18; Luke 1:37; Ephesians 3:20-21). He is also omnipresent (Psalm 139:7-10) and cannot be confined to one place. Unlike us, God has no beginning or end: 'From everlasting to everlasting you are God' (Psalm 90:2; 102:11-12; Isaiah 57:15). He is the eternal 'I am' (Exodus 3:14).

God is unchanging

Our lives and circumstances are continually changing, either for better or worse, but God himself never changes. 'I the LORD do not change' (Malachi 3:6). He does not change in his being, for he is eternal and has 'no variation' (James 1:17, NASB). Neither does God change his purposes (Isaiah 46:11; Numbers 23:19; Ephesians 1:11).

God is sovereign

'The LORD reigns' (Psalm 97:1) is the consistent message of the Bible. He reigns over the entire universe. The winds, seas, rain, sun, moon and all living creatures are ruled over by God. Even unbelievers are under his control and 'He does as he pleases with the powers of heaven and the peoples of the earth' (Daniel 4:35; 1 Chronicles 29:11; Psalm 115:3; Ephesians 1:11). Despite the rage and malice of men, the evil and ceaseless attacks by Satan and even the weaknesses of God's own people, the Lord will carry out his plans. He is the supreme being. That is why the Lord Jesus could say with certainty, 'I will build my church, and the gates of Hades will not overcome it' (Matthew 16:18). Each person chosen to salvation by God will come to him; his purposes will not fail.

God is holy

'Holy, holy, holy is the LORD Almighty...' is the anthem of praise the seraphim sing in heaven as they gaze upon the holy nature of God (Isaiah 6:3). Day and night, the choirs of heaven 'never stop saying, "Holy, holy, holy is the Lord God Almighty, who was, and is, and is to come"' (Revelation 4:8). God is 'majestic in holiness...' (Exodus 15:11) and 'There is no one holy like the LORD' (1 Samuel 2:2).

The holiness of God means that he is free from all sin (1 John 1:5) and that he hates all sin with an intense hatred (Psalm 5:4-6). Closely related is the righteousness of God, which means that God always speaks and works consistently with his own holy nature and law (Ezra 9:15; Psalm 119:137; 145:17; John 17:25; 1 John 2:29; Revelation 16:5).

WHAT IS HE LIKE?

The controlled, permanent opposition of God's holy nature to all sin is described as wrath. This wrath of God is not temper nor a bad mood, nor is it capriciousness, but the necessary reaction of his glorious and holy nature to sin (Romans 1:18; 2:5; Revelation 19:15). For this reason, wrath is as basic to the divine nature as is love; and without wrath God would cease to be God.

God is love

This is a truth which is underlined, expounded and illustrated extensively in the Bible, in both Old and New Testaments. John declares: 'God is love' and 'Love comes from God' (1 John 4:8; 4:7).

In his love, God is good towards all his creatures (Psalm 145:9, 15-16; Matthew 5:45; 6:26; Acts 14:17), but he loves believers with a special love in Christ. Christians love God only 'because he first loved us' (1 John 4:19; John 3:16). 'Herein is love,' adds the apostle John, 'not that we loved God, but that he loved us, and sent his Son to be the propitiation for our sins' (1 John 4:10, AV; cf. Romans 5:8).

Such divine love towards sinners is described as grace, for it is undeserved and completely unmerited (Ephesians 2:7-9; Titus 3:4-7). Mercy refers to the expression of the love of God in pitying sinners who desperately need the help and salvation of God (1 Timothy 1:12-16).

CHAPTER
TWENTY-FIVE

THE
HOLY TRINITY

⟨A BRIEF HISTORY⟩

Jehovah's Witnesses and several other cults claim that the orthodox doctrine of the Trinity is a false, unbiblical doctrine originating with the devil in pagan Babylon and they frequently misrepresent the doctrine. For example, they accuse Christians of believing in three gods, or in a 'three-headed God', or of accepting the mathematical absurdity that one equals three. Here, then, is some of the Bible evidence for the doctrine of the Trinity.

There is only one God, not three

This truth is clearly stated in, for example, Deuteronomy 6:4; Isaiah 44:6; and James 2:19. Besides this one, living God, there is no other. E. C. Gruss, in his helpful book *Apostles of Denial,*[1] draws attention to the significance of the Hebrew word *echad* translated 'one' in Deuteronomy 6:4: 'The LORD our God, the LORD is one.'

Far from denying the Trinity, this word and text actually support the doctrine! *Echad* expresses a compound unity, that is, a plurality within one. The same word, for example, is used in Genesis 1:5, where day and night are

united into 'day one', and in Genesis 2:24 Adam and
Eve were united as husband and wife to 'become one
flesh'. Here two individuals constitute a real oneness.
Again in Ezra 2:64 the New World Translation (NWT),
which Jehovah's Witnesses regard as the most accurate
translation, correctly gives the sense of this Hebrew
word, 'the entire congregation as one group'. What is
still more interesting is that the Hebrew word *yachid*,
denoting absolute oneness, is never used in relation to
the unity of God, although it occurs twelve times in the
Old Testament in other contexts.

Within the one Godhead, there are three distinguishable but equal persons

Not only is the plural title *Elohim* used of God (Genesis
20:13; 35:7) but God also speaks of himself in the plural,
for example, 'Let us make man in our image, according
to our likeness' (Genesis 1:26, NWT); 'The man has
become like one of us' (Genesis 3:22, NWT); 'Let us go
down and there confuse their language…' (Genesis 11:7-
8, NWT). These references indicate a plurality within
the Godhead. Again, in Zechariah 2:8-11 we find there
are two persons called Jehovah, while in Zechariah 3:1-
2 one person of Jehovah refers to another.

Some passages in the Old Testament (e.g. Isaiah
48:16; 63:8-10) bring together all the three persons and
in the New Testament the apostles are commanded to
baptize converts 'in the name' (that is, only one, single

name) of the Father, the Son and the Holy Spirit (Matthew 28:19; cf. 2 Corinthians 13:14; 1 Peter 1:2).

The Lord Jesus Christ

The crucial question, of course, concerns the deity of the Lord Jesus. Is he God, or, as Jehovah's Witnesses teach, a created angel and therefore only a god? Consider the evidence set out below for our Lord's deity.

1. The 'angel of Jehovah' in the Old Testament is also identified as Jehovah

Jehovah's Witnesses agree that 'the angel of Jehovah' is Jesus Christ in his pre-incarnation appearances. But, using their own NWT Bible, we can show that 'the angel of Jehovah' is also Jehovah himself. Consider Genesis 16:7-14. In verses 10-12, 'Jehovah's angel' speaks, but in verse 13 we read, 'She began to call the name of Jehovah who was speaking to her...' In Genesis 21:17-19 the angel of God is identified with God, then in 22:11-18 the angel of Jehovah speaks as Jehovah and Abraham knows he has seen a theophany, that is, an appearance of Jehovah himself (v. 14).

Jacob is told by the angel of God that 'I am the God of Bethel...' (Genesis 31:11, 13). Hosea

12:4-5 reveals that the man who wrestled with Jacob in Genesis 32:24-30 was the angel of Jehovah but Jacob says, 'I saw God face to face.' Other passages could be cited, such as Exodus 3:2, 4; 14:19, 21, 24; Judges 6:11-24; 13:2-23.

2. In the New Testament the Lord Jesus is identified as Jehovah

Old Testament verses referring to Jehovah are applied without hesitation to Christ in the New Testament.

Psalm 102:25-27 (the psalm is a prayer to Jehovah, see verse 1) is applied to Christ in Hebrews 1:8-12. 'Taste and see that the LORD [Jehovah] is good' (Psalm 34:8) is quoted by Peter then applied to Christ in 1 Peter 2:3. The prophet's vision of the glory of God in Isaiah 6 is explained in John 12:37-41 as a vision of Christ's glory. See also Matthew 3:3 and Mark 1:2-3 which quote Isaiah 40:3. Philippians 2:10-11 applies Isaiah 45:23 to Christ. Romans 10:13 quotes from Joel 2:32 and Romans 14:11 from Isaiah 45:23. In these and other references the Lord Jesus is identified as Jehovah.

3. The titles of Jehovah are also applied to Christ

'I am' (John 8:58; cf. Exodus 3:14); 'Shepherd' (John 10:11; Hebrews 13:20; cf. Psalm 23:1); 'Saviour' (2 Peter 1:1, 11; cf. Isaiah 43:3); 'First and the Last' (Revelation 1:8; 1:17; 2:8; 22:13; cf. Isaiah 41:4; 44:6; 48:12).

The name Jesus, which is *Jeshua* in the Hebrew, means 'Jehovah the Saviour'.

4. While worship must only be given to God, the Lord Jesus himself received worship

Consider the evidence in Matthew 8:2; 9:18; 14:33; 15:25; 28:9; and John 9:35-38. In each of these references the same word — *proskuneo* — is used and this is the word used to describe the worship of God. In Matthew 4:10 the Lord told Satan, 'Worship [*proskuneo*] the Lord your God, and serve him only.' The worship of angels and men is clearly forbidden, so the worship of Jesus indicates his deity. Like Thomas we can rightly worship him, saying, 'My Lord and my God!' (John 20:28). When being stoned to death, Stephen prayed to the Lord Jesus (Acts 7:59), but if Jesus was only a spirit-creature, as the Witnesses claim, this would have been idolatry.

5. Some claims of Christ and the apostles

John 1:1: 'In the beginning was the Word, and the Word was with God, and the Word was God.' This verse has been translated by Witnesses to prove their belief that Jesus was not the God but only a god, inferior to Jehovah-God. The main reason given by them for this translation ('The Word was a God') is that when the word *Theos* (God) occurs first of all in the verse, the definite article ('the' — Greek: *pros ton theon*) also occurs, whereas the next time the word 'God' occurs, there is no

THREE, BUT ONE

definite article at all. They take this to mean that the Word is an inferior God.

It can easily be proved that this is a wrong and deceitful translation. For example, in this same chapter the word *Theos* (God) occurs in four other places without the definite article, as it does at the end of verse 1, and yet each time in these other verses they correctly translate the word as 'God', not as 'a God' (see verses 6, 12, 13, 18). To be consistent, they should also translate the end of verse 1 in the same way but, unfortunately for them, it does not support their heresy!

John 10:30: 'I and the Father are one.' That this means more than a oneness in purpose, as the Witnesses teach, is clear from the verses which follow and also from John 5:18. The Jews understood this claim as implying deity and the Lord did not contradict them.

John 14:9: 'Anyone who has seen me has seen the Father.' Despite Jehovah's Witnesses' insistence that they only saw the Son, our Lord clearly says they did see the Father.

John 14:28: 'The Father is greater than I.' As John Calvin observed in his commentary on this verse, the Lord is not comparing the Father's deity with his own deity, nor his own human nature with the Father's divine essence. What he is actually doing is comparing his present condition with the glory which he would soon receive in his exaltation.

Furthermore, if we compare these words with Hebrews 1:4 we find confirmation of the Lord's deity here. The Greek word *meizon* translated 'greater' in John 14:28 is not the word used in Hebrews (*kreitton*) to show that the angels were inferior to Christ. If the Jehovah's Witnesses' teaching was correct, the other word (*kreitton*) should have been used by the Lord in John 14:28. But, of course, our Lord was not saying he was an inferior God; he was referring to his position as a servant, a subordinate position which he had voluntarily assumed in order to redeem sinners.

Remember, too, that our Lord's aim here is to comfort his disciples in the light of his approaching death, but there is no suggestion here that he was a created being.

Colossians 1:15-17. In the NWT the word 'other', which is not in the original Greek, has been included in their translation of these verses to twist the true meaning. Also the NWT 'first born of all creation' is wrong because the Greek word *prototokos* does not mean 'created' but expresses priority and sovereignty. Another Greek word, *protokistos*, would have been used if Paul had wanted to say that Jesus was created.

Colossians 2:9. All that constitutes God resides in Jesus Christ bodily (cf. Philippians 2:6; Titus 2:13).

There are other passages which confirm the deity of Christ, but the passages quoted provide sufficient biblical evidence to establish the doctrine.

The Holy Spirit

We also find that the Holy Spirit is a person and not an impersonal force. For example, he teaches and reminds (John 14:26), he guides (16:13) and speaks (Acts 8:29; 10:19; 13:2), and no impersonal power can do these things. He also intercedes (Romans 8:26), searches (1 Corinthians 2:10) and distributes gifts as he wills (1 Corinthians 12:11). He can be grieved (Ephesians 4:30), blasphemed (Matthew 12:31), lied to (Acts 5:3) and resisted (Acts 7:51). The Holy Spirit is associated with persons in Acts 15:28 and is identified as a person in Matthew 28:19.

Deity, as well as personality, is attributed to the Holy Spirit in the New Testament. He is omniscient (1 Corinthians 2:10-11), eternal (Hebrews 9:14), omnipresent (Psalm 139:7) and omnipotent (Luke 1:35; Romans 8:11). Peter tells Ananias that by lying to the Holy Spirit he had lied to God (Acts 5:3, 4). In 1 Corinthians 3:17 and 6:19 the phrases 'the temple of the Holy Spirit' and 'the temple of God' are used interchangeably to describe the body of the believer.

While many other biblical verses and passages could be cited in support, the foregoing references are sufficient to demonstrate that the doctrine of the Trinity is not a pagan, devilish teaching but one that is thoroughly grounded in the Bible. The deity of the Father, Son and Holy Spirit does not mean there are three gods, but rather that they are distinguishable persons, co-equal and co-eternal, within the one Godhead.

CHAPTER
TWENTY - SIX

THE WORKS
OF GOD

WHAT DOES GOD DO?

Having seen what God is like we shall now underline what the Bible says about the works of God. We shall consider four aspects of what God does, namely, the decrees of God, election, creation and providence.

The decrees of God

All that happens in the universe has been planned by God from eternity. Nothing happens by chance or accident. Throughout the centuries, God has worked according to his own absolute plan, which applies to all his creatures, not just to Christians or even to human beings, but also to animals and angels. The testimony of the Bible is that '[God] works out everything in conformity with the purpose of his will' (Ephesians 1:11).

It is difficult at times for us to understand why God works as he does in the world. There is much we cannot understand, for God's ways are past finding out (Romans 11:33; Isaiah 55:8-9). God is infinitely wise and plans all things perfectly. Nor will God fail to carry out his purposes. 'My purpose will stand,' says the Lord,' and I will do all that I please' (Isaiah 46:10).

This does not mean that God wants us to sin. Not at all. God is holy and he 'cannot be tempted by evil, nor does he tempt anyone' (James 1:13). God permitted sin to enter the world yet is not the author of sin.

Election

Included in God's eternal decrees was his choice of those who should be Christians. Too often this is a theme which Christians argue about, and not always in a loving spirit. If you look at Ephesians 1:3-6 you will see that election was not a subject Paul argued about but one that he believed and accepted with gratitude and worship.

There are many questions to ask concerning election.

- What does election mean? The word 'chose' in Ephesians 1:4 means to 'pick out' or 'choose out of'.
- Who chooses us to become Christians? God! Ephesians 1:4 says, '...he [i.e. God the Father] chose us...' While we make our personal response to God in faith and repentance, this is only as a result of God having first chosen us.

  God was under no obligation to choose and save us. Certainly there was nothing in us to attract or deserve his love. God chose us for no other reason than that he was pleased to do so (Romans 9:15-16).

- When did God choose us? 'Before the creation of the world...', that is, in eternity.
- How did God choose us? He chose us 'in him', that is, in Christ. In eternity, God the Father chose and placed his people in Christ as their representative and substitute. Christ it was who 'redeemed us from the curse of the law, by becoming a curse for us' (Galatians 3:13).
- Why choose us? The answer in Ephesians 1:4 is 'that we should be holy and without blame before him in love' (AV). This begins when we receive a new nature in new birth (Ezekiel 36:26-27) and continues as the Holy Spirit makes us more like Christ (Romans 8:13). However, it is only when the Christian dies and goes to be with the Lord that he will be without sin.

Here is good news for you. God has never refused mercy to any who have turned to him in repenting faith. All who go to Christ will be welcomed: 'Whoever comes to me', said Christ, 'I will never drive away' (John 6:37). In fact, God commands all men everywhere to repent (Acts 17:30).

Creation

The Bible teaches that God created the whole universe (John 1:3; Colossians 1:16) including man himself (Genesis 1:26-27; 2:7, 21-22). Rather than developing from a chance evolutionary process, man is a special creation of God. Consider how complex the human body is. The human mind, for example, has been described as the best and most intricate computer the world has known. Or think of the way in which a fertilized cell grows into a perfectly developed foetus and then into a child (Psalm 139:13-16). 'It is he who made us, and not we ourselves' (Psalm 100:3). Why did God create? The ultimate reason is for his own glory (Revelation 4:11).

Providence

It is not enough, however, to say that 'All things were created by him and for him' (Colossians 1:16). The Bible adds that 'In him, all things hold together' (1:17). His power alone supports, preserves and directs creation. The world does not survive because of fate or chance; it is God who holds the universe in his hand. Left to itself, the universe could not survive and all life would perish. 'For in him we live and move and have our being' (Acts 17:28). In his wise, holy and righteous providence, God upholds, preserves and governs all creatures and all their actions. He makes all things work together for the good of those who love God (Romans 8:28).

THE GUIDE

NOTES

NOTES

Chapter 1

1. J. Michael Feazell, *The Liberation of the World-wide Church of God*, inside page blurbs, Zondervan, Grand Rapids, 2001.

Chapter 2

1. G. J. Paxton, *The shaking of Adventism*, Zenith Publishers, 1977, p.55.
2. *Concise Oxford Dictionary*, Clarendon Press, Oxford, 1995, p.987.
3. *Spectrum* 9:31.
4. Published by Evangelion Press, 1980.
5. *Spectrum* 11:36.
6. *Ibid.*, 13:7.
7. *Adventist Review*, 4 September 1980; cf. *Ministry* 53, October 1980 and *Spectrum* 11:2-26, November 1980.
8. *Christianity Today*, 10 October 1980.
9. *Ibid.*, p.87.
10. Walter Martin, *Adventism*, Zondervan, 1960.
11. *Ibid.*, pp.236-7.

Chapter 3

1. Deists in the eighteenth century were people who accepted the existence of God but rejected the revealed message of the Bible.
2. Higher Criticism assesses theories concerning the compilation of Bible narratives from alleged sources, such as 'Q' in the synoptic Gospels, or J E P in Genesis, etc.
3. The first five books of the Old Testament.
4. John Urquhart, *Inspiration and accuracy of Holy Scripture*, p.iv.

5. *Ibid.*, p.iii.
6. *Ibid.*, p.89.
7. Quoted by A. C. Thiselton in *The two horizons*, Paternoster, pp.207, 214.
8. Hannah Tillich, *From time to time*, Stein & Day, 1973, pp.222-4.
9. Dave Tomlinson, *The Post Evangelical*, Triangle, SPCK, 1995.
10. The Universities and Colleges Christian Fellowship (UCCF), previously known as IVF, is an evangelical organization committed to propagating biblical truth in the colleges and gathering Christian young people together in Christian Unions for the purpose of fellowship and witness.
11. The Evangelical Movement of Wales has known considerable blessing on its work, e.g. annual youth camps, conferences, preaching meetings, ministers' fellowships and literature, etc.
12. Urquhart, *Inspiration*, p.38.
13. John A. T. Robinson, *But that I can't believe*, Collins, 1967, p.86.
14. Urquhart, *Inspiration*, p.14.
15. *Ibid.*, p.25.
16. *Ibid.*, p.31.
17. *Ibid.*, p.32.
18. *Ibid.*, p.79.
19. *Ibid.*, p.41.

Chapter 4
1. D. M. Lloyd-Jones, *Maintaining the evangelical faith today*, IVF, 1951, pp.10-11.
2. M. Tinker (ed.), *The Anglican Evangelical Crisis*, Christian Focus Publications, 1995, p.117.
3. Eds. B. Meeking + J. Stott, *The Evangelical Roman Catholic Dialogue on Mission 1977-1984*, Paternoster, 1988, p.10.

4.   W. Hendriksen, *Matthew*, Banner of Truth Trust, p.301.

Chapter 5
1.   John R. Hughes, *The background of Quakerism in Wales and the Border*, 1952, p.39.
2.   Quoted by George H. Gorman, *Introducing Quakers*, FHSC, 1979, p.10.
3.   *Ibid.*, p.25.

Chapter 6
1.   F. E. Raven, *New Series*, v. 12, pp.136-7.

Chapter 7
1.   *Light to London*, vol.6, no.7, July 1987, p.3, Douglas Jacoby, 'Immersion for salvation'.

Chapter 9
1.   *Doctrine of the New Apostolic Church,* p.1.
2.   See *New International Dictionary of Pentecostal and Charismatic Movements*, revised edition, 2002.
3.   *Evangelical Dictionary of Theology,* p.65.
4.   *New Concise Bible Dictionary*, pp.379-380.
5.   *Doctrine*, p.1.
6.   Article 4, *The New Apostolic Creed.*
7.   *Doctrine,* p.3.
8.   *Ibid.*, p.4.

Chapter 10
1.   *Pentecostal Press Trust, 1998, First Edition.*
2.   *Power Divine,* vol. 2, No. 2, Oct.-Dec. 1997, p.1.
3.   *Voice of Pentecost,* vol. 28, No. 8, May 2000, p.14.
4.   *The Biography of Pastor Paul*, p.1.
5.   *Ibid.*, pp.4-5.

NOTES

6.   *Ibid.*, p.22.
7.   *Ibid.*, p.80.
8.   *Ibid.*, p.81.
9.   *The Message of Acts*, p.74.
10.   *Pentecost,* February 2000, p.6.
11.   *Ibid.,* May 2000, p.15.
12.   *Ibid.,* August 1998, p.16.
13.   *Power Divine,* Oct-Dec 1997, p.13.
14.   *Pentecost,* June 2000, p.15.
15.   *Ibid.*, February 2000, p.15.

Chapter 12
1.   *Judgement,* p.19.
2.   *Omitted Warfare Against Evil Spirits*, p.17.
3.   *Judgement,* p.35.
4.   *Ibid.*, p.22.
5.   *Ibid.*, p.25.

Chapter 13
1.   Indiana University Press.
2.   *The Pentecostals*, 1972, p.354.
3.   *Dictionary of Pentecostal and Charismatic Movements*, 1988, p.96.
4.   See *Following a man?*, p.1.
5.   *This is the Way Walk Ye In It*, p.10.

Chapter 15
1.   *The Father and His Family,* p.118.
2.   *Advanced Bible Course,* p.279.
3.   *Identification,* p.12.
4.   *What Happened from the Cross to the Throne,* pp.20, 33, 44-45.
5.   *Zoe: The God-Kind Life,* p.35.
6.   *Word of Faith*, Dec. 1980, p.14.
7.   *The Name of Jesus*, pp.29-31.
8.   *Word of Faith*, Aug. 1977.

9. The Endtime Manifestation of the Sons of God',
audiotape 1.
10. Quoted by Hanegraaff, p.33.
11. Hagin in *Word of Faith*, p.14, Dec. 1980.
12. Kenyon, p.12, *Identification*.
13. Kenyon, *Advanced Bible Course*, p.279.

Chapter 16
1. To trace the movement of individuals and
congregations from Presbyterianism to
Unitarianism in England in the early period
especially, read: Eds. G. Bolan, J. Gong, H. L.
Short, R. Thomas, *The English Presbyterians*,
George Allen & Unwin, London, 1968, pp.219-
252.
2. *The Unitarians*, pp.2-3.

Chapter 18
1. In the early church period this teaching
was known as Modalism, Modalistic
Monarchianism and Sabellianism. Sabellius
lived in the third century A.D. and taught
in Rome about A.D. 215. His teaching was
condemned there but flourished in other
areas, especially in Egypt and Libya. Sabellius
argued that the Father, Son and Holy Spirit are
all one and the same although manifested in
different forms at different times.
2. Gordon Melton, *Encyclopedia of American
Religions*, McGrath Publishing Co., 1978, vol.
1, p.288.
3. Led by Raymond P. Virgil, this is a small group
with its head office in Pueblo Colorado; its
work is among Spanish-speaking Americans.
4. The first local congregation was established

in Honolulu in 1923-4 by Rev. and Mrs Charles
Lochbaum. Their influential radio ministry was
launched in 1969.

5.   Plans to form this group were first made in 1933
but implemented about ten years later. The group
is pacifist by conviction and congregational in its
church government; its main aim is to encourage
fellowship between 'oneness' Pentecostal churches,
particularly those refused fellowship by trinitarian
Pentecostal churches.

6.   This group was established in 1952 after a merger
of three separate 'Jesus only' groups. Doctrinally,
this group is in almost complete agreement with the
larger United Pentecostal Church; it also has an active
missionary work in Uruguay and Colombia.

7.   Formed in 1919 by G. T. Haywood, this is the oldest
'oneness' Pentecostal denomination. Since 1924 its
work has been restricted to coloured people, and it is
now active in countries like Nigeria, Jamaica, Ghana,
Egypt and Britain. The headquarters of the group is in
Indianapolis.

8.   They are led by a bishop and observe the sabbath on
the seventh day of the week. Their name arises from
the conviction that Jesus is the 'new and proper name
of God, Christ and the Church'.

9.   A former black minister in the Methodist Episcopal
Church, Alabama, W. T. Phillips, formed the Ethiopian
Overcoming Holy Church of God in 1919; the name
was changed in 1927.

10.   An early 'oneness' group established in 1919 by R. C.
Lawson.

11.   This was formed in 1957 by members of various
congregations within the Church of Our Lord Jesus
Christ of the Apostolic Faith who wanted a more
democratic form of church government.

NOTES

12.   Rev. A. D. Bradley was warned by the bishops of the Church of God in Christ in 1927 to stop preaching the 'Jesus only' heresy. When Bradley refused to comply, he helped to establish this new group and became its first presiding bishop.

13.   Founded by Rev. Donald Abernathy in 1963 in California. They identify Jesus with the Father, prohibit the use of medicine or surgery and have strict rules concerning dress for both men and women.

14.   Two groups formed this new body in 1945. The head office and publishing house are in St Louis; their magazine, *Pentecostal Herald*, has a wide distribution. They undertake missionary work in twenty-one countries, including Britain.

15.   John Montgomery, for example, shows conclusively how the Churches of God denomination in Ulster changed from a trinitarian to a 'oneness' doctrine about 1955 through the influence of Gordon Magee. An Ulster man who had emigrated to the United States, Magee embraced the 'Jesus only' teaching and felt he should share this 'new revelation' with the Churches of God in Ulster. See his *Evangelical or heretical: an examination of the Church of God in Ulster*, Burning Bush Publications, 1985, p.64.

16.   Quoted by James Bjornstad in duplicated notes dated 16 December 1983 and entitled *The oneness and threeness of God*', p.9.

17.   *Truly Pentecostal? A critique of the United Pentecostal Church*, (leaflet), p.2.

18.   *Calvin's Commentaries, Acts of the Apostles*, Eerdmans, 1949, vol.1, p.120.

Chapter 20
1.   *The Christian Warfare: An Exposition of Ephesians 6:10-13*, pp.121-132, Banner of Truth Trust, 1976.
2.   *Ibid.* pp.79-93.
3.   *Ibid.* pp.94-107.
4.   *Ibid.* pp.124-125.
5.   *Ibid.* pp.126-127.
6.   *Ibid.* p.128.
7.   *Ibid.* pp.128-132.
8.   *Ibid.* p.130.
9.   *Watchtower*, 15 Jan. 1995, p.6.
10.   *Ibid.*, 15 June 1978, p.24.

Chapter 25
1.   E. C. Gruss, *Apostles of denial*, p.127.

THE GUIDE

INDEX

INDEX

INDEX